YOUNG OVID

YOUNG OVID

An Unfinished Biography

DIANE MIDDLEBROOK

Literary Executor's Note by Leah Middlebrook
Foreword by Maurice Biriotti
Afterword by Carl Djerassi

COUNTERPOINT
BERKELEY

Portions of the Chapter "Ovid Is Born" first appeared in: *Feminist Studies Journal*, 38.2 (Summer 2012), 293-329.

Library of Congress Cataloging-in-Publication Data is available

ISBN 978-1-61902-331-4

Cover design by QUEMADURA

Interior design by VJB/Scribe

COUNTERPOINT

2560 Ninth Street, Suite 318, Berkeley, CA 94710

www.counterpointpress.com

Distributed by Publishers Group West

Printed in the United States of America

10 9 8 7 6 5 4 3 2 1

To Professor Dr. Rainer Engemann
For the following words:

"Mrs. Middlebrook—now finish your book!"

CONTENTS

When Diane Middlebrook died, the world of letters lost an extraordinary guiding voice. Diane was a teacher before she was a biographer, and everything she wrote, from *Worlds into Words* (W.W. Norton, 1980) through *Anne Sexton* (Houghton Mifflin, 1991), *Suits Me: The Double Life of Billy Tipton* (Houghton Mifflin, 1998), and *Her Husband: Ted Hughes and Sylvia Plath—A Marriage* (Viking, 2003), was designed to draw the reader into the world of the writer, and especially the poet. At the time of her death, she was working on her most richly imagined project to date, a biography of the poet Ovid, and a desire grew among Diane's admirers, family, and friends to publish the fragments of this text in order to perpetuate her life's work of introducing the general reader to the psyche of the artist.

Maurice Biriotti and Carl Djerassi explain in more detail the chapters that follow. My role here is simply to offer my deepest thanks to them, and to the great circles of friends who convinced me that this work should come into print. Carl Djerassi, as well as Charlie Winton, Rolph Blythe, and Jack Shoemaker of Counterpoint Press, were crucial to that decision, and the press made some well-judged editorial interventions—in particular, the inclusion of the relevant selections from Ovid, which should add to the experience of reading this book.

We have chosen not to dot every i and cross every t. Had my mother lived, the few missteps that the keen-eyed classicist may encounter would no doubt have been pruned with the same care she applied to the laurel trees on her London patio: She cut them with nail scissors, leaf by leaf, and she applied the same meticulous attention to her manuscripts. The fluidity of her prose masked an exacting scholarly rigor. But *Young Ovid* represents great work, interrupted.

Leah Middlebrook
Literary Executor for the Estate of Diane Middlebrook

Diane Middlebrook had originally set out to write a biography of the whole of Ovid's life. When she died, this work was far from complete. For those who knew Diane Middlebrook, that is a tragedy both personal and artistic. For those who did not but who love Ovid, or poetry, or language, or pondering the supreme mystery of creativity, it is a deprivation they may never be aware of. The history of culture must be full of such missed opportunities; this essay is a celebration of what might have been.

When she died of cancer in 2007, Diane Middlebrook had been in the process of trying to do something that was as breathtaking in its audacity as it was daunting in its implications for the writer. The aim was plainly laid out: By gathering the tiny shreds of available biographical data, amassing the known scholarship on the daily life and politics of the Augustan era, and above all applying the full force of shrewd literary interpretation to inspired conjecture, she would bring Ovid back to life for us. She would infer the psychology of a man we know almost nothing about from the human traces buried deep in his literary masterpieces.

In some ways, one can see Diane Middlebrook's professional and creative life as having built toward the culminating achievement of the Ovid project. As Carl Djerassi shows in the afterword to this volume, her record reads like the CV of a perfect candidate for the task. In her life of Anne Sexton, she had asked what complex psychology lay behind the poet's persona. She had broken new ground—and taboos—by using transcripts of psychoanalytic sessions, and told a rich and compelling story. What emerged was a new level of meticulous and subtle literary brushwork to construct a portrait of a human being in all her complexity. Later, she told the true story of a jazz artist who lived as a man and married three times, but turned out to have been born female (*Suits Me: The Double Life of Billy Tipton*, 1998). She delved deep into big questions: How do people come to transform themselves? How does the intimate space of a private life coexist with public performance? *Her Husband: Ted Hughes and Sylvia Plath—A Marriage* (2003), a double portrait of Sylvia Plath and Ted Hughes, had laid bare the peculiar mysteries of the writer's vocation. How do creative people come to do what they do? In that last completed work especially, Middlebrook had mastered the art of exhuming human motivations and frailties not only from letters or memoirs but from the complex soil of poetic language.

We can add to those achievements Diane Middlebrook's sensitivity to poetry and her own creative gifts, not only as biographer but also as poet (*Gin Considered as a Demon*), as well as her lifelong dedication, as a teacher, to Ovid.

Young Ovid is a fragment, but it is also a self-contained text. Apart from the fact that some portions of the originally conceived piece were not attempted, the work in front of us is still not as Diane Middlebrook wanted it to be. Texts, like people, undergo metamorphoses—revisions, reworkings, variations. This was a process as familiar to Diane Middlebrook as to her hero, Ovid. Diane Middlebrook wrote like a poet, whether her medium was verse, biography, or an academic paper. The creative process mattered. Here she cites Ovid from Book 6 of the *Metamorphoses*, describing the nymphs gazing in wonder at Arachne:

> [They were] equally eager to watch her handwork in progress
> (her skill was so graceful) as much as to look at the finished
>   article.
> Perhaps she was forming the first round clumps from the
>   wool in its crude state,
> shaping the stuff in her fingers and steadily teasing the
>   cloud-like
> fleece into long soft threads.

> (*Metamorphoses* 6.17–21)

This is art as metamorphosis—something Diane Middlebrook

explicitly links to Ovid's literary craft and something that can surely be applied to her own. Except that in this case the wool is not yet fully teased. What we have is an unfinished attempt, caught in midtransformation. She would certainly have continued to spin its threads of language with deft skill and tireless attention to detail.

Her respect for the craft and the sheer genius of the original was evidenced by Latin lines from the master painted in gold letters around the walls in the London apartment she shared with her husband, Carl. Their majestic domination of the space was, for visitors, a testament to Diane Middlebrook's unshakable belief in the power of the written word and the writer's craft.

So what does the unfinished, semipolished manuscript of the shorter project tell us? Above all, it speaks of a bold and startling ambition. That is its legacy. To answer the questions: How can the life of the author emerge from the writing on the page? How can poetry do exactly what Ovid claimed: secure eternal life for its creator?

It is perhaps not surprising that the model for this sort of procedure comes from Ovid himself. In the *Metamorphoses*, he tells us of the way things come to be what they are. Immanent in everything around us is the story of how each thing came to be. The traces of how it came into being still mark each thing we perceive around us—a fountain, an echo, a tree.

Take a simple story from the poem, the story of Perdix from the *Metamorphoses* (8.236–259). Forced to plunge to his death from a great height, the boy Perdix is about to be killed by the impact of his fall when a god takes pity on him and saves him. He turns him into a bird. But the bird in question, the partridge, is able to fly only for a tiny while, reflecting the boy's understandable and eternally enduring fear of heights. To look at a partridge is to see the trace of the story in its being. The process of transformation marks the object forever, remaining encoded within it like a narrative trace waiting for an expert investigator to unearth its secret meanings.

And that was Diane Middlebrook's proposed procedure with Ovid's own text: to mine its rhythms, its linguistic quirks, its unique literary signature, to reveal the code to the ultimate enigma: Who, or what, created it? And how did he in turn come into being?

Such an undertaking has many risks. Principal among them is the danger of descending into wild and unsustainable conjecture. That Diane Middlebrook was alive to this possibility is evident already from the existing manuscript. Her proposed solution was an ingenious balance of textual features that signaled a new departure for her.

First, she realized that this undertaking put great emphasis on a principled and detailed reading of the text. Second, the undertaking had to be rooted in fact and scholarship. Diane Middlebrook could be as rational and clear-sighted as a scientist, as skeptical as a historian. If detective work was to be done, then its foundation needed to be the forensic certainty of the expert witness. She consulted books and living scholars with all the zeal of the police inspector in hot pursuit, as shown in the numerous endnotes of her unfinished text.

Third, she would come clean about her guesswork, laying out the leaps, the doubts, the questions, for readers to see. The reader is left in no doubt as to the status or the provenance of the conjecture.

And finally, Diane Middlebrook added outright fiction—or fictionalization—to her armory: "I have written a few illustrative scenes into each chapter, scenes that dramatize significant episodes that must or might have occurred in Ovid's life. Those scenes are presented in italic type, to signify their fictional status. They are based on my research into Roman social history, but the application to Ovid's life is my own."

None of these features is unique. Perhaps their combination is not unique either. But the coming together of supreme authority in reading poetry, the rigor of a great scholar, the shrewd psychological insight of a biographer at the height of her prowess, the writerly craft of a poet—it is this striking coming together of focus for one project that surely would have broken new ground in the field of biography.

In Ovid's *Metamorphoses*, transformations happen suddenly, violently, unexpectedly. Even when they are benign, they speak of processes outside our control, at the whim of the gods. Ovid himself was subject to a whim—of the all-powerful emperor Augustus—and was treated to a cruel and unexpected exile. He continued to write, but life was never the same. Transformation can be tragic, brutal, or hard.

Diane Middlebrook's cancer, turning her life upside down and ending her huge project, had that sudden and terrible feeling of an Ovidian metamorphosis in all its cruel suddenness.

One big transformation comes to us all. We can only hope to achieve all we set out to before its day comes.

Maurice Biriotti

Now I have finished my work, which nothing can ever destroy
    ...
The finer part of myself shall sweep me into eternity,
higher than all the stars. My name shall never be forgotten.
Wherever the might of Rome extends in the lands she has
       conquered,
the people shall read and recite my works. Throughout all ages,
if poets have vision to prophesy truth, I shall live.

(*Metamorphoses* 15.871, 875–9)[1]

This extravagant claim ends the epic poem *Metamorphoses*, by the poet who flourished during the tumultuous years of Roman history that ended the Roman Republic and made the soldier Octavian into the emperor Augustus. The poet's name was Publius Ovidius Naso. We modern readers call him Ovid and tend to find such self-promotion distasteful. Naive, as well. The conquered lands have shaken off the conquerors: We are all postcolonials now. Yet Ovid's prophecy has proved true. The Latin language survived the fall of Rome, and that language was Ovid's posthumous habitat. Amazingly, his work has never been out of circulation since he first began reading it in public when he was about eighteen years old, around the year 25 BC. It made a powerful impact on its earliest audiences, and its celebrity never waned. It has been preserved, admired, quoted, translated, imitated, illustrated, excerpted, reinterpreted, and steadily transmitted for more than two thousand years.[2]

To a biographer, Ovid's declaration "I shall live" can feel like a glove slapping a cheek across twenty centuries. Quite aside from its embarrassingly self-promotional aspect, the phrase can be dismissed as empty convention: Ovid's most celebrated contemporaries incorporated lines like this in work of their own they most admired. But what if Ovid meant it? What could support a writer's belief that works of poetry could be immortal and that his own was destined for this rare elevation?

Biography is a medium for working out solutions to such puzzles. Yet Ovid is not an obvious candidate for biography; there is almost no documentation of Ovid's life outside his poetry.[3] The evidence *inside* his poetry is all we have to go on. But it is enough, for Ovid was an unusually autobiographical writer for his time. His voice comes toward us like a plucked string, immediate and recognizable across two millennia, partly because he made frequent use of an effective rhetorical strategy: accosting us readers as if we were present in the room with him. At one point he even calls us, his heirs, by name: "Who is this I you read . . . ? / You want to know, posterity? Then attend" (*Tristia* 4.10.1–2).[4]

And the story of his life, as he tells it, comes across as a *story*, with an exciting plot. Publius Ovidius Naso, a provincial boy from a good family, was born in 43 BC in rustic Sulmo, a town in the Apennines of central Italy, and went to Rome at around age twelve with his older brother to complete their education and embark on the *cursus honorum*, the series of public offices that could eventually lead to a position in the Roman Senate. But Ovid defied his father by becoming a poet, and succeeded precociously. He gave that first public reading at age eighteen under the sponsorship of a wealthy patron; his reputation soared. Eventually he became Rome's foremost living writer.[5] Then, at the peak of his fame, at age fifty-one, he was summoned to a private meeting with the emperor, who was furious with him for some misbehavior that Ovid was forbidden to specify. Ovid learned that he would be punished, by exile. He spent the next ten years in Tomis, a settlement on the Black Sea—now called Constanța, in Romania—at the very edge of the empire. He died in exile, at around age sixty.

During his ten years of forced absence from Rome, hoping to regain favor with Augustus, he addressed eighty verse epistles to influential friends, reminding them of his highborn status and his exemplary life as an artist and citizen. Ovid's hope for pardon was not entirely groundless, because his punishment was a form of exile called relegation; he retained his property and his citizenship.[6] The poems were not private letters, however; they were written for publication. Ovid wished to put himself on record for his future readers, and he believed that his words would survive. Ovid's very early rise to celebrity was assisted by an aristocratic benefactor acquired before he was sixteen years old. That first patron was Marcus Valerius Messalla Corvinus, who discovered Ovid's talent while the poet was still an adolescent and encouraged Ovid to take it seriously. Once Ovid had been drawn into the circle of poets around Messalla, he treated his obligations to the *cursus honorum* as a kind of day job and threw his energy into developing his talent for writing. His first book, the *Amores*, was completed while he was in his twenties[7] and became the equivalent of a bestseller. Appearing at the time that Augustus, having ended the Civil War, was consolidating his power as Rome's postwar leader, the *Amores* captured the spirit of its time: Young Romans were ready to make love, not war, and they dismissed the abstemious values of their elders with immense self-confidence.

Several other books of love poems followed the *Amores*: *Ars Amatoria* (*The Art of Love*); *Remedia Amoris* (*Cures for Love*); *Heroides* (each poem the epistle of a mythological heroine or hero to a lover); and *Medicamina Faciei Femineae* (*Facial Treatment for Ladies*, an instruction manual)—all of which were instantly popular. At some point Ovid probably wrote a tragedy, *Medea*, for one of the newly built theaters.[8] Then, in his midforties, Ovid undertook the ambitious project of writing an epic, as his great predecessor Vergil had done. Vergil's epic, the *Aeneid*, was a continuation of the *Iliad* and the *Odyssey*, Homer's poems about the legendary war in Troy. The *Aeneid* told how the hero Aeneas escaped from the ruins of Troy. From Aeneas's struggles evolved the founding of Rome and its emergence as a world power under Augustus. Vergil represented Rome as an Eternal City, a gloriously permanent contribution to civilization.

Vergil had been dead for twenty years when Ovid began the *Metamorphoses* (*Transformations*), which he appears to have conceived as a counter-epic to the *Aeneid*. Ovid's *Metamorphoses* represented a complete change in the conception of an epic. It had no plot; it was a collection of approximately twenty-five hundred stories running "from the world's beginning / down to my own lifetime"

(1.3–4). He called it a *carmen perpetuum* (1.4), "ongoing song." Its theme would be *everything changes*. Most significantly, it had no heroic protagonist—no Aeneas, no Achilles, no Ulysses whose conflicts and triumphs gave emotional power and focus to the traditional epic. Instead, Ovid's epic had a narrator, whose role was to anchor the storytelling in the knowledge and ingenuity of a single mind. Differing from all of his great antecedents in the epic, including Vergil, Ovid's narrator in the *Metamorphoses* speaks in the first person throughout the poem—not intrusively, just often enough to remind the reader that the story has a story*teller* who manages the flow of narrative rather in the way a conductor leads an orchestra through a complex musical score. The most radical shift in Ovid's new work is this mature point of view from which it is narrated.

Who is that narrator? Ovid provides an image of him early in the *Metamorphoses*, in the section dealing with the creation of the universe. After the heaven and earth had been created, and the sky and the sea, Ovid tells us,

> A holier living creature, more able to think high thoughts,
> which could hold dominion over the rest, was still to be found.
> So Man came into the world. Maybe the great artificer
> made him of seed divine in a plan for a better universe . . .
> Where other animals walk on all fours and look to the ground,
> man was given a towering head and commanded to stand
> erect, with his face uplifted to gaze on the stars of heaven.

> (*Metamorphoses* 1.76–9, 84–6)

Ovid's image of the creative human being is a portrait of the artist who has undertaken the making of the *Metamorphoses*. He is a creature shaped like a god, "able to think high thoughts." His talent, the trait Ovid often calls *ingenium*, is ingenuity. He will spin his epic poem line by line, just as it comes to mind. No external source directs the action of *this* story, no preexisting history or legend.

This biography of Ovid explores the sources in life of that literary persona, "the great artificer" who steps forward at the opening of the *Metamorphoses*.

To compensate for the unavailability of a full historical documentation of Ovid's existence, I have chosen to account for four exemplary milestones at the beginning of young Ovid's life—a period that has hardly been touched upon.[9] To assist this effort, I have written a few illustrative scenes into each chapter, scenes that dramatize significant episodes that must or might have occurred in Ovid's life. Those scenes are presented in italic type, to signify their fictional status. They are based on my research into Roman social history, but the application to Ovid's life is my own.

As a biographer I am interested in the question of why Ovid became a poet rather than a Roman magistrate, as his father intended he should do. I find the answers to this question buried in some of the rich symbolisms of poems in Ovid's masterpiece, *Metamorphoses*: in the passages about the universe's creation, about Phaethon, about the daughters of Minyas, about Daphne, about Minerva and the Muses, about Arachne, and in the epilogue. The search for answers requires establishing the psychological validity of speculation about emotional dynamics to be found in Ovid's work. For example, Ovid's poetry conveys an unusual kind and degree of interest in women, which I attribute to the influence of a hypothetical young mother with a certain amount of literary education and a talent for storytelling. While such assumptions are not based on direct historical evidence, I show that they have emotional soundness.

But the instigating source of this biography was the remarkable confidence that Ovid had in his own survival. He knew that the artistic strategy by which he had created a narrator in his work was a guarantee that it would outlive him; he even believed that it would never die. He said so, repeatedly, in his most ambitious poems, but never so intimately as in the poem he wrote from exile, apparently to his stepdaughter, urging her not to give up the art in which he had been one of her instructors:

> In brief, there's nothing we own that isn't mortal
> > save talent, the spark in the mind.
> Look at me—I've lost my home, the two of you, my country,
> > they've stripped me of all they could take,
> yet my talent remains my joy, my constant companion:
> > over *this*, Caesar could have no rights. What if
> some savage's sword should cut short my existence?
> > When I'm gone, my fame will endure,

and while from her seven hills Mars' Rome in triumph
   still surveys a conquered world, *I shall be read.*

(*Tristia* 3.7.43–52)

How did Ovid know that his grandiose ambition could be realized? And how closely did he identify the speaking persona with
himself, the condemned man? The genre of biography offers a template for investigating just such mysteries about a work of art.

CHAPTER 1

Ovid Is Born

The midwife watched the laboring woman discreetly from a chair in the corner of the room, resting and readying herself for what was to come. The mother had by now undergone many hours of acute and exhausting discomfort before entering this current stage of transition, in which the cervix was approaching its full dilation, accompanied by ferocious pain. Strangled cries rhythmically escaped her clenched teeth as she writhed, wringing her hands.

The midwife, a well-trained Greek freedwoman, had seen many a child into the world and knew that success in delivering the baby would depend partly on psychological preparation of the mother, who needed to be surrounded by expectations that she would survive this ordeal, though the midwife knew all too well the possibility that she would not survive it. So the birthing room had been arranged to promote an atmosphere of normalcy. There were two couches in the room: the low, flat bed on which the woman lay in labor, and the other, piled with soft cushions where she would rest after delivery. The light was dim, its only source the brazier; water and oil stood warming on a nearby shelf, a sign of trust that the baby too would survive.

The birthing couch was hard, and the hour was late, and the laboring woman, fixated on her pain, was now barely aware of her surroundings. How much more delay could she tolerate before weakening and giving up? The midwife oiled her left hand once again and reached up into the birth canal—she had previously cut her nails very short, to increase the sensitivity of her fingertips and to avoid scratching the woman's tender membranes. Yes, the cervix was ready: dilated by a full handspan. It was time to invoke the power of the gods. Dramatically, she rose from her seat and signaled to the three attendants she had brought with her into the birthing room, selected from the large staff of household slaves and freedwomen in the

Ovidius family villa—literate women, well-spoken, well-groomed, and well-mannered. That they had no training in midwifery was irrelevant: They were the mother's work companions in daily life.

During the early hours of labor, these attendants had distracted their mistress with local gossip, while the midwife herself ministered to her physical comfort. They now began a soft repetitive chant, casting incense into the brazier while imploring gods and goddesses to hasten safe delivery of the child: Dispater, Mena, Lucina, Diana Hythia, Egeria, Prosa, Manageneta, and the dii nixi, all protectors of women. The prayers culminated in a libation to the goddess Latona, whose own struggle giving birth to the glorious twins Apollo and Diana had made her the principal divine overseer of human childbirth.

The midwife did not take part in these devotions; hers was a more practical role. She raised the mistress in her arms and stripped the sweat-stained, bloody coverlet from under her body. She cleansed the woman's nether parts with warm water and wiped her with a damp sponge, then brushed the drenched hair away from her eyes. These ministrations had a ritual purpose too, marking the point of transition into the last stage of labor. The midwife told her mistress that she must now move to the birthing stool that stood ready nearby.

The attendants helped the mistress rise to her feet, then seated her on the crescent-shaped stool. They covered her belly and feet with cloths warmed in oil. Then they strewed the floor with crushed, sweet-smelling plants that were abundant at the vernal equinox: barley grass, apple blossom, quince flowers, lemons, cucumbers. The scent of these juices were thought to revive a person's strength.

Meanwhile, the midwife had donned a large linen apron. Seating herself on a low chair opposite the woman's knees, she locked her eyes on the woman's face, speaking in a low, comforting voice while reaching with her left hand deep into the aperture of the birth canal, massaging and dilating the cervix. For the next hour, after each contraction had passed, accompanied by the mother's screaming and groaning, the midwife again massaged the orifice, to keep it fully dilated, always telling the laboring woman when to push, when not to push. The attendants assisted from either side, gently pressing the mass of the belly downward after the muscles unclenched.

The high, solid back and stout armrests of the birthing stool gave leverage as the woman braced herself to bear down, but its most important feature was the access it permitted to her lower body. When the midwife's fingers at last located the amniotic sac that encased the fetus, she guided it forward and downward, then waited for the next contraction. "Now," she said, in a firm voice, and the laboring woman once again gripped the armrests and pushed hard, and harder still, shouting in pain, until the flesh of the peritoneum tore with a gush of blood and the womb's waters poured between her legs, mixed with urine and feces. Now the crown of the baby's head could be felt in the opened passageway. Luckily, this was the mother's second child, and this last part of her labor was likely to be short. Another and another powerful push from the mother, and the head appeared, its black hair slicked into damp waves. The midwife gently groped her way back into the birth canal and found a shoulder, then pulled and turned the little body while arms and trunk and crotch and legs emerged, streaky with shredding vernix and swathed in blood. The midwife lifted him away from his mother's legs, and the cool air passing over his body caused him to gasp, then expel a gratifying howl.

She laid the wailing infant on a pillow in her lap while she stroked the mother's breasts to induce contractions of the womb, to deliver the afterbirth, and stanched the heavy bleeding that could kill the postpartum mother in minutes. Then she motioned the attendants to wash the mother and move her to the comfortable couch. Meanwhile the midwife prodded and stretched the newborn's limbs for evidence of deformities and investigated all of his orifices for defects. It was she who would determine whether he was worth rearing or should be removed at once from the family home, for exposure on some outlying midden. When she had finished her inspection, she nodded assent, severed the umbilical cord, then stripped the blood from the stump and tied it off with a short length of wool thread. At last she turned to her mistress, holding the baby up to view and lifting her own voice above his cries: "Praise the gods, you have another son." And high over the villa, Lucifer, the morning star, shone in the dawn sky—a heavenly recipient of that newborn voice, which was now firmly in the world, once and for all.[10]

This was a story he liked to hear again and again, a few years later, standing at his mother's shoulder while she sat at her spinning and weaving. The tale was as gory as any battle. And it was a story he really shouldn't have been told, since the birthing process was a woman's mystery, never witnessed nor discussed by male members of the household. He wanted to be the exception, to know exactly what had happened, and she would tell him, amused by his persistence, talking while she worked. Holding a clump of wool in one hand while the thumb on her other hand pushed out and twisted a single thread, blending one strand with another, she could wind it long and unbroken onto a spindle, just the way she spun a story, making it last as long as she wished. She would recite passages from the epics of Homer, having memorized them in childhood herself. She would tell him the myths and legends about Rome that children were supposed to hear at an early age, to shape their ideas about the world that they would govern. When she told the little boy about the day he was born, she would point at his belly button to prove that the story he liked so much was absolutely true, *not a myth. A human body had grown inside another human body, then burst forth whole and perfect, to be tied off in a knot: There it was, the permanent evidence of an amazing transformation.*

Inevitably, the story of how Ovid transformed himself into an immortal begins on the day he was born: March 20, 43 BC.

In ancient Rome, more women died in childbirth than men died in war.[11] The infants too were at great risk of early death; and half who survived infancy would not reach puberty.[12] A good deal of what might be described as magical thinking—fine-tuned transactions with the deities who governed a household—accompanied childrearing; but a good deal of practical experience would have gone into the midwife's ministrations to baby Ovid during his first hours of life, as well.

Immediately after his birth, he would have been thoroughly bathed, his whole body sprinkled lightly with salt, then washed in lukewarm water two or three times. While he was immersed in the last ablution, the midwife would remove the mucus from his nostrils and throat, clean his ears, and open his anus for the excretion of meconium. The tied-off umbilical cord would be doubled over and covered with a clump of fleece dipped in olive oil, then centered on his body to encourage a well-shaped navel.

Now he was ready for his first swaddling, a process that was meant to complete the process begun in the womb, of shaping a well-proportioned adult body. Swaddling was a complicated task that needed practice and concentration, because some parts of the body would require compression in order to achieve their "natural" form, while other parts required looseness. The binding began with the infant's hands. Long strips of soft woolen cloth were wound over the fingers—extended to keep the hand flat—and up the middle of the hand to the forearm and upper arm; compression was applied at the wrist, looseness at the armpit. Broader strips would be wrapped around the thorax. Then the legs were bound, loosely around the upper thighs and calves, more tightly at the knees, instep, and ankles. The bandage would cover the very tips of the toes, as it had covered the very tips of the fingers. Pieces of wool were wrapped into the joints at the ankles, the knees, and the elbows, to avoid ulcerations. Then the whole body would be wrapped into a fairly tight package that held the arms at the infant's sides and joined the legs and feet together in a straight line. Finally, the head would be wrapped: either encircled by a bandage or draped with a small shawl. The baby would continue to undergo just such swaddling after a bath, for as long as the first sixty days of its life.

The process of unswaddling would be equally deliberate and methodical. First the right hand would be unbound, to encourage right-handedness. Other parts of the body would be unbound gradually, depending on the state of firmness each had achieved.

This practice was not only fundamental to the "shaping" theory of childrearing practiced by Romans but was also the crucial, very first step in the process of integrating the newborn with its family. In effect, the first swaddling expressed the midwife's vote of confidence in the soundness of the child she had delivered. Having swaddled the baby, she would seek out the presumptive father and lay it on the ground before him. The father would then take the infant up into his arms. The name for this ritual was *tollere liberos*—literally, elevating or raising the child. If for any reason the father refused, the baby would not be permitted to enter the family. It would be exposed outdoors, in some location where it might well be found and raised as a slave, or treated as the child of parents themselves unable to bear children. In any case, its fate would be of no further interest to this father. But once the infant had been "raised," its acceptance into the family was assured. A flame could now be lit on the family altar, and prayers initiated with the hope of keeping the newborn alive. And a wreath could be hung on the door of the villa to announce the birth to the whole community.[13]

Since a woman's main responsibility was to produce a male heir for the family into which she married, it is perhaps not surprising that midwifery was highly valued, and its best practitioners regarded as professionals. We extrapolate this assumption from a gynecological treatise dating to the first century AD. Its author, known only as Soranus of Ephesus, practiced medicine in Rome.[14] The midwife who delivered Ovid may have been just such a professional, whose services had been called upon because Ovid's was a family with the means to pay for the best help on offer. She would be responsible for delivering the baby and overseeing the immediate care of the mother.

To a modern mind, the midwife would not have put the washed and swaddled baby at his mother's breast that day. Since breastfeeding interferes with the production of hormones necessary to a woman's fertility, it is most likely that Ovid's mother did not nurse the children herself—she would not have become pregnant with this child, Publius, had she breastfed the older baby longer than three months, whereas Roman babies were usually not weaned for two or three years. A child's principal supplier of nutrition for the first years of life was a usually a wet nurse, and this role too required professional training, judging from the length and character of Soranus's instructions in his tract, *Gynecology*. Soranus strongly advises against maternal breastfeeding, on the grounds that it exhausts the mother and ages her prematurely, making her less fit for further childbearing.

He takes great pains in providing advice regarding procedures for selecting a wet nurse. A primary concern, in addition to his explicit counsel about the condition of the breasts and of the milk the candidate should possess, is her age and character. The wet nurse should be a healthy woman between twenty and forty years, able to bring both experience and mature emotions to her work. She should exercise regularly and should eat the kinds and amounts of food that Soranus prescribes exactly. She should drink no alcohol until the child has attained a certain age and strength, and she should abstain from sex, lest her sympathies be drawn away from the infant. Plus, the nursing infant should become accustomed to more than one nurse, lest he reject the milk of a replacement if his primary feeder falls ill or is otherwise unavailable.

The mere thriving of the newborn baby in the house of the Ovidii was not enough to make him a member of the family, however. A ritual was required. Nine days after the birth of a son (eight days after the birth of a daughter), a bloodless sacrifice would be conducted at a gathering of friends and extended family, with offerings burned before the family's household gods. This religious ceremony, called the *dies lustricus*—day of purification—was meant to purge the infant of the pollution associated with birthing. The *dies lustricus* was a major family celebration but also involved the elite members of the town in which the child was born, and the guests would have brought the family abundant gifts of congratulation.[15]

The ritual would culminate in bestowing a name on the baby. Publius Ovidius Naso was the name given to this newborn son on that day. Freeborn Romans had three names. The *praenomen* was the personal name, used at home and among intimates. The Romans had very few first names to choose from—only about eighteen were in existence in the year 100 BC—so there were already many Publiuses (or Publii) in the world. Ovid may have received the name as a tribute to another family member, but the *praenomen* Publius would at the very least differentiate him from his brother, who, being the firstborn son in the family, was likely to have been named after the father. Had there been girls in the family, they would be given, as *praenomen*, the feminine version of the father's *nomen*; so all of Ovid's sisters would very likely have been named Ovidia and known around the house by a nickname (though Ovid mentions no sisters).

The last two of these three names were common to the family. Ovidius referred to the family's *gens* or clan. Ovid's *cognomen,* Naso, meant "nose," which suggests that some ancestral Ovidius had a big endowment of that feature, or maybe a too-curious disposition, nosiness, and that the family carried the comic burden ever after.

At the name-day ritual, a son or daughter also received a *bulla.* This was a large, round pouch-shaped pendant in which good-luck charms had been sealed. In an affluent family, the *bulla* night be made of gold, but its purpose was not ornamental; it enabled anyone who looked at the wearer to identify, even at a distance, a child's status as freeborn. Baby Publius Ovidius Naso would wear his *bulla* steadily until reaching manhood, at around age sixteen. Along with the *bulla,* he might also receive on his name day a number of other protective amulets by which the family hoped to keep him alive. Despite the educated Roman's skepticism toward magical thinking, charms were employed along with every other protective device.

With the bestowal of his name, the arrival of Publius was official: The family's hereditary line had been extended by a son exactly one year younger than his brother. The family records would have dated the year of Publius's birth by the names of the men who held the consulship in Rome. In Ovid's case, those consuls were Aulus Hirtius and Gaius Vibius Pansa Caetronianus, both nominated by Julius Caesar (Caesar having been assassinated only five days before Ovid's brother was born). The date would also have referenced the Roman calendar of festivals: Both boys had been born on the second day of Quinquatrus, the five-day festival dedicated to Minerva, March 19 to 23. In addition, the hour of each birth would have been noted for the purpose of casting their horoscopes.[16]

THE BABY IN THE FAMILY

I was born, in the year both consuls perished
    at Antony's hands; heir (for what that's worth)
to an ancient family, no brand-new knight promoted
    just yesterday for his wealth.
I was not the eldest child: I came after a brother
    born a twelvemonth before me, to the day

so that we shared a birthday, celebrated one occasion
  with two cakes, in March, at the time
of that festival sacred to armed Minerva.

(*Tristia* 4.10.5–13)

This is Ovid's account of his arrival spelled out in the *Tristia*. "Not the eldest" was an important detail in this concise account. To be the firstborn son in "an ancient family" would have influenced the psychological climate of his upbringing. The core of every ancient family was the presence in the household of three generations of males: the *paterfamilias*, his son, and the son's son. That is why Vergil made this triad central to the *Aeneid*, his epic account of the founding of Rome: Aeneas escapes from the burning city of Troy with the household gods in his baggage, carrying his elderly father on his shoulders and leading his son by the hand. Along the way, his wife disappears and is mourned, but her loss does not disrupt the integrity of the family; the surviving trio of males constitutes the foundation of a new household. Yet the two boys were equally cherished within the Ovidius Naso family, it would seem, and Roman legal statutes decreed that they (along with any other siblings, male or female) would inherit equal shares of property at the time of their father's death.[17]

The twelve-month gap that separated the Ovidius sons would have been a distinction without much difference for the next six years of their lives, though, since their proximity in age would have made it efficient for the household to treat them as if they were the same age. Once the ceremonies were over, baby Publius would have joined his toddling brother in the care of a staff of women, overseen by their mother.

The two little sons in the house of Ovidius Naso therefore would have formed their first significant relationships with the several female attendants into whose care they were entrusted. A swarm of household slaves, mainly female, would also have surrounded them from birth, and, in addition, they were watched over by a host of divinities, all of them female. The goddess Opis (or Ops) oversaw the way the midwife laid the child on the ground, to be raised by the father; Levana was at hand when the child was lifted. Cuma rocked the cradle, Carmenta lullabied him, and Vegetanus hushed him when he cried. Rumina made sure the baby took the breast; later on, Polina helped him drink from a cup, and Edura taught him how to eat solid food. Osslago and Carna worked within the baby's growing body, giving it strength. Stilinus or Statanus showed toddlers how to walk, Fabulina showed them how to talk, and Camaena taught them how to sing. Paventia protected them from childhood terrors.[18] From an early age, the children would have been taught stories about the ways these invisible goddesses influenced the human world, and they would have been shown the proper ways to pay respect. It was all part of shaping them into Romans.

ANCESTRY

It was early morning, still more dark than light, when the little boys were shocked awake by the sound of screaming. It came from the room in which their grandfather lay. Three days earlier he had been carried down from the mountains on a litter, unconscious. Riding over the narrow track in the Apennines that was the rough version of a road from Sulmo to the Via Valeria, his horse had slipped and cata-pulted him headfirst onto the rocks. From the moment he'd arrived at the villa, doctors had been attending him, and the boys had been told to keep out of everyone's way and to remain absolutely quiet. Publius was only five years old, but he had already learned to obey. If he forgot what he had been told, his brother was sure to remind him.

Now, suddenly, the silence of the household had been broken by the shrill and awful sound of a voice they had never heard before, though they knew it was their mother's voice: a terrifying wail, rising and falling—no words, just a horrible keening, repeated again and again. It wakened the servants, who ran to the grandfather's room, and soon the other women too were screaming.

This was the grandfather who had begun teaching the little boys to ride a horse as soon as each of them was able to sit without sup-port. He would put them on the horse's back and balance them with his own hands; he wanted them to learn the feeling of responsive horseflesh even before they could toddle. As they grew older, he took them along when he inspected the vineyards and orchards, talking to them as they walked. He told them stories about the tribe of the Paeligni to which they belonged and about the escapades of their great-grandfather, who was a hero in the Italian War, in which the Paeligni had won Roman citizenship. The great-grandfather had refused to wear the iron ring that signified citizenship once the battle had been won. He did not want to be a Roman: He wanted freedom from Roman exploitation. Their grandfather had fought alongside his father in those wars, as soon as he came of age. But he was the younger generation, and he gladly wore the iron ring of citizenship: Why not? It was the insignia of an important victory. Yet he did not wish his own little grandsons to glorify military combat. Peace was better than war, he told his grandsons, and the best life of all was spent tilling the soil in their mountain-guarded valley, far from the precincts of Rome. The little boys did not yet understand much of his description of how the Paeligni figured in Roman history, but they felt proud to be in his company, to be spoken to in such a serious way about their family.

Something bad had now happened to this grandfather, they had no doubt. Hours passed, and feet hurried to and fro among the rooms that morning; they could hear everything from the cubicle they shared. Then the house grew strangely quiet, but still no one came to raise them from their beds and wash them, and give them food. They played listlessly at games of knucklebone, and then at building words with the little ivory tiles they had been given on their birthday, on which letters were carved. Eventually, they both fell asleep.

They were wakened by footsteps approaching their room. A hand pulled the curtain aside, and to their amazement, their father was standing in the doorway. He had never, ever, since they were born, entered the back rooms of the house where the women and children and slaves had their quarters. At ages six and five, the boys were too young to interest him very much; aside from feast days, he spent no time with them at all. Their father was greatly taken up with the business of running the large estate. He occupied a room just off the garden, beyond the large tablinum, which was their grandfather's reception room and sleeping room.

Now their father knelt by their couch and spoke to them kindly.

He told them that their grandfather was dead—a great man, known for his bravery in battle and his good sense as a man of justice, serving his municipium. He had also been the family's paterfamilias for many years, their father told them. So, though the boys were not quite old enough to participate in the strict formal rituals by which the family served the household gods, they were old enough now to share in the family's mourning. He took them by the hand and led them to the atrium at the front of the house.

The room was open to the sky, and strong midday sunlight poured down on the long table that stood beneath this opening. The table had been covered with the best tapestry. On it lay a long wooden box, heavily garlanded with sweet-scented flowers woven into branches of greens. At the foot of the coffin their mother stood quietly with her hands folded. The peculiar passion of the morning, which they had witnessed only in her screaming, had left its strange vestiges on her appearance. Her cheeks were scored by long bloody scratches, like the swipe of an animal's claws, and her long dark hair was snarled and tangled. The garments she wore had been torn and smeared with ashes from the hearth.

The boys were too small to see over the coffin's edge, but their father lifted each in turn, to look for the last time at their grandfather's face. On the following day, they were told, their father would lead a funeral procession bearing the body of his father to its pyre in a burial ground outside the city. Many, many mourners would join this procession—all the dignitaries of Sulmo and the far-flung acquaintances of the grandfather, along with any relatives who lived close enough to attend. At the end of that long day, the grandfather's bones would be collected in an urn and placed in the family mausoleum, and the death mask that had been made before the body was burned would be carried back to the family's villa and placed in a box near the family altar.

The family's ceremony of mourning would be a household affair, however, and would take place immediately. In preparation for the ritual, the boys were sent away with their nanny to bathe. Their hair was dressed, and they donned the garment reserved for special occasions, the toga praetexta, its purple stripes signifying their status as freeborn children. They returned with their nanny to the kitchen *hearth, where the rest of the family and the slaves were gathered, for the slaves too were part of the household that the spirit of the grandfather had now abandoned.*[19] *Their father first killed a lamb from their own herd, using the ritual knife that always stood by the hearth, catching its blood in a large bowl. Expertly, he slit the lamb's belly, removed the entrails, and laid them on the fire, offering them and the lamb's blood to the gods with ritual prayers. The family and the slaves joined in these prayers while the entrails crackled and burned in the flames. Then their father moved to a small brazier standing in a niche where images of the household Lares and Penates had been painted on the plaster: two dancing boys in festive costume, flanking a sober figure in a white toga. This was the image of the genius of the household, protector of their longevity. Incense and saffron had been piled in votive dishes, and a filled wine bowl stood at hand. When they had all assembled at this altar, their sorrowing father began speaking the consecrating ritual words in a low voice. At the end of his prayers, he asked for protection of the little boys on whom the future of the family depended, and each in turn cast incense into the flames before their father quenched the fire with wine, a libation to the genius. In that gesture he asserted his role as the new* paterfamilias.

The ancestral home of Ovid's family was Sulmo, a town that lay seventy-three miles northeast of Rome, in the area of central Italy now known as the Abruzzi. Encircled by mountains that rise to eight thousand feet, Sulmo was situated on a high fertile plateau "rich in chilly springs," Ovid tells us (*Tristia* 4.10.3–4), a place of hilly grazing land and terraces where vineyards and orchards and olive groves flourished. Today in the Abruzzi, as probably in ancient times, truffles are found in abundance, and saffron is grown, and fine mozzarella produced. Hannibal had passed through Sulmo on his march to Rome during the Second Punic War. The historian Polybius claimed that the local Montepulciano had greatly revived the Carthaginian soldiers and horses after their exhausting battle.[20]

Sulmo was settled by a tribe called the Paeligni, which enters the annals of Roman history toward the end of the fourth century BC, when they were loosely affiliated with their tribal neighbors the Marsi, the Marrucini, and the Vestini and made common use of the port town of Aternum on the Adriatic.[21] Oscan was their mother tongue; for religious and private purposes at least, the Paelignian dialect lasted down to the middle of the first century BC.[22] Throughout the early history of the Roman Republic the Paeligni proved themselves to be "first class fighting men."[23] In the wars Rome waged with the Samnites, their aggressive neighbors, the Paeligni took the side of Rome when the Roman army needed a back door into Samnite territory.

Their loyalty had not been repaid by Rome. By the second century BC, with Rome pursuing colonial expansion, the "Italic" communities suffered egregiously from their lack of citizenship. Large numbers of local men were siphoned into the huge armies Rome required to pursue its military aims; as noncitizens, these troops were subject to "gross and flagrant discrimination" and were used as cannon fodder.[24] Meanwhile, the provinces were being invaded by another kind of Roman army, the wealthy class of *equites*, whose citizenship also gave them prerogatives to confiscate land held by the Italians. Lands were also confiscated to reward the thousands of soldiers who served in the numerous armies mustered by Roman generals. Many provincial aristocrats formed alliances with Roman senators who could offer them protection from the confiscations. It is not known whether the Paeligni were endangered by the threat of proscription; possibly, they were already under the protection of the Valerii, one of whose descendants was later to become Ovid's patron.

The locals could not pursue justice or compensation; they had no legal right even to appeal. Provincial leaders began rallying in Rome to protest and to campaign for citizenship. In response, in 95 BC the Senate passed the Lex Licinia Mucia, a draconian law that barred any noncitizen from entering Rome.[25] In 91 BC,[26] resistance against these conditions came to a boil. Local aristocracy in the Italic tribes that occupied the Adriatic side of Italy formed a coalition and undertook a campaign for independence, the Bellum Italicum. Large, strong armies were amassed by the tribal leaders—Ovid's great-grandfather, being a member of the Paelignian aristocracy, probably fought in this war and conceivably could have been one of its instigators. The Italian alliance seceded from Rome, then rapidly set about developing Italia, a state to rival that of Rome. Its capital was the fortress town of Corfinium, about eight miles north of Sulmo. The rebels renamed the town Vitellio, the Oscan form of Italia. This name appears on coins struck there, one showing eight fighters swearing an oath; presumably, they symbolize the tribes of the confederacy.[27]

The Bellum Italicum lasted, officially, for two years, ending with Rome's agreement to citizenship for all populations in the Italic territories. Among the tribes that won their citizenship was the Paeligni, and one of the local towns that was upgraded from *oppidum* (a settlement) to *municipium* (a city full of Roman citizens and their institutions) was Sulmo.[28]

"Romanization" was a standardized method of reorganizing municipal life once the Roman army had subdued local resistance and introduced Latin as the language of affairs. Shrewdly, the Romans left decision making about the new township to local leaders, who were also expected to contribute their wealth to rebuilding the city according to the standard Roman plan. If the existing tribal township was judged unsuitable for development as a *municipium*, a whole new town would be laid out alongside it, permitting the installation of essential features. These were, chiefly, a grid of streets that provided the necessary conditions for creating a water supply and the proper distribution of public buildings: forum, basilica for the courts of law, baths, theater, amphitheater. Men such as Ovid's grandfather and his cohort, as the largest landowners in the region, would have been in charge and would therefore have had to become fully conversant in Latin. Just as Ovid's great-grandfather and grandfather had been of age to fight in the Bellum Italicum, and presumably to win substantial benefits by their involvement, so Ovid's grandfather and his father were of age to participate in the Civil Wars that began forty years later, in 49 BC, when Julius Caesar took his legions across the Rubicon and headed for Paelignian territory.

Ovid's father, at around age thirty-six in 49 BC, when Mark Antony entered Sulmo in Caesar's name, was more than likely one of the men in arms that day, and laying down those arms in welcome to Caesar later paid off when a grateful Octavian, the adopted son of

Julius Caesar, rewarded the Ovidius family with equestrian status in gratitude for their loyalty.

Participation in two great wars and the acquisition of Roman citizenship were the most significant legacies of Ovid's family to the poet's own later fortunes. His grandfather's generation and his father's generation had both come to manhood under ideal historical circumstances for changing social class. Because they were local aristocrats, and because they were warriors, they reaped rich rewards from Caesar's success and then from Octavian's policy of widening membership in the Senate to include highborn men from Italian municipalities.[29] Ovid recalled those glorious moments in the history of his family and his *patria* at the end of his first book of poems, *Amores* (*Loves*).

> . . . I shall become the pride
> of my fellow Paelignians—a race who fought for freedom,
>   freedom with honor, in the Italian wars
> that scared Rome witless. I can see some visitor to Sulmona
>   taking in its tiny scale, the streams and walls,
> and saying, "Any township, however small, that could breed so
>   splendid a poet, I call great."

(Amores 3.15.8–14)[30]

Not a trace of the township Ovid celebrated remains in present-day Sulmo, except, possibly, a few Roman walls a few miles out of town that the local citizens refer to as the Villa Ovidio.[31] As the setting for Ovid's childhood, then, we have to imagine a thriving provincial Roman *municipium*—a town built to the standard Roman plan and organized by Roman institutions of governance—in which the villa of this highborn family was a notable feature. "Highborn" is a relative term in social life, though. It appears that Ovid's ancestors were citizen-farmers, in the Roman manner, which is to say, stewards of a property on which they worked alongside their slaves, all common laborers together.[32] Ovid mentions vineyards and orchards and gardens.[33] These fields would have produced vegetables for the table, and staples such as wheat, olives, and wine grapes. The chickens and sheep and goats and pigs were preferred for sacrifices in the home.³⁴ A portion of the animal sacrifice would be offered to the gods at the domestic altar on festival occasions, and the remainder would be consumed at a banquet in the *domus*, the family home.

Since the Paeligni were known as able horsemen, Ovid's family very likely bred horses as well; in Rome, Ovid enjoyed going to horse races, and he frequently used metaphors about riding. Ovid's family probably didn't own herds of cattle, since cattlemen raised their herds for profit, without owning the lands they grazed. Citizen landowners such as Ovid's father considered themselves not laborers but cultivated men who depended on their lands for their own use. Other aspects of the cultivated life that rural Roman citizens pursued included the establishment of a home; attention to maintaining a healthy body and an educated mind; and, somewhat surprisingly, "the art of cookery."³⁵

Ovid's father's Paelignian estate supported just such a life, and in the warm months it was idyllic, if we can believe Ovid's description in a verse love letter printed in the *Amores*:

> I am here in Sulmona, my own Paelignian riding,
> a small place, but lush with streams:
> though the ground parch and crack under a blazing summer
> sun, though the Dog Star glares
> like brass, clear rills still wander through these fertile meadows,
> the grass remains fresh and green.
> Wheat yields well in this soil, the vine still better; in places
> you can glimpse an olive grove,
> and along the slow river-bank, by knee-deep pastures,
> the turf grows rank and moist.
>
> (*Amores* 2.16.1–10)

But the most interesting imprint of Ovid's provincial upbringing is not nostalgic. It can be found in the pages of his great epic poem, *Metamorphoses*. That world is full of forests, and of animals whose lives are intimately understood by the poet; they have been in his world from boyhood. Some of them are dangerous. (Wild boars, bears, and wolves are still found in the forests of the Abruzzi.) The Paelignian landowners would hunt in those forests with nets and spears,[36] in the same way that, in the *Metamorphoses*, the mythic prince Actaeon hunts game on the slopes of the unnamed mountain where he meets a dreadful fate at the hands of the goddess Diana. Ovid also writes, in the *Metamorphoses*, of a chilly spring called Hippocrene on Mount Helicon, to which the militant goddess Minerva retreats after leaving the sickening carnage of a battle. He describes a fenced orchard passionately tended by the nymph Pomona. Ovid's narrator bathes the mythic landscapes in the warmth of familiarity. We can hear this warmth in the playful voice of the narrator describing the way Jove oversaw the restoration of Arcadia after a catastrophic fire came close to destroying heaven and earth:

> Then the Almighty Father conducted a tour of inspection
> around the walls of the sky, in case the great fire's impact
> had caused them to weaken and crumble down. When he saw
>   they were still
> as strong and stable as ever, he turned his attention to earth
> and the works of mankind. Arcadia, where he was born,
>   engaged
> his particular care. He revived the fountains and rivers
>   which still
> were reluctant to flow, put grass on the soil and leaves on
>   the trees,
> and ordered the blackened forests to burst once more into green.
> As he busily came and went, an Arcadian virgin suddenly
> caught his fancy . . .

> (*Metamorphoses* 2.401–10)

The image of Jove as an ad hoc farmer would have amused Ovid's contemporary readers, since spending weekends and hot weather in a country villa enabled prosperous city-dwelling Romans to retain a sense of maintaining a living connection to their idealized past. The centuries that separated the Roman Empire under Augustus from the wellsprings of myth had not changed the countryside very much—or so Romans liked to think. For Ovid's family, this connection was ongoing, and quite real.

FATHER AND MOTHER

Partly as a consequence of growing up in the provincial setting of
Sulmo, Ovid probably spent a good deal of time in the company of
his parents. A Roman father was expected to take an active role in
shaping a son, particularly in helping the young boy acquire the
kinds of self-control that Romans associated with rectitude. The few
but pointed remarks Ovid makes about his father in his poetry indicate that an old-fashioned ethos was preserved in the family governed by the senior Ovidius Naso. "My father's plain middle-class,
/ and there aren't any squads of ploughmen to deal with *my* broad
acres— / my parents are both pretty thrifty, and need to be," he
wrote in one of his early poems (*Amores* 1.3.8–10). Ovid's father
was, of course, a soldier-farmer. In addition to book learning, he
would have encouraged horsemanship and the skills necessary to
managing large estates. Ovid's poetry suggests that he, the poet, was
a skilled horseman, and, as we have seen, he also took pride in his
knowledge of cultivating the land.

Much instruction is also conveyed *unconsciously* by parents.
Rank is communicated, and judgments are handed down. Yet parents are also subject to violent passions and furtive urges; punishment is administered, sometimes unfairly. Children absorb, and cope
with, these aspects of their parents' behavior without necessarily
understanding them. And they must not question the authority that
looms over them from on high.

Ovid's epic poem is a repository of complex family relationships
among the gods, many of which are set forth with great psychological insight. Notably, it contains a small population of interesting fathers. Two in particular stand out when we are trying to think
about Ovid's biography because each departs from a well-estab-
lished Roman code of fatherly conduct. One occurs in the tale of
Phaethon (Book 2), reputedly the son of Apollo, the sun god. The
boy approaches the god with a question about his origins: Is Apollo
really his father? Apollo, to prove his authentic claim to paternity
of this tender boy, brashly promises Phaethon that he will grant
any request. Being a god, Apollo cannot revoke a promise, and so
Phaethon gets his wish to drive the chariot of the sun across the sky

for one day. Phaethon comes close to destroying the whole heaven and earth before he crashes and burns.

Another parent is the river god Peneus, father of the nymph Daphne (Book 1), a young beauty who loves to roam the woods capturing animals. She has just become of marriageable age; for a Roman girl, that would be about twelve years old. Her father reminds her that she owes him a son-in-law and that she owes him a grandson. Daphne hates the prospect of marriage, but rather than resist openly, she offers a shrewd argument. The goddess Diana's father—Jove—has permitted his daughter to remain a virgin; can't Peneus—who is after all a god himself—regard this as a precedent and grant her the same privilege? If Peneus were a strict Roman father, he would not have been susceptible to this flattering comparison. Unwisely, Peneus grants Daphne's wish and lets her continue to roam the woods as unhampered as though she were a mere girl, not a desirable young woman. She crosses the path of the young god Apollo, who, instantly smitten, chases her down. Daphne throws up her arms and appeals to Peneus to take away her body, and she is turned into a laurel tree.

In both of these stories, parents and children are shown to be foolish. Apollo desires to taste the simple pleasure of a status denied to the gods; thus, as Phaethon approaches the throne, Apollo removes the dazzling diadem that signifies his divine status. He wants to embrace Phaethon as a mere father may embrace his son. Peneus is also blameworthy in permitting himself to be made a coconspirator in his daughter's unsuitable desire. The children are shown to be foolish too, but merely because they are adolescents; in asking to be exceptional, each is undergoing a failed metamorphosis into an adult. Phaethon is obsessed with the adolescent fantasy that his parentage is other and better than the world believes, and he seduces Apollo into proving he is right. Daphne clings anxiously to the vanishing freedom of girlhood while puberty overtakes her body.

Observing these specific fathers and their children in Ovid's poetry does not give us anything so welcome as insight into the workings of Ovid's family, of course. Rather, it conveys to us something unusual about Ovid's imagination—unusual in the art of Ovid's time, that is. Ovid was interested in the psychology of fathers.

In each of these stories, the father is made vulnerable by the fact that, since he can choose to do anything, he can choose to do the wrong thing. Each of these all-powerful fathers destroys a child as an unintended consequence of an impulsive decision, and suffers spectacularly.

> What of [Phaethon's] father? Wretchedly stricken and sick
>   with grief,
> he had covered his face with his robe. If we can believe what
>   is said,
> the Sun went into eclipse for a day . . .
> Phaethon's father, unkempt in his mourning, had lost
> his accustomed splendour, as though there had been a solar
>   eclipse.
> Detesting the daylight and so himself, he surrendered his spirit
> to grief. He was angry into the bargain, and therefore refused
> to work for the world any longer.
>
> (*Metamorphoses* 2.329–31, 381–5)

Apollo's indulgence is in conflict with his duties, and the other Olympian gods have to engage in a delicate negotiation to bring Apollo back to his duties as sun god.

For Peneus, Ovid chooses a different method of expressing such grief: He displaces it into a metaphor. The lines following the description of how Daphne became a tree return to Peneus—not in his character as Daphne's father, but in the form of a torrential river speeding toward a precipice.

> Thessaly boasts a ravine called Tempe, enclosed on each side
> by a rock face covered with trees; and down it the river Peneus
> pours and rolls on his foaming way from the foot of Mount
>   Pindus.
> Powerfully tumbling, the cataract leaps into clouds of a
>   wandering,
> wispy vapor; the spray sprinkles the trees on the clifftops
> like showers of rain; and a constant roar is returned from
>   the distance.

This is the dwelling, the mansion, the innermost shrine of
    the mighty
river-god . . .

(*Metamorphoses* 1.568–75)

Peneus as a deafening waterfall casting its mist high as the tops of
trees: This is an image of irrepressible emotion erupting from its
inmost source. The daring metaphor communicates a depth of feeling that cannot successfully be represented in actions such as the
covering of the face.

Ovid's references to his own father suggest he was the next best
thing to immortal: He lived to the ripe old age of ninety. He was
probably already in his late forties by the time Ovid was born and
his authority in the household was unquestionable. In Roman law,
he held absolute power over every member of the family, the *patria
potestas*; he even had the right to kill or order the deaths of those
who were related to him, or were his property. Though the absolute power was rarely exercised, it remained alive in the culture of
Romans as a valuable symbolic legacy from the ancient past.[37] Striking exhibition of this power occurred when an infant was — or was
not — ceremonially lifted off the ground and held in its father's arms
on the day of its birth.

Usually, however, a very young child had little contact with
its father. It wasn't until a child lost its baby teeth, at around age
seven, that it would be turned over to men to be educated. Prosperous Romans normally delegated that responsibility to a peda-
gogue who lived with the family — often a literate slave, preferably
Greek. Ovid's father saw to it that the education taking place under
his roof was of a high standard. That he was also actively involved in
his children's education and spent time hearing their lessons is suggested in a joke Ovid tells in one of his poems. His father had chas-
tised him for playing around writing verses when he should have
been studying. Ovid begs forgiveness and promises never to write
another verse — in a line of verse. He just couldn't help it. However,
his gift was one that Roman society held in low esteem; it was not
to be encouraged in a boy destined to occupy a seat in the Senate.

For the first seven years of life, however, children were educated
by their mothers and nurses. Ovid's brother would have moved

on to being tutored by men a year before Publius did, leaving the younger boy alone with his mother for an important year in his development. No references to his mother appear in Ovid's work, aside from a remark that she died after his father's death. But a few things about her can be assumed with confidence. First, she was younger than her husband, very likely by a whole generation, probably no older than twenty and perhaps as young as eighteen when she married; though women were eligible as soon as they began menstruating, they did not normally marry until their late teens. She was probably not the father's first wife, and perhaps Ovid had half siblings, sisters born to an earlier mother, whom he does not mention. His own mother probably bore only two male children who survived: Ovid and his brother. Ovid's mother would not have lived a life of luxury in Sulmo. She would have been responsible for managing the household. If she brought a large dowry into the family, she might also have occupied herself with business interests. One of her most important roles was overseeing the early education of her children. She would have guided them in correct usage of Latin and Greek while they learned to talk (all wellborn Roman children were bilingual), and she would have introduced them to reading, writing, and arithmetic at elementary levels.

Just as important was her role in shaping their sense of what it meant to be a freeborn Roman. In the early years of a child's life, the inculcation of Roman values was likely to have been accomplished via stories with moralizing messages in them. Such storytelling could have become a painless accompaniment to one task that almost all Roman women performed: spinning and weaving. Women were responsible for manufacturing all the clothing, draperies, and linens in the household.

Roman girls learned these complex skills while they were young and practiced them all their lives; demonstrating proficiency was an aspect of a young woman's bridal ceremony. The night before her wedding, the bride dressed ceremonially in a tunic and a yellow hairnet she had woven herself on a special loom; the next day, after the marriage ritual, a member of the bride's entourage would carry her spindle and distaff to her husband's home, indicating that this was now the setting of her life and work.[38] Roman poetry suggests that popular courtesans replaced their incomes by spinning and weaving when they began to age and were no longer supported by young men — working the distaff provided one of the few other occupations by which a woman could earn a living. It was also one of the occupations that caused their deaths. Women often used spittle to moisten the thread, inhaling small fibers and lint that could eventually produce pulmonary diseases.

Spinning and weaving was work that women sometimes performed collectively. Ovid has given us a lively picture of their activities in *Metamorphoses* Book 4, where the daughters of Minyas decide to sit at home with their work while the rest of the women in the community take part in violent rituals honoring Bacchus.

> Only the daughters of Minyas
> stayed indoors and marred the feast with their untoward
>   housecraft,
> drawing the wool into thread and twisting the strands with
>   their thumbs,
> or moving close to the loom and keeping their servants
>   occupied.
> One of the daughters, while deftly spinning, advanced a
>   suggestion:
> "While others are idle and fondly observing their so-called
>   festival,
> we are detained by Minerva, who better deserves our attention.
> But why don't we also relieve the toil of our hands by telling
> stories of different kinds and take it in turns to speak,
> while the rest of us quietly listen? The time will go by
>   more quickly."

> (*Metamorphoses* 4.32–41)

The storytelling of these sisters occupies many pages, and Ovid has shrewdly represented the plots and themes as those most beguiling to women: romances. The tale of Pyramus and Thisbe is followed by the tale of how Leucothoe and Clytie both fell helplessly in love with the sun god, Apollo, and how he rewarded their infatuation. The next storyteller offers the well-known account of how the cuckolded Vulcan entrapped the adulterous lovers, Venus and

Mars, with a cunning golden net. Finally, there comes the tale of the nymph Salmacis, who, maddened by passion for a beautiful boy, was changed into a part of his body, creating a being who "couldn't be fairly / described as male or as female . . . neither and both" (4.378–9) — a hermaphrodite.

We *overhear* these stories, seated as we are by the narrator amidst the storytellers at their looms; we are permitted to watch each deciding aloud which tale to tell. And we also witness the way the storyteller sets up her audience and how the audience responds. To the tale of Mars, Venus, and Vulcan, they behave rather like enthusiastic members of a book club, as if the gods were actual people:

> [The sister's] wonderful tale had entranced her audience.
> Some said, "It couldn't have happened"; but others declared,
>   "Real gods
> Can do anything!"

> (*Metamorphoses* 4.271–3)

At some time in his life, Ovid must have listened to women talking to each other in the absence of men. Was it in childhood that Ovid's imagination was captivated by what went on among women sitting together over their spindles and their looms? Ovid's poetry is unique in ancient literature in its representation of the social world that women created for themselves within the household, a world largely concealed from the attention of men. Women of all ages and kinds enrich the world of Ovid's work by broadening its emotional and social reach to include women interacting with women. If an unwelcome man should arrive on the scene, interrupting the women, this world would immediately fold itself up and away out of sight. A male child of under seven years, however, might have been a tolerated exception.

Quite often, the protagonists of these stories are competitive women, none more so than the character of the goddess Minerva, patroness of all crafts, but especially of weaving, which might be an argument for the influence of Ovid's mother on the development of his art.

Also, Ovid's birthday, March 20, fell on the second day of

Quinquatrus, the major Roman holiday dedicated to the goddess. Ovid uses the name Minerva and her epithet Pallas interchangeably in his poetry. By the first century BC in Roman culture, the identity of Minerva had been merged with the identity of a Greek counterpart, Pallas Athena, on the basis of her intellectual skill at making war—as distinguished from the mindless aggression represented by Ares, who was called Mars by the Romans.

Ovid's commentary on Quinquatrus in the *Fasti*, his poem about ancient Roman religious holidays, doesn't mention that his own birthday fell on the day after the birthday of Minerva. No: In the *Fasti*, he ducks under her mantle, in an undisguisedly personal argument that his own work belongs to the category of handicraft along with that of weavers, cobblers, carpenters, and other artful makers of useful objects:

> The first day lacks blood, no sword-fights are lawful.
>   The cause: Minerva was born on this day . . .
> Now make your prayers to Pallas, boys and gentle girls:
>   skill depends on placating Pallas well.
> After placating Pallas let the girls learn
>   to card wool and unload the full distaffs.
> Pallas, too, teaches how to shuttle the standing warp
>   and to pack the straggling work with combs.
> Worship her, cleaners of stained and damaged garments,
>   worship her, workers of the bronze dye-vats.
> No one will make good sandals against Pallas' wish,
>   though he outrank Tychius [the maker of Ajax's shield]
>   in skill.
> Even if a craftsman surpass ancient Epeus [builder of the
>   Trojan Horse],
>   the anger of Pallas will maim him.
> You, too, who remove sickness with Phoebus' art,
>   reserve the goddess a few of your fees.
> And teachers, a class often cheated of your pay,
>   no rebuff (she attracts new pupils),
> nor from you engravers and encaustic painters
>   and sensualist masters of stone.

Hers are a thousand tasks: she must be goddess of song.
If I'm worthy, may she be my work's friend.

(Fasti 3.811–12, 815–34)[39]

Pallas Athena/Minerva and Apollo are patrons of the art of poetry. Their instruments, the bow, the lyre, the loom—all three require the management of strings or threads. Ovid was an avid pursuer of etymologies and may well have known these subtle underground connections in the Greek language: "The word [lyre] itself probably derives from the Indo-European word *kerkolyra*, which in turn originates from the verb *krekein*, to pass a shuttle across threads."[40] In addition, the Latin word for a loom's sley (*pecten*) is also the word used for the plectrum, the lyre's plucking device.[41]

There is nothing stereotypically maternal in the symbolism of Minerva/Pallas that appears in the *Fasti*. In the *Tristia*, however, we find an image of Minerva that *is* maternal. Crossing the Gulf of Corinth in a ship called *Minerva*, heading toward Thrace on his way to exile, Ovid personifies the ship *Minerva* and makes of her an indomitable and comforting protector:

I have (may I always keep!) blonde Minerva's protection:
    my vessel
  bears her painted casque, borrows her name.
Under sail she runs well with the slightest breeze; her
    rowers
  speed her along when there's need for oars.
Not content with outstripping any companion vessel
  she'll somehow contrive to overhaul any craft
that's set out before her: no storms will spring her timbers,
  she'll ride tall waves like a flat calm;
first met at Cenchreae, harbor of Corinth; since then
  the faithful guide and companion of my flight,
kept safe by the power of Pallas though countless hazards,
  across endless gale-swept seas. Safe still—
I pray!—may she thread vast Pontus's entrance-channel
  and enter the waters of the Getic shore.

(Tristia 1.10.1–14)

The imprint of the mother in Ovid's poetry has been displaced into his representations of Minerva; in the *Metamorphoses*, she is a character with a complex psychology, one that references the mother in striking ways.

The emergence of Minerva as an important character in the epic occurs midway through *Metamorphoses* Book 5. In the preceding pages, Pallas has been a silent observer of her brother Perseus as he wreaks bloody havoc at his own wedding with Andromeda and amuses himself by turning the guests to stone by baring the head of Medusa to their helpless eyes.

> Minerva supported her brother, born in the shower of gold,
> throughout these trials. But now . . .
> she made for Thebes and the mountain of Helicon, home of
>   the Muses.
> Here she landed and spoke to the sisters who govern the arts:
> "A rumour has come to my ears of a fountain that started
>   to gush
> when the earth was struck by the hoof of the winged horse
>   sprung from Medusa.
> Hence my arrival. I wanted to see this amazing spring,
> as I witnessed the horse's birth from the blood of his Gorgon
>   mother."
> Urania answered: "Whatever your reason for coming to
>   visit us
> here in our home, kind goddess, we feel great pleasure.
> The story you heard is correct: the winged horse Pegasus
>   started
> our spring"; and she took Minerva down to the sacred fountain.
> Slowly admiring the waters which Pegasus' hoof had created,
> the goddess surveyed the clusters of grand, primeval trees,
> mysterious caves and grass bejewelled with myriads of flowers.
> She declared that Memory's daughters were truly blessed in
>   their dwelling
> as well as the arts they ruled. Then one of the sisters
>   addressed her:
> "Minerva, goddess who fitly could join our musical
>   company,

had not your own fine qualities marked you out for yet greater
tasks, your praise of our arts and our home is truly
        deserved."

(*Metamorphoses* 5.250–1, 254–71)

This Muse goes on to tell how the artfulness of her sisters has
recently defeated the strategies of Pyreneus, a violent rapist. After
listening to the account of their victory, the militant auditor wants
more! The goddess asks about birds she hears calling in human
voices from the trees.[42] Clearly, her attention has been captured, and
another narrative—a poetic battle story—is forthcoming. The Muse
interrupts herself to ask Minerva slyly whether she is bored.

> "But perhaps you haven't
> the time or the leisure to lend an ear to our own performance."
> "I've plenty of time," Minerva replied, as she took her seat
> In the shade of the forest. "Now sing me your song from
>   beginning to end."

(*Metamorphoses* 5.333–6)

So indeed does Pallas stay seated for the rest of this long book of
the epic, hearing time and again how female artfulness has overcome myriad challenges to female interests; and the longest story of
all is a mother story, the tale of how the goddess Ceres rescued her
daughter Persephone from the king of Hades (5.341–71).

Why is this normally impatient goddess so susceptible to the
influence of her surroundings? Maybe because the Muses—who
are given the epithet "daughters of Memory" by Ovid—were all
fathered by Jupiter, as was Minerva. But according to the tradition,
Pallas herself knew no mother. She had been conceived by Jupiter
with the goddess Metis ("intelligence"). But Jupiter, having received
a warning that his next offspring would be a son who overthrew
him, swallowed Metis so that her pregnancy could not come to term.
In the fullness of time, however, Jupiter experienced a great head-
ache; his head was split open and out sprang Minerva, fully grown
and armed. And though she could claim no mothering, she had
received a great endowment of intelligence.

It is one of the beautiful ironies of the *Metamorphoses* that at this point in the epic Minerva becomes the recipient of tales told by daughters who are her sisters by paternal lineage but in no other way; and that through these sisters is transmitted a female world Pallas does not share; and that the makers of these grand poems are those great patronesses of the arts, the Muses themselves.

When Pallas finally leaves Helicon, at the beginning of Book 6, Ovid makes the lingering effects of the storytelling she has heard the substance of his transition:

> Minerva, who'd lent an attentive ear to the Muses' narration,
> commended their song and their justified anger against
>   the Pierides.
> Then she said to herself: "Is praising enough? I also
> need to be praised in turn. No mortal shall scoff at my power
> unpunished." She therefore considered how best to dispose of
>   a Lydian
> girl, called Arachne, who claimed (so she'd heard) to equal
>   herself
> in working with wool.

> (*Metamorphoses* 6.1–7)

Thus opens one of the great stories about art making in Western literature: the challenge of a goddess by a mortal artisan.

Arachne is a young, unmarried woman from the working class. Her father is a dyer of wool; her mother is dead. Arachne was born into a family of *plebs* or plebeians (6.10), the Roman name for the class of citizens without political rights: Romans who can't vote or hold office. By this anachronism, Ovid breaks Arachne out of the frame of mythic time and places her in his own. For Arachne's is not merely a suspenseful and cautionary tale about the need for respecting the gods;[43] it is about the standards by which art is evaluated, and it is a story—like Ovid's own—about how a talented young person from the provinces, an "outsider," trumped a socially disadvantaged class position through artistic mastery. Arachne, too, lives for her art and is ambitious to make a name for herself by her talent as a weaver. Indeed, so great is her skill that even the nymphs—who are demigods—come from field and river just to watch her:

The nymphs used often to leave their haunts, Mount
       Timolus's vines
or the banks of the river Pactolus, to gaze on Arachne's
       amazing
artistry, equally eager to watch her handwork in progress
(her skill was so graceful) as much as to look at the finished
       article.
Perhaps she was forming the first round clumps from the
       wool in its crude state,
shaping the stuff in her fingers and steadily teasing the
       cloud-like
fleece into long soft threads. She might have been deftly
       applying
her thumb to the polished spindle. Or else they would watch
       her embroider
a picture. Whatever she did, you would know Minerva had
       taught her.

(Metamorphoses 6.15–23)

Pallas has learned that Arachne not only denies owing her skill to anyone, including the goddess, but also boasts that she would gladly enter a competition with the goddess, if the challenge would be accepted. So Pallas decides to test Arachne. Disguised as a feeble old woman, she cleverly scolds Arachne both for disrespecting old age and for impiety toward the goddess. Her taunts tease out Arachne's specific vulnerabilities: as a young woman who has no mother; as an unmarried woman in a world where childbearing is a woman's most significant obligation; and as an artist from a small town in the provinces. The defiant girl should know her place (as a woman) and give credit where it is due. But Arachne sneers, "You can give your advice to what daughters you have / or the wives of your sons" (6.39–40). Once the competition is under way, the two contestants are represented as equals. The narrator describes, at some length, the way that identical looms are set up and furnished with materials identical in delicacy and coloration. When he tells us in great detail about the pictures they make, we find that they are equal in mastery, though very different in formal characteristics.

Minerva weaves the story of how she won a competition with Neptune and became the patroness of Athens, in a contest witnessed by all the other Olympian gods. She is a formalist whose imagery reflects the hierarchies of power among the deities. In the background Jove stands in the middle of the grouping, with the other Olympians ranged to left and right. In the foreground stand the protagonists: Neptune on the left is balanced by Pallas on the right. He cleaves a rock with his trident, and seawater gushes forth. She strikes the ground with her spear, and an olive tree springs up, in the very center of the picture: the cause of her victory, mirrored in the amazed expressions on the faces of the gods. In each corner of the tapestry is a small depiction of mortals who have come to grief through transgression against the gods. The whole design is framed in olive branches.

Arachne's design is based on an opposite aesthetic and an opposite point of view, with forms swirling into and around each other, though each is cleanly shaped. Taken together, they convey a clear enough theme: the sexual transgressions of gods against mortals and against one another.

> Arachne's picture presented Europe seduced by Jove
> in the guise of a bull; the bull and the girl were convincingly real.
> The girl appeared to be looking back to the shore behind her,
> calling out to her friends she was leaving, afraid of the surging
> waves which threatened to touch her and nervously lifting
>   her feet.
> Asterie also was shown, in the grip of a struggling eagle;
> Leda, meekly reclining under the wings of the swan.
> And there was Jove once again, but now in the form of a satyr,
> taking lovely Antiope, sowing the seeds of her twins . . .
> All these scenes were given authentic settings, the persons
> their natural likenesses.

(*Metamorphoses* 6.103–11, 121–2)

Jove, Neptune, Apollo, Bacchus, and Saturn are all depicted as deceiving seducers, of goddesses as well as mortal women. Arachne's imagery is meant as a confident chastisement of these male deities, yet the whole tapestry is bounded by a garland of twined flowers and ivy, its energetically fierce movement framed by a reminder that this is only a work of art.

Pallas looks at the splendid work of Arachne and flies into a rage. First she destroys the tapestry. Then she begins beating the artist with her shuttle. Arachne, "too proud to endure it" (6.134), attempts suicide. But Pallas prevents Arachne's death—she shrinks Arachne's head into a tiny ball and swells her abdomen, rimming it with legs. The genius-endowed mortal artist has become an instinct-driven arachnid, from which mortals instinctively withdraw with disgust.

The goddess, then, has proved that she is more powerful than Arachne. But she does not win the contest: "Not Pallas, not even the goddess of Envy could criticize weaving / like that" (6.129–30). It is irresistible to see in this story a defense of the mortal artist—indeed, an artist such as Ovid himself. Notably, several of the episodes depicted in Arachne's tapestry have been subjects in Ovid's epic up to that point, which makes it possible to compare versions and to see that Arachne's highly artful depictions are expressions of an explicitly female outrage.

Pallas breaks the rule of the contest. Her rage at Arachne is impulsive and exorbitant rather than merely punitive. It arises from wounded pride and is not at all dignified. Why? Is it because she, being female herself, recognizes the justice in Arachne's outrage against the masculine gods, among whom Pallas stands as a kind of ambiguous exception? Is it because she, being motherless herself and knowing that Arachne is too, hoped to win Arachne over to accepting a daughter's position toward her?

Arachne, too, is at fault. Arachne claims she has had no instruction, but this cannot be true, for she has grown up in a community of dyers who work in a most precious commodity, extracting (from murex shells) the purple dye used to signify social rank in Rome. This is a highly specialized craft, of which her father is a practitioner; she cannot have grown up in this environment without learning the required skills. And though Arachne's mother is dead, somebody must have begun inducting Arachne into the female activity of weaving at an early age.

How can this story be an outlet in Ovid's work—possibly, probably, an unconscious outlet—for Ovid's relationship with his mother? No one will ever know anything at all about Ovid's relationship to his mother, except through observing closely the way he treats a complex of representations in his art. That complex includes, first, major stories in which the principal characters are motherless; second, major stories in which the social world is almost entirely female; and third, the presence of female artists in his work. Aside from the Muses, all the female artists in the *Metamorphoses* are weavers, and in all the stories that significantly figure weaving, the weavers are competitive storytellers.

The most brutally violent tale in the entire *Metamorphoses* is the story of Tereus, Procne, and Philomela (Book 6). King Tereus of Thrace is the husband of Procne, daughter of Pandion, the king of Athens; Procne has borne Tereus a son, Itys. But on a visit to the court of Pandion, five years after his marriage to Procne, Tereus conceives a mighty lust for Pandion's younger daughter, Philomela. He takes her back to Thrace with him, and when an occasion presents itself, he savagely rapes Philomela. She curses his treachery with all her might. To stop her voice Tereus cuts off her tongue, then rapes her again and again. He abandons her in a little hut, securely guarded, then returns to Procne with a sad story about how Philomela died on the trip to Thrace. Meanwhile, Philomela sets up a loom that is at hand in the house where she is held captive, and in purple thread she weaves into the white warp a depiction of Tereus's crime. She rolls and ties the tapestry and gives it to her one attendant, an old woman, with instructions to present it to Queen Procne. The old woman arouses no suspicion when she carries the tapestry past Philomela's guards or when she puts it directly into Procne's hands: How could an old woman be dangerous? Procne reads the tapestry and understands it. Enraged and bent on punishing Tereus, she conceals her intentions to rescue Philomela under cover of participating in a Bacchic ritual. Procne brings her sister back to the home she shares with Tereus and casts about for a cruel form of revenge. When little Itys enters her chamber, seeking to embrace her, she makes up her mind what to do. With Philomela's assistance, Procne murders her son, cuts him into pieces, and cooks him. After Tereus eats the stew, the sisters reveal their crime. But Ovid's narrator does not permit consummation of another cycle of vengeance. He calmly interrupts the action with three metamorphoses into birds. The attacking Tereus becomes a hoopoe, the fleeing Philomela becomes the swallow who nests in the eves of houses, and Procne becomes the nightingale who conceals herself in the darkness of the wood and sings only at night.[44]

In the *Metamorphoses*, then, weaving is sometimes used as a metaphor for song making and storytelling; and it is the way that female characters assume the identity of artists. Through her representation of his crime, Philomela has defeated her rapist and is now protected by Minerva, patroness of the arts.

But the narrator in the *Metamorphoses* also has an overtly unusual relationship to the character he has created, Pallas Athena or Minerva. Whenever she appears in the *Metamorphoses*, she is much more interesting than is necessary to the role she plays as an agent in the narrative. She is large, majestic, beautiful, and willful and has a penchant for inflicting unfair punishment—like all the gods. She is unlike the other gods, though, in behaving mysteriously. Why does she stand silent and nonparticipating at a wedding where her brother enacts savage slaughter? Why does she flee that place so deliberately to investigate the fountain of Helicon? What emotions trigger her decision to seat herself under a tree, attentive to the Muses' stories of motherly love and sisterly collaboration against scheming men? Later, why does she pick a fight with Arachne, over whom she has an unfair advantage, and lose her temper when she cannot win the contest she insists on? The poem does not answer such questions, but their tantalizing existence leaves us with a feeling for the enigma Pallas represents to the narrator, enigma like that felt by the grown-up child remembering a woman adored, admired, and feared. I venture to guess that the goddess embodies Ovid's relationship to his first teacher, who, while working at her loom, set him on the path of the kind of storytelling so brilliantly on display in the *Metamorphoses*, the craft of thumbing the turning threads into one endless strand.

CHAPTER 2

Ovid Becomes a Roman

They were crossing the mountains in snow. The two boys and their father rode horseback, accompanied by the boys' tutor. Ahead, a guide looked out for bandits and for wild animals that had an appetite for corpses, a legacy of the battles that had been fought over this territory. Behind, a horse-drawn baggage wagon bumped along, accompanied by four slaves on foot. The party on horseback kept to the sandy track at the side of the road, to protect their horses' feet from the metaled paving. Their father wanted no accidents to subvert his plan of settling the boys in Rome by the Feast of Liberalia, the seventeenth of March, when the nephew of their great friend and patron Marcus Valerius Messalla Corvinus would receive his toga virilis.

The Valerii were among the oldest nobility in Roman society, and in that year Messalla held the post of consul. In recognition of their long-standing association, Messalla had invited all three of the male Ovidii to be present both at the formal ceremony, in the midst of Messalla's family, and at the great feast that followed, where hundreds would gather to honor the new citizen, a boy only a few years older than Publius. There would be a religious ceremony at the family shrine at their home on the Palatine Hill and a public procession to the Forum; then a climb up the Capitoline Hill to make an offering at the Temple of Jupiter and attend the augury. These were places and ceremonies the boys had read about in their lessons on Roman history.

Publius and his brother would stay on in Rome, at a school governed by a grammaticus that Messalla had chosen for them. Their father was still ambivalent about this decision. At thirteen and twelve, the boys were young enough to worry about. Why not keep them in Sulmo for another couple of years? Let them grow up a bit more, study at home until they were ready to enter a school of rhetoric. They were getting perfectly good training under the grammaticus who lived in the family villa as their instructor, a self-assured young Greek, schooled in Athens, the finest money could buy. On the other hand, if the boys went to Rome now, they would begin to profit from the rank of eques that had been conferred on them by Octavian—no doubt on advice from Messalla. They would at least begin to associate with boys from aristocratic families and make important friendships. So their father had argued with himself.

Messalla had settled the question by arranging admission to the school where his own nephew had studied. He was a kind man, too tactful to criticize the way the Ovidii pronounced Latin, but to his ears they sounded like Oscan peasants—the Paeligni had been slow to adopt Latin, except as the language in which to conduct business. It was high time that the boys begin learning to speak like Romans. At this age their speech could still be reshaped by pressure from scoffing peers.

Reluctantly, their father had succumbed to Messalla's counsel and organized the boys' first trip to Rome: more than ninety miles, at least a week of hard traveling at this time of year. They had first ridden quickly up the valley to Corfinium, where they spent the first night of their journey with a branch of their mother's family. The boys had often been to Corfinium on such visits, because their father conducted business there; it was a seat of municipal government in the region. It had amenities not to be found in Sulmo, including a real theater, which Publius loved. It was also a necessary stage in their journey. From Corfinium they could enter the Via Valeria, which would carry them west across the Apennines. This road was named for an ancestor of Messalla and had for centuries been a main corridor connecting Rome with the Adriatic Sea.

The Greek grammaticus, who accompanied the boys, shared the family's excitement. He was traveling with them as far as Rome, with good prospects for finding a new position with an urban patrician family, and leaving the provinces for good. He had taught the boys well, his greatest contribution to their education being the library he had insisted on acquiring upon assuming his post at their villa. Along with the Greek authors always studied in the curriculum of a grammaticus, he had assembled a large library of works by contemporary poets who wrote in Latin. His enthusiasm for Roman authors *expressed a youthful optimism that Rome might eventually catch up with Greece in producing poetry of the highest caliber. The boys' father, usually so frugal, had not challenged this expensive taste but had relinquished the choices of texts to the tutor.*

One thing their father had not guessed was the role this library played in the tutor's encouragement of the younger boy's gift for writing verse. Publius's talent had been obvious to the tutor, who regarded writing poetry as an ideal medium in which to grasp the intricacies of written language. By reading the newest work in circulation along with the required textbooks, the boy had developed a startling facility for working in the signature meters of writers such as Catullus, Horace, and Vergil.

As the miles passed under the horses' bellies, their hoof-taps sounded a steady meter, the only diversion on the steep mountain road that carried the travelers through sparsely populated territory punctuated only by sentinel camps that had been strung along the Via Valeria thirty kilometers apart by the army. Along the way the family stayed with acquaintances, such as the host at Carsioli, whom Ovid would remember warmly many years later when writing the Fasti. It was only at the end of their third day on the road that they reached a real settlement, the old city of Alba Fucens, a real municipium gridded on the Roman plan, its neatly crisscrossed streets replete with temples, fora, grand houses, an amphitheater, and the most welcome of all amenities, a proper public bath. And just outside the city walls, the scenery changed. Tracts of wilderness had given way to "centuriated" allotments of land, on which many of the local citizens lived, the city walls encompassing too little space to hold the entire population. Alba, they would come to understand, was an exemplary city in this regard.

These dim footprints of Roman colonization in the Italic lands now grew thicker with every passing mile: Near the municipium of Arsoli, they were joined by the tall arches of the Aqua Marcia, the first aqueduct the boys had ever seen. A milestone told them that they were now only thirty-six miles from Rome. But not until their seventh day of travel did they complete their descent of the treacherous mountains. Descending with them was the river Anio. In deafening spate at this season of snowmelt, it roared and tumbled in its deep gorge for miles, sending spray as high as the treetops, before plunging over a high rocky lip to lose itself in a series of waterfalls, approaching the city of Tibur. Large villas with terraced orchards could be viewed at a distance, and the ancient Aqua Anio Vetus swung into view. Tibur was a fashionable resort where rich Romans gathered. That night the father and his sons slept in luxury. Here, the Via Valeria became the Via Tiburtina, which would carry them through the Porta Esquilina into the city. By picking up their pace next day, they would be in time for the toga ceremony at Messalla's mansion.

Jolting along on his horse, with the world of his childhood at his back, Publius had plenty of time for daydreaming. Unbeknownst to his father or his brother, he had sequestered in the baggage a scroll of his own work, selected with the help of his tutor, to show—maybe!—the fabled Messalla, whose many desirable attributes included a deep knowledge of literature and a reputation for making himself the patron of promising poets. Presenting his own work to this magnificent personage was audacious and might be regarded as an impertinent affront. Ovid would wait and see—he would choose his moment.

THE PATRON OF THE OVIDII

Consul Messalla belonged to the class of *gentes maiores*, who traced their lineage far back in Roman history, to the time of the kings. In Messalla's full name, Marcus Valerius Messalla Corvinus, the *praenomen* Valerius indicated his affiliation with the house of the Valerii. Altogether the true *gentes maiores* were a surprisingly small group of families—the Valerii, Aemilii, Claudii, Cornelii, Fabii, and Manlii—and they constituted an aristocracy among the patricians themselves. Romans were fixated on genealogy. Some noble families, mainly social-climbing provincial families, claimed to be descendants of gods; the Valerii more modestly named the Sabine hero Titus Tatius, who ruled over Rome with Romulus, as their great forebear.[45]

The other patricians, called *homines nobiles*, consisted of families in which some member had held a consulship. Achieving the consulship was a tremendously expensive and politically complicated undertaking for those not of noble birth, but the rewards were permanent.[46] Together, the *gentes maiores* and the *nobiles* were the ruling class in Rome, a caste referred to as *optimates*. Third in status came the *equites,* sometimes translated loosely as "knights"—a class of men sufficiently propertied to undertake the *cursus honorum,* which would prepare them for political careers. This was the case with Ovid's family, who were provincial landowners; their two sons might in due course qualify for election to the Senate. This is the reason the boys were brought to Rome at ages twelve and thirteen: to enable them to enter elections for various magistracies.

But how did Ovid's family acquire its access to this important family of Messalla? Ovid's poetry provides no answers; but the connection between the Valerii and the Ovidii may have originated under the momentum of the military conquests that were rapidly transforming Rome into an empire. Any would-be officeholder was under pressure to muster troops. The imperative of acquiring military glory in short-term campaigns forced Roman patricians to forge relationships with influential provincial landholders by becoming patrons. Ovid's family was an example: a prominent family that could muster both votes and military recruits when called upon, or levy taxes, or promote a favorable opinion locally in support of a patron's legislative initiatives in Rome.[47] Patronage could be inherited, on both sides; it seems likely that Messalla was born into his obligations toward the Paeligni, and Ovid's father into service for the Valerii. In the background, for Ovid's father, was there a debt of protection by the Valerii from confiscations of Italic lands during the proscriptions that followed the Italian War? In any case, Ovid's father would have felt obliged to consult Messalla on matters as important as the conduct of his sons' educations.

A ROMAN EDUCATION

In Rome, Ovid and his brother would study Greek and Latin poetry under a *grammaticus.* The boys' education reflected its derivation from the Greek model imported by Rome in the second century BC, and it privileged Greek sources, especially Homer and Menander.[48] The course in Latin relied heavily on translations such as the Latin *Odyssey* of Andronicus. But by Ovid's time the reading list also included *Annales,* the Latin epic based on Roman history, by Ennius; works by the comic playwrights Plautus and Terence; and more recent writings in Latin: love lyrics by Catullus, histories by Sallust, the philosophical poem *De Rerum Natura* (*On the Nature of Things*) by Lucretius, a range of writings by Cicero, Vergil's *Georgics*, and some of Horace's early odes.[49]

The teaching was conducted through recitation, in a manner most tedious and embarrassing to undergo. The master read a passage aloud, explaining the main difficulties. Then a pupil, or a number of pupils in turn, read the same passage aloud—from a text (a roll) on which there were no intervals between words. After this the detailed construe started. To "construe" the grammar in a Greek or Latin sentence in a poem meant to subject every word to scrutiny—to figure out which words modified which other words in the making of sense. It also meant determining the sonic value of each syllable within its metrical position. When a boy made a mistake, he might be punished with blows or caning.

Even the Romans found Latin grammar daunting, partly because there were so many exceptions to every rule, and so much license was granted to the poets. The point of the exercise was to teach young minds to be analytical, though as a side effect of reading poetry, students acquired an extensive knowledge of Greek and Latin mythology as well as geography, history, and cosmology. In certain schools a boy might also be offered the option of courses in astronomy, geometry, music, or even philosophy, though the Romans were dubious about philosophy.

No doubt Ovid could have been as bored as any other boy by parsing the grammar of Greek and Latin sentences. But by his own account he was wholly attuned to the workings of poetic language. It is hard to imagine a more relevant education than one in which the maddening exactness of his two native tongues was set before him like a puzzle to be solved day after day. Equally relevant was the required attention to the workings of meter, a pursuit both intellectual and auditory. As he tells us in the *Tristia*,

> but I, even in boyhood, held out for higher matters,
>   and the Muse was seducing me subtly to her work.

> (*Tristia* 4.10.19–20)

Moreover, attending instruction by the *grammaticus* provided the boys with an introduction to Roman life in all its chaotic diversity. Classes under the *grammaticus* were normally conducted in rooms on the edges of fora, or under the colonnades—separated by a mere curtain from the bustling world outside and around. In the years 31–29 BC, Rome was an overgrown, overcrowded jumble of narrow, unpaved streets, choked with buildings whose ground levels were a hodgepodge of tiny shops, bars, and eating houses, and whose projecting upper levels often nearly met above the heads of pedestrians. Pity the pedestrians! Chamber pots were freely emptied from the upper-story cubicles that served as bedrooms; garbage choked the passages. Yet despite the stench and ordure, a great deal of business was conducted in the open by barbers, prostitutes, moneylenders, food vendors, and thieves. There were no police; only the unlucky citizen ventured out after dark, when criminals controlled the streets. There were no firefighters, though fires were frequent, and once ignited they could not easily be extinguished. The poor occupied rooms in rickety multistory tenements, if they had homes at all, while the rich lived in thick-walled houses that opened onto quiet, light-filled courtyards but had no windows onto the noisy, smelly streets. Clamor was a twenty-four-hour constant, since commercial traffic was permitted access to city streets only after dark, by order of a law Julius Caesar had imposed on the city during his dictatorship as an effort to mitigate congestion. All night, wheeled vehicles trucking every kind of commodity vied for space in streets too narrow to allow them to pass each other. The one amenity Rome possessed in abundance was water, and it was freely available. Small public squares punctuated the streets of Rome, as they do today, each with its fountain where citizens without plumbing in their houses could collect what they needed or could order from water sellers.[50] The public baths accommodated even the poor, at a low cost; for the rich, there were large, beautifully appointed buildings that served as social clubs and fitness centers, available to both women and men.

One year after arriving, as we know from the *Tristia*, Ovid and his brother left the *grammaticus* and proceeded to a school of rhetoric. The *rhetor* occupied a much higher social status than the *grammaticus*, and the location of instruction reflected this higher status: The *rhetores* had actual classrooms. So illustrious were some reputations that their names have come down to us. Students of a *rhetor* spent much of their time on rigorous exercises, in preparation for giving public declamations—performances, we would call them. The *rhetores* too gave declamations, and had their fan groups. For the Roman, a recitation was fashionable entertainment. Since all educated Romans were educated by *rhetores*, they could enjoy displays of style. Even the emperor Augustus was known to attend such recitations.

Appropriately, the student of a *rhetor* was referred to as an auditor, for the *rhetor* taught mainly by example. Ovid had two favorites. He first studied with Arellius Fuscus, who reveled in extravagant effects of speech.[51] It is said by Seneca that Ovid eventually outdid his own master, Fuscus, in the skillful deployment of ingenuity. Ovid then moved on to study with Marcus Porcius Latro, whose stylistic hallmarks were self-restraint and a talent for pithy formulations: *Sententiae* was the technical term. Ovid displays this technique in an early poem of the *Amores*, where the lover is speaking to Cupid:

> Shall I give in? To resist might just bank up the furnace—
>   all right, I give in. A well-squared load lies light.
> Flourish a torch, it burns fiercer. I know, I've seen it. Stop the
>   motion, and pouf! it's out.
> Yoke-shy rebellious oxen collect more blows and curses
>   than a team that's inured to the plough.
> Your restive horse earns a wolf-curb, his mouth's all bruises;
>   a harness-broken nag scarcely feels the reins.
> It's the same with Love.
>
> (*Amores* 1.2.9–17)

Sententiae were admired ornaments in declamation; but *paraphrasis* was also admired and was characterized as "efforts 'to surpass oneself' in successive variations on a single theme."[52] There was no end to the subtlety of the rhetorician's dissection of the spoken word; *rhetores* classified "every theme and its development, every turn of thought and expression, known to man."[53]

Under the *rhetor*, students learned two types of oratory: *suasoriae* (persuasion) and *controversiae* (debate). Ovid claimed that his brother far outdistanced him in *controversiae*, the aggressive form of advocacy practiced by lawyers. It required carefully researching and working up a case, then organizing the materials into a persuasively logical argument, then delivering the argument with passionate conviction. His brother displayed this talent at an early age: "from his green years [he] had the gift of eloquence, / was born for the clash of words in a public court" (*Tristia* 4.10.17–18). Ovid much preferred *suasoriae*,[54] advice-giving declamations that were often performed as speeches in character. *Suasoriae* too required research, but it was literary research, and inventiveness, not logical coherence, that made it persuasive.

According to an expert eyewitness, Ovid became an excellent platform orator in this mode of declamation: Seneca called him *bonus declamator*. But Ovid's intention to become a poet was not swayed by such success. Evidently, Ovid used the education in rhetoric to shape his gift of linguistic fluency into a conscious instrument of poetic expression — and, far from stultifying his artistic powers, formal training enhanced them. If Ovid had not lived at a time when the art of effective speech was intensively cultivated, more for its own sake than for civic use, his best would have been less good. But he gave to rhetoric as much or more than he got: "Within a very few years it was Ovid the poet who had created a stock of erotic commonplaces (*sententiae*) on which would-be declaimers were encouraged to draw."[55]

THE ROMAN REPUBLIC BECOMES THE ROMAN EMPIRE

Remarkably, Ovid was cloistered in Roman schools during five of the most tumultuous and historically significant years of Roman history, 31 to 27 BC: the years that ended the Roman Republic and established the era of empire. To capture the significance of this period for Ovid and his brother, it is enough to follow the career of Messalla as he negotiated a dangerous shift of loyalties while Mark Antony and Octavian were each vying to become absolute ruler of Rome.

In 44 BC, a core group of *nobiles* conspired to assassinate Caesar. Messalla was twenty years old and living in Athens, completing his studies under one of the prominent philosophers. In 44–42 BC civil war was renewed, with the Caesarian faction, led by Octavian and

Antony, opposing the Republican faction, led by Caesar's assassins Cassius and Brutus. In 43 BC, the triumvirs decided to raise money for the Caesarian faction's armies by seizing the property of wealthy members of the Republican faction via proscription—loss of citizenship, seizure of property, even death. Two thousand *equites* and three hundred senators were singled out; these included the families of Messalla and of the poets Horace and Tibullus. Messalla clearly had protection in high places from the worst effect of the proscriptions, but he was no Caesarian; his aristocratic status identified him with the Republican cause, by default. By 42 BC, at age twenty-two, he had completed the military training that upper-class Romans began receiving at around age seventeen, but was untried in battle; it was high time he began acquiring military honors. Bearing one of the oldest patrician names in Rome, he was already a darling of the Republicans. Casting his lot with Brutus and Cassius, Messalla went to Macedonia, as did Horace, who became a military tribune under Brutus. Both the Republicans and the Caesarians had acquired huge armies. When the Republican legions finally engaged the Caesarians at Philippi, in October, Messalla was fighting alongside Cassius. As an aristocrat, Messalla held rank immediately under the two commanders, despite his lack of military experience. But he also participated as a man of letters. Notes Messalla recorded about serving with Cassius eventually contributed to Plutarch's account of the Civil War. These included a description of the suicide of Cassius, who deduced, incorrectly, that the Republicans under Brutus had been defeated. Antony's troops did in fact defeat the Republicans in the second battle at Philippi three weeks later. Brutus committed suicide, and the remaining Republican troops turned to Messalla as their leader.[56] But Messalla refused the role, engineered "a general capitulation to Antonius,"[57] and transferred his allegiance to the Caesarians.

Messalla and Antony were members of more or less the same class, *optimates*. And Antony was now the surest bet as a successor to Julius Caesar: first among equals in the new triumvirate Antony and Octavian had formed (with the lusterless general Marcus Aemilius Lepidus as a shaky third) to impose martial law again on Rome. Absolute power was shared equally by the triumvirate, at least in principle, but Antony commanded the biggest legions, possessed the greatest number of ships, and ruled the wealthiest provinces. Very significantly, his victory at Philippi made him the most admired military hero in all of the Roman Empire.

Throughout the years between 42 and 33 BC, Messalla retained a certain detachment from the rivalry of Antony with Octavian. The tensions between the two commanders offered Messalla opportunities for diplomatic service.[58] He apparently shuttled between Antony's home base in Alexandria and Octavian's home base in Rome, where Octavian was attempting to establish himself as the legitimate heir of Julius Caesar's authority. In 38 BC, Octavian, a borderline aristocrat, had married a woman with a rich pedigree: Livia Drusilla, who descended from a minor branch of the *gens Claudii*. Messalla, of course, had already declared his loyalty to Antony, but in 36 BC he made a separate alliance with Octavian, and he was among three patricians who joined Octavian's campaign for Sicily.

But during 33 BC, when by law the triumvirate expired, Messalla dropped Antony and transferred his loyalty entirely to Octavian, whom he assisted in attacking Antony's character. Messalla, like many—most—Romans, was revolted by Antony's affiliation with Cleopatra. Writing with the intimate knowledge of a former friend, Messalla produced at least three pamphlets in which he condemned the depraved excesses of Antony's personal life and his practices as governor of the eastern provinces.[59]

When, in September of 31 BC, Octavian achieved a military victory over Antony in a sea battle at Actium, Messalla was one of Octavian's admirals. Antony withdrew his ships from the battle and returned to Alexandria. The Senate responded by stripping Antony of his rights and privileges and allotting to Messalla the consulship that was to have been Antony's.[60]

Messalla reaped other large rewards from his bond with Octavian. Following his year as consul, Messalla was appointed governor of Syria,[61] the opulent province that had contributed greatly to the personal wealth of many an ex-consul. Messalla was next dispatched to Gaul, an important military province, where he won a significant martial victory. He declared war on Egypt in late July of 30 BC, refused Antony's offer of hand-to-hand combat, and dispatched Antony's demoralized armies. Antony committed suicide, and Cleopatra quickly followed him, dreading the fate of being paraded through Rome as Octavian's prize captive.[62] Her death ended the rule of the Ptolemies and brought Egypt entirely under Roman control. Octavian made sure there would be no dispute over succession by ordering the murder of Caesarion, Cleopatra's son by Julius Caesar; he also insured that her two children by Antony could cause no trouble. In January of 29 BC, Octavian ceremonially closed the gates of Janus, which by tradition stood open in time of war, symbolically inaugurating the Pax Romana, the Roman Peace.

Octavian was poised to acquire the dictatorship that had eluded Julius Caesar. For this, he needed the support of popular opinion. He acquired it later that year through a manipulative use of public works and spectacles, beginning with a series of "triumphs" to celebrate his victories in three wars: in Illyricum, Actium, and Egypt. Messalla's victory in Gaul entitled him to a triumph, too;[63] but it cannot have been comparable to Octavian's. Rome had never seen the likes of it, in costliness and splendor. To underscore the meaning of his victory, Octavian had commissioned an assertive monument to the Battle of Actium in the Forum: an arch with columns made of bronze from the prows of Cleopatra's ships.

On every popular front, Octavian, the victor at Actium and at Alexandria, was driving home a point: While Antony had squandered his wealth and dignity in Egypt, Octavian was dedicating his own wealth to the glorification of the gods, the beautification of Rome, and the well-being of a grateful people. Octavian, the heir of Julius Caesar in more ways than one, was renamed Augustus, the sole governor of Rome. The political impact of the ruling class was disappearing. Their former powers were replaced by ceremonial roles with spectacular costuming; during the era of the republic, freeborn Romans wore the uniform of the white toga. A new world order had begun.

OVID'S DEBUT

It was during those political transformations that Ovid appeared in the literary world. Sometime during the completion of his schooling in rhetoric, Ovid became a member of the salon of literary artists hosted by Messalla. It seems to have occurred before his sixteenth year.[64] Ovid recalled this period in his life directly in two of his poems from exile, where he reminds Messalla's son Cotta Maximus,

> From my earliest years . . .
> I honored your father; he esteemed
> my talent—you may remember—even more highly
> than in my own opinion I deserved, and would
> discourse on my verses with that rounded eloquence
> in which one element of his nobility lay.

(Tristia 4.427–32)

> Your father, whose eloquence in Latin
> was no whit inferior to his noble birth,
> first urged me to commit my verse to public judgment,
> was my talent's mentor and guide.

(Epistulae 2.3.75–8)

Messalla was one of the most admired cultural figures of his generation. He is remembered most prominently as a master of oratory in Rome.[65] Cicero, Rome's foremost orator, had written fondly to Brutus in 43 BC that Messalla possessed many qualities for preeminence in rhetoric, among them eloquence (*eloquentia*), judgment (*iudicium*), skill (*ars*), and innate talent (*ingenium*).[66] He was also a master of the written word, in several genres, and was "known to have written grammatical treatises of a specialized nature."[67] Messalla produced an influential memoir, late in life, which furnished Plutarch with much of the content of his *Life of Brutus*. He was a connoisseur of Roman and Alexandrian poetry and wrote verse in both Greek and Latin; in conjunction with that interest, he gathered around himself an array of talented poets. The star performers in this salon were Propertius and Tibullus, poets still esteemed today, plus several others whose work has barely come down to us: Lygdamus, Valgius Rufus, and Aemilius Macer. In the *Tristia* Ovid defines the importance of this salon in his own development as an artist:

> The poets of those days I cultivated and cherished:
> for me, bards were so many gods.

> Often the aging Macer would read me what he had written
>   on birds or poisonous snakes or healing herbs;
> often Propertius, by virtue of that close-binding
>   comradeship between us, would recite
> his burning verses. Ponticus, noted for epic, and Bassus,
>   pre-eminent in iambics, both belonged
> to my circle; Horace, that metrical wizard, held us
>   spellbound with songs to the lyre.
> Vergil I only saw, while greedy fate left Tibullus
>   scant time for our friendship.
>
> (*Tristia* 4.10.41–52)

It is also known that a niece of Messalla, named Sulpicia, participated in this salon; some of her poems in elegiacs were preserved in
a manuscript of Tibullus, the *Corpus Tibullianum*, and provide a rare
glimpse of verse written by a woman.[68] Sulpicia addresses a lover
named Cerinthus in a fresh voice—sometimes very passionate, at
other times a wry witness to male vanity:

> I'm pleased you're so liberal to yourself through confidence
>   in me,
>   unafraid that I may foolishly come to grief in female vanity.
> Care more for your toga, then, or some wool-basket-
>   burdened whore,
>   more than for Sulpicia, daughter of Servius!
> But some are worried on my account, who could be pained
>   by nothing more,
>   than that for a strange woman's bed I should take second
>   place.
>
> (*Corpus Tibullianum* 3.16 = *Sulpicia* 4)[69]

The surviving poems of Tibullus and Sulpicia—whom Tibullus
does not mention as author—often celebrate a birthday or some
other domestic occasion. They imply both intimacy with the Messallae and acknowledgment of their superior social status. Poetry written by this circle was an exercise of talent in the service of refined,
upper-class amusement.[70]

During the interminable dinner, Ovid selected politely from every dish he was offered, only to slip each morsel into the large napkin he had brought to the table. Romans were expected to carry food home with them after a banquet, so his napkin attracted little notice. But he hoped no one could guess what was stifling his appetite: the shuddering stage fright he felt most keenly in his stomach. When the last course had been served he would be asked to rise and entertain the august company with a few of his own verses. Would his knees buckle? Would he muff any lines? Nothing in his past experience of declamation had quite prepared him for this debut. Those were school exercises witnessed by teachers and fellow students. This was the real thing: an invited recitation at the home of his father's friend Messalla, with Messalla's circle of poets as audience. Ovid had dressed with care, in his finest clothes, but these too were a cause of anxiety. He was fifteen years old, but had not yet acquired the toga virilis; the broad purple stripes on his fine wool toga praetexta and the gold bulla hung around his neck identified him unambiguously as a boy.

He might doubt himself, but the approval of his host Messalla was not in doubt. For over a year now, Ovid had been welcome to join the select group of poets that gathered occasionally in Messalla's grand house to show their work and discuss their craft. There was always an excellent dinner, and plenty of wine—Messalla loved wine. After they had dined, one or another of the poets would set off a discussion by reciting recent work. It was courteous of the other guests to offer words of praise before settling into the learned and niggling forms of criticism they loved. They would often debate fine points of style far into the night.

Tonight it was Ovid's turn to present his work to this discriminating company of poets. He had been a member of the circle long enough to understand that his youth would not be considered an excuse for inept writing. In fact, Ovid was precociously good at forming poetic lines; he produced complex technical effects as easily as he rode a horse. No, the problem presented by this coveted invitation was coming up with a subject. The acknowledged masters in this circle, Propertius and Tibullus, were bearded youths in their twenties and had lived to the hilt. Tibullus was no soldier, but he had seen battle with Messalla—generals liked to take a semiofficial cohort of amici *and* clientes *along on their marches. While some of Tibullus's poems made polite reference to Messalla's military prowess, his typical verse spoke affectionately of life in the countryside, and of passionate love as a retreat into trustworthy consolation. Propertius, on the other hand, wrote wild and crazy erotic verse that made falling in love seem horrible, like an onset of madness. Yet his characterization of his mistress Cynthia presented Ovid with a kind of woman he had never seen in real life: sophisticated, learned, passionate, absolutely beautiful, full of devilment—and married to a high-ranking Roman.*

Ovid had never been in love, and had never been in battle. But discussions in Messalla's circle had revealed to him that poetry evolved out of poetry, not out of life. Specifically, you put into poems the kinds of life required by the poetic form. Ovid thought that what Tibullus and Propertius described in their poetry had probably happened in their lives; yet the men stretched out nearby on their dining couches bore little resemblance to the images of themselves presented in their poems. The literary form they deployed required a first-person speaker, so each of them created a stand-in for himself and selected from experience what might work best in art, then made up the rest.

This insight had given Ovid courage. That night he had a surprise for all of them, a clever poem in which the hero was a boy. It had a dramatic opening, riffing on the Aeneid *(who didn't riff on the opening of the* Aeneid *these days?):*

Arms, warfare, violence—I was winding up to produce a
    regular epic, with verse-form to match—
hexameters, naturally. But Cupid (they say) with a snicker
    lopped off one foot from each alternate line.
"Nasty young brat," I told him, "who made *you* Inspector of
    Meters?"

(Amores 1.1.1–5)

The poem made a little bow to Tibullus, whose favorite topic was the war; and it made another little bow to Propertius, who frequently referred to Cupid dismissively as "that boy." The age of "I" in the poem is not specified, but he talks like a smart-ass kid; what we hear is his cheerful taunting of that other kid, Amor, whose reply is an arrow. The speaker is shafted. Now he's ready to write:

I'm on fire now, Love owns the freehold of my heart.
so let my verse rise with six stresses, drop to five on the downbeat—
goodbye to martial epic, and epic meter too!
Come on then, my Muse, bind your blonde hair with a
wreath of
sea-myrtle, and lead me off in the six-five groove!

(*Amores* 1.1.26–30)

Elegiacs—hexameter plus pentameter—were a capacious form for use by a first-person speaker; the effect could range from uplifting lyricism to informality, even chattiness. It did not take Ovid very long to master this form.

His father was not enthusiastic about Ovid's skill in writing verse. Messalla, in offering his support to the young poet, was acting against the judgment and prerogatives of Ovid's father. Only Messalla's status as a patrician could have trumped a father's *patria potestas* in this way; but what was his motivation? Perhaps Messalla, who only dabbled in poetry himself, did not expect Ovid to devote his life to poetry and did not consider it a dangerous pastime in a public man. After all, Octavian had appointed the poetry-writing *eques* Cornelius Gallus as governor of Egypt. Or perhaps Messalla was merely arrogant in the manner of the highborn, and competitive: Recognizing Ovid's talent, Messalla wished to secure Ovid's loyalty by putting him forward at an early age, before Messalla's rival Maecenas lured the boy away. After the publication of his first book, Propertius had migrated from the salon of Messalla to that of Maecenas, at the prompting of Vergil.

THE GRAND *DOMUS*

Messalla, like all Romans, conducted the business of his life within the precincts of his *domus*. The year the boys arrived in Rome, 31 BC, Messalla moved into a mansion on the Palatine Hill that Mark Antony had previously owned.

This house had an interestingly politicized history. The Palatine Hill was the favored residential quarter of Roman aristocrats.

Located at the center of the seven hills of Rome, surrounded by marshes, the Palatine's twenty-five acres commanded spectacular views. Magnificent homes had been built by families profiting from the conquest of Asian provinces.

Octavian also lived on the Palatine, in a rather modest house formerly owned by the wealthy orator Hortensius. In 36 BC this house had been hit by a thunderbolt, indicating the will of Jove that it should become a temple site, according to the augurs.[71] Octavian decided to make his own *domus* the center of public life by incorporating it in a group of buildings that would include temples, walkways, and a grand library; its focal point would be a temple to Apollo.[72] Around the same time Octavian announced his intentions to build the temple complex, Mark Antony built a house in the same area. Apparently, Antony's appropriation of the site was yet another expression of his rivalry with Octavian, for the house was positioned atop what later became the steps to that Temple of Apollo. When the Roman Senate stripped Antony of his powers in 31 BC, they presented Antony's grand house to Messalla, to share with Marcus Vipsanius Agrippa, Octavian's most prized military commander and boyhood friend. Apparently this was a mansion large and gorgeous enough to house the extended families of two Roman grandees. When the Ovidius brothers arrived in Rome to take up their schooling, it was to this house that they probably came to pay their respects to Messalla. No description of Antony's mansion exists in literature from that period, but the boys must have been impressed, just like the young lad Phaethon in Ovid's *Metamorphoses* as he approaches the palace of the sun god, Apollo.

> Picture the Sun's royal seat, an imposing building with towering
> columns, resplendent in glittering gold and blazing bronze;
> its pediment proudly surmounted by figures in burnished ivory;
> the double doors at the entrance a sheen of shimmering silver.

> (*Metamorphoses* 2.1–4)

The story of Phaethon is based on a boy's search for his "real" father, a tale that embeds a powerful childhood and adolescent fantasy. To a reader familiar with Messalla's role in Ovid's adolescence, it will not seem unlikely that Ovid drew, in his description of Phaethon's admission to the palace of the sun, on memories, conscious or unconscious, of the way his personal relationship to Messalla was formed. Like Phaethon, Ovid was a mere boy when this occurred, not yet wearing a toga; twelve years old, he feels himself ready for the duties and glories of Roman manhood. And maybe Ovid even shared a little bit of Phaethon's desire to be acknowledged by his "real" father: not the one who looked after him in the world, but the one who looked down on him from a kind of heaven.

THE TOGA CEREMONY[73]

It was decided in a family counsel that Publius and his brother should receive their togas on the same day, in late September, 27 BC, a half year before their birthdays: Publius would be going on sixteen, and his brother would be sixteen and six months. Their rituals and feasting would take place at Messalla's mansion in Rome, rather than at the family shrine in Sulmo, and their retinue would include boys and youths they had met at school. The date was set for two days after Messalla's triumph, which all of the Ovidius household would attend. In preparation for the toga ceremony, their father removed the family Lares from their shrine in Sulmo and carried them to Messalla's domus *in Rome.*

The morning began with a simple breakfast of figs and bread, followed by a visit to the private bath that was one of the luxuries of Messalla's mansion. The household barber awaited the boys and their father in the men's quarter of the bath, to give the brothers the first trimming of their beards. But first they all bathed: in a warm pool scented with jasmine, then in the hot pool where they scraped one another with strigils. Then their straggly facial hair was snipped off, and their unkempt manes trimmed and dressed: short at the neck, ears exposed, brushed forward onto the forehead. Ovidius, who wore a beard, permitted his hair to be trimmed a little but seemed embarrassed by such intimate attention.

Fresh from the bath, the brothers went to the dressing room to don the new tunics and togas that awaited them, each piece of clothing now featuring the broad purple stripe that indicated their status as future senators. Messalla's dresser expertly arrayed the togas, arranging the folds to fall in the correct manner, to drape across the right shoulder and lie across the left arm.

Meanwhile, the other members of the two families had assembled at the shrine of the Messallae. In a solemn procession, the paterfamilias Ovidius and his sons slowly entered the room and approached the shrine. Together they chanted the ritual prayers, and together the two young men laid their boyhood togae praetextae at the feet of the Ovidius family Lares. Each brother removed from the other's neck the bulla that had protected their boyhoods, and those too became offerings to the household gods, all of which would be carried back to Sulmo by their parents.

Messalla had summoned a large array of friends and clients to the garden party that followed the family ritual. A red canopy had been spread over the garden to shield the guests from the morning sun; gorgeous dining couches had been set under the portico. A lavish spread of delicacies was laid out on small tables near the couches, and also passed by slaves, to be consumed by attendees more interested in one another than in the food. These guests included all who would become part of the invited retinue accompanying the family to the Forum, where the names of the Ovidius brothers would be inscribed in the roll of citizens. When they began assembling for the procession, Messalla's freedmen and even the household slaves joined the party, to swell the number of well-wishers and to create a public stir as the procession made its way through the streets.

Messalla led the way, followed by Ovidius and his sons, and a long jostling escort of men—women were not included in this phase of the ceremonies. Messalla was now swathed in the vivid ceremonial robes of his priesthood, the trabea, with horizontal stripes of purple and saffron. The brothers, stepping onto the Sacred Way and taking their first walk to the Forum as citizens, could hear onlookers excitedly identifying Messalla. The crowds of people passing through the Forum fell back to let them pass.

When they had walked the length of the Forum, most of the retinue disbanded, leaving only the four principals to make their way up the Capitoline Hill. They first visited the Tabularium, where the *names of Publius and his brother were entered in the list of citizens.*[74] *A short walk away was the paved* auguraculum, *where the augur stood to make his observations, which looked toward the Alban Mount and also commanded a view of the horizon. With the wand of his office, Messalla marked out a quadrant of the sky from which he would gather the auspices. The day was clear and hot: not a leaf stirring, and for a long time nary a bird. At last a small flock of crows ascended, cawing loudly, from a garden overlooked by the Capitoline. As if on cue, two crows parted from the others, wheeled once, and set off to the west. Messalla announced that the portents could not be better. Crows were birds sacred to Apollo; their cries expressed his divine approval, Messalla said. That two crows had separated from the flock reflected that the boys had flown west from their family home and would continue to be joined in the enterprises they had embarked on. They would be lucky in Rome.*

The last stage of the day was a banquet to which the circle of poets around Messalla had been invited, along with the rhetores *with whom the boys had studied. Messalla had also invited guests Publius did not recognize. Casual introductions were made over predinner drinks, but everyone knew that the occasion was important, no matter how informal the presentation of guests to each other. This was a debut sponsored by Messalla, whose invitations were highly prized.*

The group was so large that three sets of dining couches had been arranged in the banqueting room overlooking the garden. Ovid's father was given the honor of dining at Messalla's right; one of Messalla's friends—father of another family—sat at Messalla's left, and Publius's brother dined at the same table, flanked by the rhetores.

Publius had a place at the poet's table, where Propertius and Tibullus occupied the central couch. The dinner exemplified the principle of "one birthday, two cakes." Following the first course, each of the rhetores *delivered a warm declamation for the newly togated brothers. Great expectations were elaborated. Following the second course, each of the poets delivered poems they had improvised in honor of the brothers. Propertius cleverly worked in an account of the auguries, which had furnished a lively topic at the table where the poets reclined; his poem made witty use of the conversation that was still warm in the minds of the guests at the table, and Propertius was* applauded for his quick wit. Tibullus, not to be outdone, paraphrased the poem he had previously written in honor of Messalla's triumph, adapting it to the procession of the boys and their retinue to the Forum that morning. Messalla listened with emphatic attention to this parody: It skirted insult to his dignitas.

As the dinner progressed through the third course, Publius became overwhelmingly drowsy; the rounds of wine, the long day with its spasmodic excitements, had taken their toll. But he snapped awake at the end of the meal when his father rose from his seat to address the guests. Publius knew that his father's rough Latin made him shy of oratory.

But Ovidius had a message that could not be delegated. In his plain-speaking way, he said that this important occasion, for which his friend Messalla's hospitality had been so generously extended, had seemed to him a fine opportunity for the announcement of the betrothal of his sons to the daughters of the guest seated at Messalla's left hand. This decision had been taken by the elders of the two families, without consulting his sons, he explained; and he turned to them with a sober expression that they well recognized—the face that told them there were to be no second thoughts on the matter. If today they had become men, and Romans, Ovidius said, it followed that they were ready to marry. True, it was not the Roman custom to betroth at this early age, but he considered it opportune and fitting for his sons. They would pass from boyhood directly into a suitable affiliation with an important family whose Roman pedigree matched the pedigree of these new young men from the provinces, whose future—as all had proclaimed tonight—was indubitably so bright. Ovidius asked Messalla, as host, to lead forth these ladies, who had dined separately with their mothers and were now awaiting a summons.

The guests rose from their dining couches, and two richly arrayed young women stepped through the door.

CHAPTER 3

Marriage, Divorce, Vocation

The household is quiet; everyone permitted to rest at midday is taking a siesta. A very young woman rises from the couch in her sleeping chamber. She tells her maid not to accompany her as she walks barefoot to a nearby room and quietly moves the curtain aside. She pauses on the threshold, letting her eyes adjust to the dim light filtering through the shutters. She knows he has heard her approach, and she is sure he must have scented the spicy oil brushed into her hair when the maid unpinned and loosened it for the siesta. But, naked on his couch, he feigns sleep. Sexual pleasure is still new to both of them, and they compete in devising games. Today she has decided that they will act out the little drama they call "modest maiden." She unfastens a jeweled brooch at her shoulder, letting the long silk tunic slither open, baring a breast, but clutches the rest of the garment close to her body. The drooping hem of her skirt rustles over the tiles as she enters the room—his cue to rouse himself. Whispering her pet name over and over, he tries to pluck the tunic out of her grasp; she struggles playfully to elude him. At last he captures her, and with his free hand he opens the other shoulder brooch and sweeps her clothing to the floor.

CORINNA

This is an embellished reconstruction of the story told in the most famous poem of the first book of Ovid's *Amores*. The poems of the *Amores* were the earliest Ovid published, and he was very young when he began reading them in public. There is no evidence external to the poems that the character called Corinna in the *Amores* was Ovid's wife. Were the *Amores* based on the marriage arranged for Ovid at the time he received his toga? That is the tantalizing biographical question raised by several ambiguous features of this enduringly interesting book, and the most truthful answer to that question is *maybe not, but maybe so.*

The *Amores* are an example of a very popular kind of love poetry invented by the Romans—books featuring the presence of a beautiful, clever married woman who generates the poet's helpless adoration and eventually abandons him. Catullus named the heartbreaker Lesbia, evoking Sappho of Lesbos, on whose erotic poems he modeled some of his own. Tibullus wrote elegiac verse about not one but two mistresses: Delia and, after they parted, another he amazingly called Nemesis, which is the name of the goddess of vengeance in Greek myth—his Nemesis seems to be nothing but trouble. Propertius named his mistress Cynthia, one of the epithets for Diana, the goddess of the ever-changing moon.[75] In each case, the actual name and social rank of the adulteress was known to the literati. Then as now, the aspect of gossip clinging to the books promoted their popularity with the poet's contemporaries, but they have survived the centuries because of the remarkable quality of the poetry.

The name Corinna places Ovid's heroine in a neatly literary frame from the outset: It was the name of a Boeotian poet well-known in Rome as Corinna of Tanagra, a contemporary of Pindar, whose apparently archaic voice was a stylistic posture of the kind attractive to poets in Ovid's day. So Ovid's literary audience would have understood the name Corinna as code for a type of woman the Romans called *docta puella* or "learned girl": educated but still desirable. Propertius had alluded to this ancient Greek Corinna in one of his most ardent poems to his beloved Cynthia: When Cynthia takes up the lyre, "she rivals the texts of bygone Corinna" (2.3.21).[76] Probably, Ovid picked up the name of his mistress from this line, fashioning himself as a junior colleague to Propertius.

For most readers, such esoteric insider information is of secondary interest at best. Most of us read love poetry to read about love, and we assume that the poet's account of love is based, however circumspectly, on experience as rapturous and painful as any we have lived through or fantasized. We also assume that it originates in feelings for a real person. Naturally, we prick up our ears when the name of Lesbia or Cynthia or Corinna recurs in a book of

Roman love poems. The repetition functions like points on a graph; we want to connect the dots and discover a plot in which these fascinating women function as central characters. We want the love story, replete with sexual consummations.

In the Roman love elegies based on adulterous alliance, that story is always loosely the same: a bell curve of rising desire that ascends to ravishing fulfillment, then slopes into mistrust, anxiety, and an obsession that ends only with the poet's resolve to let go. The sketchy outline of just such a plot can easily be found in Ovid's *Amores*. In Book 1, the poet revels in Corinna's beauty and in the force of their desire, but he also begins teaching her to lie and cheat, strategies for eluding the eye of her husband and other guardians. The poet's voice registers these experiences as all very fresh and exciting. By the middle of Book 2, the poet begins to fear that his mistress has learned these lessons too well—that she is unfaithful. When she becomes pregnant, she wants to have an abortion; miserable, he does not know for sure whether he is the father. By Book 3 he is desperately trying to persuade himself that she may be merely teasing to keep his ardor alive. Unfaithful himself, he tries to rationalize her infidelities as an expression of their shared urbanity as Romans: "It's so provincial / to object to adulterous wives—a deplorable lack / of that *ton* for which Rome is famous" (*Amores* 3.4.37–9). All of these efforts to restore his confidence in her fail. He considers breaking off the affair but finds he cannot do so. At last he reaches a compromise position: He won't ask if she won't tell. "Lay them all," he says, "but allay my suspicions, leave me / in ignorance, let me cling / to my foolish illusions" (3.14.29–31). This solution is, of course, emotionally intolerable. The sequence ends on a note of exhaustion, with the poet bidding farewell to Venus in her role as the Muse and (interestingly) mother of his work: "Mother of tender loves, you must find another poet" (3.15.1). He resolves to take up "weightier efforts" (3.15.17) in the future of his art.

BEARDLESS YOUTH

In contrast to the love elegies of Catullus, Tibullus, and Propertius, the first-person speaker in the *Amores* is very young, just receiving

his initiation into adult life. It is thought that Ovid may have completed the *Amores* in 15 BC, around the time he was twenty-eight
years old;[77] but he began writing the poems much earlier, probably
during the days of his apprenticeship in the circle of Messalla. The
Amores have to be regarded in part as a coming-of-age story, a portrait of the artist as a young man, in which the protagonist's challenges, successes, and failures as a poet are embedded in the story of
his development into a sexual swordsman.

Sexual freedom was one of the privileges granted to the young
man who had just been launched into adult society with the acquisition of a toga. For the period of "beardless youth,"[78] while a man's
facial hair retained its light downiness and was trimmed rather than
shaved, he was expected to experience as fully as possible his new-
found freedom from childhood constraints. This expectation was
supported by the belief that adolescent males were driven by uncon-
trollable urges. The wealth and luxury of Rome presented tempta-
tions they were not expected to resist: gambling, drinking all night,
whoring, thuggery, squandering money—these were predictable
vices in youths who had barely emerged from childhood. They
often roved in packs and gangs, and they were considered to be easily swayed by glamorous reprobates. Horace exemplified the type in
his *Ars Poetica*:

The beardless youth, finally free of his guardian,
rejoices in horses and hounds and the sun-drenched grass
of the Campus Martius: he is putty in your hands to mold
to evil courses, resentful of warning advisers;
slow to provide for his needs but recklessly fast
to spend his money, enthusiastic, intense,
but quick to transfer his affections.

(Horace, *Ars Poetica* 161–7)[79]

But, gradually, the down on the youth's cheeks would thicken
into a full beard. Its first real cutting—usually when a man reached
his early twenties—might be marked by another ceremony: the
depositio barbae. Snips of hair from the full-grown beard would be
placed in an ornamental box and dedicated to the household gods
in a religious rite that was followed by feasting, to which the whole

family was invited.[80] By this time in the young man's life, all that was boyish would have melted away like baby fat, leaving a solid citizen in its place. When he reached age twenty-five, he would be expected to have married and set his aims on becoming a father, and to have settled into the role in public life suited to his birth and talents. Cicero, an authoritative register of Roman morals, put it this way: "When he has listened to the voice of pleasure and given some time to love affairs and these empty desires of youth, let him at length turn to the interests of a more domestic life, to the activities of the Forum and public life" (*Pro Caelio* 42).[81]

An adolescent in beardless youth is the principal character in the *Amores*; we watch him, like in a movie, going through the early stages of attaining manhood. The opening poems establish that the *Amores* are not just about "loves," but first love. Cupid's arrow—call it the shock of testosterone—smites the poet before any girl shows up to be a cause of his feelings. Nor does he seem to have had any experience of sex: The second poem shows him in a generalized and unfamiliar state of misery, caused by acute desire: "What's wrong with me? . . . If Love were my assailant, surely I'd know it . . . Yes, that must be it: heart skewered by shafts of desire" (*Amores* 1.2.1–7). When, in the third poem, we find him alone with a girl, she's anonymous, called merely "you"—ironic, in the context of his aspiration to make her as immortal as the goddesses that ornament his verse. But the point of this third, very comic poem is his naivete. These are early days in his development as a lover:

Say yes, pet. I'd be your slave for years, for a lifetime.
  Say yes—unswerving fidelity's my strong suit . . .
  Honestly, all I want is to look after you
till death do us part, have the two of us living together.

(*Amores* 1.3.5–6, 16–17)

We know he doesn't have a strong suit of any kind at this point in the story—but he's practicing the rhetoric of seduction, getting an act together. Then, in the fifth poem,

In stole Corinna, long hair tumbled about her
  soft white throat . . .

when at last she stood naked before me, not a stitch of
      clothing,
  I couldn't fault her body at any point.
smooth shoulders, delectable arms (I saw, I touched them),
      nipples inviting caresses, the flat
belly outlined beneath that flawless bosom,
      exquisite curve of a hip, firm youthful thighs.

                          (*Amores* 1.5.9–10, 17–22)

This detailed description of Corinna's beauty early in the first book
of *Amores* anchors the poet's developing sexuality, right away, in his
relations with a person presented to us as "real." And from this point
on, Corinna's behavior provides the curriculum of the poet's sexual
education. Corinna is an avid participant in their sexual pleasure:

In one short night, I remember, she made me perform
nine times, no less.

                          (*Amores* 3.7.26–7)

But she also graces his life as the warm companion of ordinary hours:

I love to lie in my mistress's tender
  embrace, feel her close by my side,
at this cool hour of deep sleep, with liquid bird-song
  tremulous in the air.

                          (*Amores* 1.13.5–8)

She can rage horridly with jealousy; she can be moody, unpre-
dictable. At one point she affects independence and scares him by
preparing to take a sea voyage without him—women frequently
traveled without their husbands. He implores her not to leave him:

Safer to stay in bed, read books, and practice
      fingerwork on your lute—
but if your mind's made up, if I'm wasting exhortations
      on the wind, then may all marine
deities grant you smooth sailing—I'll hold the whole lot
      of them
      responsible if you drown.

                          (*Amores* 2.11.31–6)

Later, when *he* in turn takes a journey without *her*, he mopes and sulks:

> Why must my mistress and I
> be parted so often? You swore you'd stay with me always,
>   on my life you swore it, by
> your eyes, those stars of my heart; but a girl's oath is lighter
>   than leaves in autumn, whirled
> away by wind or wave.

> (*Amores* 2.16.42–7)

Though she's "a spoilt beauty" (*Amores* 2.17.11), whose "loveliness makes her / treat me like dirt" (7–8), she is also the apparently inexhaustible inspiration of his poems:

> None but you shall be sung
> in my verses, you and you only shall give my creative
>   impulse its shape and theme.

> (*Amores* 2.17.32–4)

Nonetheless, within the couple they have formed, each begins to detect signs of infidelity in the other. Interestingly, the young poet cannot tolerate the discovery that his partner has also been undergoing an education—and, apparently, she has been using some of his poems as a textbook. We learn about this in the last book of *Amores*, where the genres of tragedy and elegy appear personified. In the course of their conversation with the poet, Elegy lets slip that it was she who taught Corinna various strategies of deceit:

> Corinna took lessons from me, how to hoodwink porters
>   or spring the most foolproof lock,
> how to slip out of bed in her nightdress and move with
>   unerring
>   feet, like a cat, through the night.

> (*Amores* 3.1.47–50)

How ironic that the poems she inspires should turn around and serve as an instruction manual. But the lover is not amused. Her deceitfulness brings extreme heartache to him.

> A fugitive from your vices, I'm lured back by your beauty:
> your morals turn me off, your body on.

(*Amores* 3.11B.5–6)

Eventually, the developmental path carries the beardless youth away from Corinna and into his destiny as a worldly—that is to say adulterous—Roman man-about-town. When he at last gives up the affair, he appears to have outgrown the girl and also the overwhelming passion that first hurled him into an amorous relationship and fueled the delusion that it would last forever. He has grown up.

THE SOLDIER OF LOVE

The *Amores* are not only about the sexual maturation of the poet, however. They also convey the poet's anxiety regarding the need to establish himself in an occupation. One unappetizing option was military service. When a freeborn youth in Rome reached age seventeen, he became eligible for the army, which he would enter as an officer. Training unofficially began in spates of rigorous exercise in the Campus Martius, a recreational field of about six hundred acres just outside the old boundary of the city in a bend of the Tiber. From Rome's earliest years it had been used for this purpose—youths showcasing their strengths and skills. In the second century BC, the Circus Flaminius had been built there for chariot racing, and in 55 BC, Pompey had built the first stone theater in Rome there. By Ovid's day the area was rapidly filling up with monuments, villas, apartment blocks, and parks, but there was still plenty of open land on which to ride horses and race chariots. During the years of his marriage, Ovid probably spent time there with other men his age, engaging in activities such as those he describes in later poetry: throwing the javelin and discus, fencing, rolling a hoop, playing ball, riding; then rinsing off sweat, oil, and dust with a cold swim in the Tiber.[82]

Adolescents built muscle during such workouts and presumably attained a certain amount of pride in watching their youthful bodies acquire the shapes of men. But most of them probably also understood these rigorous activities as preparation for the military training they would undergo in their early twenties, after they had studied public administration and law under a senior practitioner.[83] At twenty-seven, seasoned by participation in the major Roman institutions of the law court and the army, they were qualified to stand for the office of *quaestor* (overseeing finances), the preliminary office required before seeking the Senate.

In the early days of the republic, service during the summer for a short campaign was required of all young men; disinclination to fulfill such political or military obligations had become fairly widespread. But Ovid managed to avoid this duty, possibly by swapping military service for a few minor magistracies during the years when his peers were in the army. That is, when the time came, Ovid was willing to substitute boring paperwork for the rigors of an army camp in which his rank would have been fairly high. As a wearer of the "senatorial" toga, he would automatically have stepped into the role of military tribune of the legion and taken command of the auxiliary horse.

In the *Amores*, Ovid cleverly "justifies" his draft evasion by thematizing military service as analogous to the physical fitness, strategies, risks, and benefits involved with the successful pursuit of women.

> I can stand the strain. My limbs may be thin but they're wiry;
> > though I'm a lightweight, I'm hard—
> and virility feeds on sex, is boosted by practice;
> > no girl's ever complained about *my* technique.
> Often enough I've spent the whole night in pleasure, yet
> > still been
> fit as a fighting cock the next day.
>
> > > > > (*Amores* 2.10.23–8)

> Every lover's on active service, my friend, active service,
> > believe me,
> And Cupid has his headquarters in the field.
> Fighting and love-making belong to the same age-group—

In bed as in war, old men are out of place.
A commander looks to his troops for gallant conduct,
    A mistress expects no less.
Soldier and lover both keep night-long vigil,
    Lying rough outside their captain's (or lady's) door.
The military life brings long route-marches—but just let his
      mistress
    Be somewhere ahead, and the lover too
Will trudge on forever, scale mountains, ford swollen rivers,
    Thrust his way through deep snow . . .
So if you've got love written off as an easy option
    You'd better think twice . . .
                      Take
My own case. I was idle, born to leisure en déshabillé,
    Mind softened by lazy scribbling in the shade.
But love for a pretty girl soon drove the sluggard
    To action, made him join up
And just look at me now—fighting fit, dead keen on night
      exercises:
    If you want a cure for slackness, fall in love!

                            (*Amores* 1.9.1–12, 31–2, 40–6)

In addition to finding an occupation during those early years of maturation, Ovid would have been expected to fulfill his family's obligation to pay regular respect to their patron. It was a pressure that Ovid, and his brother, may have experienced daily, fulfilling their duty as Messalla's clients to perform the *salutatio*. This peculiar Roman ritual, which originated during the republic, required the patron's clients to wake early, don their togas, and crowd into his *domus* at sunrise, waiting the emergence of the patron. They might also form an entourage while he walked to the Forum to conduct the day's business. From the early empire and onward, each client would receive from servants the small basket of food or money (*sportula*) that signified the client's dependency on his patron, and he might, possibly, exchange a word or two with the great man and ask a favor or be asked one in return.[84] Only after the tedious rituals of the *salutatio* had been completed in a public display of deference was it courteous for the client to return home.

MAYBE SO

The *Amores* do not say much about the pressures of daily life, though Ovid's representation of sexual pursuit as a full-time occupation for a beardless youth was to some extent inflected by autobiography. Toward the end of *Amores* Book 3, the poet teases us readers about our tendency to expect that he was writing about himself. But in the autobiographical *Tristia*, Ovid tells us that Corinna was a real person, with a different name:

> She fired my genius, who now is a Roman byword
>   because of those verses, the girl to whom I gave
> the pseudonym of "Corinna."

> (*Tristia* 4.10.59–61)

A number of poems in the *Amores* reinforce that implication that the familiar bed the poet shares with Corinna is the marriage bed; the domestic setting in many poems provides the lovers with unusually easy access to one another. The poem in which Corinna seeks out her lover's bedchamber (*Amores* 1.5) is a strong example; in another, the poet makes frequent early-morning visits to the boudoir where the maid is dressing Corinna's hair (1.14); in yet another, he rejoices in a sensual entanglement that lasts far into a morning on which everyone else scurries to work (1.13).

But most significant of all are the two poems about Corinna's pregnancy and abortion. The love elegies of Ovid's fellow poets do not allude to such subjects, presumably because a pregnancy would have been entirely unwelcome in the adulterous relationship. In Ovid's two poems about Corinna's abortion, the emotions of worry, suspicion, disapproval, and hope for Corinna's survival mingle in a way that implies the anxiety of a husband. The poems make an interesting pair. The first seems to be spoken at Corinna's bedside:

> Corinna got pregnant—and rashly tried an abortion.
>   Now she's lying in danger of her life.
> She said not a word. That risk, and she never told me!
>   I ought to be furious, but I'm only scared.
> It was me by whom she conceived—or at least, I assume so:

I often jump to conclusions . . .
Look, sweetheart, I know how you're feeling, I know it's no
      time for
recriminations—but *never* try that again!

(*Amores* 2.13.1–6, 27–8)

The second is a general diatribe against abortion (it's unnatural and if practiced too freely would have extinguished the human race, including its Caesars), but it also contains a nugget of explanation about what Corinna's motivation might have been:

What's the point of a girl being exempt from active service—
      no shield-drill, no column-of-route
marching away to the wars—if she uses weapons against her
      self, suffers hurt from her own hand?
. . . Would you *really* chance your arm in that bloody arena
      just to keep your belly unwrinkled?
. . . Yet tender young girls do this—though not with
            impunity: often
the uterine murderess dies herself . . .
Be merciful, Gods. Let her first offence go unpunished,
      that's all I ask. If she errs again—then strike!

(*Amores* 2.14.1–4, 7–8, 37–8, 43–4)

The emphasis on Corinna's youth and inexperience is conspicuous: A "tender young girl" might well want to avoid the disfigurements of pregnancy; the poems present her as merely naive. The practice of abortion is thought to have been widespread among women of the upper classes, the only women about whom we know anything. The poet himself seems well aware of procedures and does not spare us the gruesome details:

Why probe your entrails with lethal
instruments? Why poison what's still unborn?

(*Amores* 2.14.27–8)

A well-born Roman male had one inarguable purpose in marrying: to produce a legitimate male heir. Of course, the poet does not charge Corinna with failing in her duty to bear him a child: Throughout, she is referred to as a mistress, a woman married to somebody else. Yet even in those poems the feeling of possessiveness is not out of keeping with the emotions of a husband. If you assume that the mistress is Ovid's own wife, it is quite easy to read these lines as the inner monologue of a jealous husband observing his wife's byplay with a guest. The *Amores* describe dinner parties at which the mistress is stretched out alongside her husband on a dining couch but manages to signal her preoccupation with her lover:

> Nudge my foot
> as you're passing by. Watch out for my nods and eye-talk,
>   pick up my stealthy messages, send replies.
> I shall speak whole silent volumes with one raised eyebrow,
>   words will spring from my fingers, words traced in wine.
> When you're thinking about the last time we made love
>   together,
>   touch your rosy cheek with one elegant thumb.

(Amores 1.4.16–22)

Ovid would not have wished to publicize the fact that the married woman in these poems was married to *him*. "Since tradition demanded an elusive mistress rather than a legally available wife," Peter Green remarks, "imagine the literary snickers if the truth got out!"[85]

MARRIAGE

It is possible to construct a backstory about this ill-fated teenage marriage by applying what is known about conventions governing Roman marriages in general. First, the alliance was almost certainly arranged by male elders in the two families. They were probably of equal status, since difference in rank was avoided by Romans of every class.[86] A poem toward the end of the *Amores* (3.13) suggests that Ovid and his bride may also have shared similar backgrounds: strong roots in the rural culture of Italy. It describes a journey to Falerii, his wife's hometown, to celebrate the Festival of Juno, presumably a family occasion. (Of course we have to assume that the wife in question was his first wife—indeed, was an actual wife.) Falerii was a city in Etruria, fifty kilometers north of Rome, "good orchard land" (3.13.1), the poet comments approvingly. Ovid's father's estate in Sulmo held orchards, we recall.

Whatever the circumstances that might have brought the bride and groom together, a significant aspect of the elders' negotiation was an exchange of assets. Ovid's father would have been expected to establish the newlyweds in a suitable home. The bride's father would have agreed upon a dowry paid to Ovid's family, not to Ovid himself, since during the life of his father Ovid could have owned nothing as an individual.[87] The bride might have been chosen in the first place not only for whatever wealth she would contribute but also because she possessed valuable social connections, such as kinship in a *gens* of high status and affiliation through friendship and family networks with members of the political elite. If she was the original of Corinna, she was also endowed with great beauty. A thick mane of fine hair fell below her waist, its color black with golden lights: "neither dark nor blonde, but a brindled auburn, / a mixture of both, like some tall cedar when / the outer bark's stripped off" (*Amores* 1.14.9–11). Her handsome profile and lovely face were remarkable enough to make her vain and haughty.[88]

As Ovid tells, he and his bride were given to one another not long after the toga ceremony. The marriage ceremony itself normally took place in the house of the bride's father, decked with garlands and wreaths. The bride would be dressed in clothing she had made, including a tunic with a woven belt tied in a special knot, to be undone by her husband on their wedding night, and a crown of flowers she had picked herself. She would also for the first time don a veil, which would indicate her status as a married woman. The bridal veil, however, was special: Saffron-colored, it covered the bride's body from head almost to foot.

After her female relatives had dressed her, sacrifices were performed before the household gods. The bride's parents would then present her to the groom, and their hands would be joined by a *pronuba*, a once-married woman. Roman iconography employed joined hands, the gesture that closed a business deal, and the marriage ceremony was unquestionably a business deal. Once the couple's hands were joined, the contracts dealing with the dowry would be witnessed—sometimes the signers were honored guests. The groom would depart to their new home, in order to welcome his bride with an entourage that carried her possessions. She was also accompanied by a torch lit at the hearth of her family home.

One of the intangibles she bore personally into her new home was the family name, her father's *nomen*; a woman did not take the name of her husband's family.[89] But in all other ways, she transferred her life into the new setting of her husband's house. Arriving, the bride daubed the doorway with oil and strands of wool—a member of her entourage carried the distaff and spindle she would use in her new role as a wife. Attendants lifted the bride over the threshold, and her husband greeted her with fire and water, an essential part of the ritual because water symbolized life and fire symbolized the Roman home.[90]

A decorated bridal bed would have stood in the reception area of the husband's house or apartment for all to see and joke about, but for the wedding night, the couple withdrew to the husband's cubiculum and was left alone. A wedding feast took place the next day, with the bride serving as hostess for the first time in her new life. She made her first offering to the household gods at this party,[91] certifying her role as *domina* and *matrona*. She was no longer a *virgo*.

These generalizations about Roman marriages may or may not have applied to the wedding ceremony Ovid underwent. And in any case, they do not explain the most interesting aspect of Ovid's marriage: the extreme immaturity of the groom. Roman men tended to marry around twenty-five or older, while women tended to marry after fifteen; this customary age gap of a decade tended to support the husband's authority and justify his preferences and tastes.[92] In Ovid's case, parental arrangement for an early marriage into a Roman family possibly made sense as yet another contribution to his Romanization: He would have entered the protection of another family just when he was undergoing the hazardous transition from boy to man, as well as continuing his evolution from rustic into Roman. Equally, if his bride was a very young woman, and a virgin, her family would have had much to gain from marrying her early to a man with good prospects.

Possibly, each father would have wanted to keep tight hands on the family's wealth. In the *Amores*, Ovid implies that Corinna has no money of her own, putting a speech in the mouth of a procuress who is trying to persuade Corinna to have sex for pay. While the poet listens through a crack in the door, the procuress argues shamelessly that Corinna should put herself on the market and become an adulterous gold digger:

> I'd like to see you become as wealthy as you are good-looking—
>   once get you in the money, I shan't ever starve . . .
> That poet of yours, now, what does he give you, except his latest
>   verses? Find the right lover, you'd scoop the pool.
> Why isn't he richer? The patron god of poets
>   wears gold, plays a gilded lyre.
> Look, dear, stop worshipping genius, try generosity
>   just for a change.

(*Amores* 1.8.27–8, 57–62)

By the time of the late republic in Rome, it was customary for a woman to retain her status as the daughter of her father when she married. This meant that her father retained *patria potestas* over her and that she would inherit property through her father's family, not her husband's. It also meant that she had no rights in any children produced in the marriage.

Two poems in the *Amores* suggest that the young poet had no money of his own either. His father probably would have settled on Ovid an allowance considered sufficient to the needs of a young man of his status when he married; and of course Ovid would have been perceived by his bride's family as the eventual heir of a major landowner. But in the day-to-day life of the young couple, limited funds, however generous, may well have provided grounds for anxiety and contention. Ovid and his bride circulated at a level of society where riches were incessantly on display, where luxuries beyond their own means were casually taken for granted. Where did *they* fit in? The *Amores* register the poet's consciousness of his own relative lack of a disposable income. One poem (1.10) harshly scolds the mistress because she has been nagging for gifts. Another poem (1.3) characterizes the poet's prospects for a grand inheritance as pretty dim. His beautiful companion will have to provide the human capital on which his art will draw; that's what he's banking on.

> I may not have top-drawer connections, I can't produce
>> blue-blooded
> ancestors to impress you, my father's plain middle-class.
> And there aren't any squads of ploughmen to deal with *my*
>> broad acres —
> my parents are both pretty thrifty, and need to be.
> What *have* I got on my side, then? Poetic genius, sweetheart,
>> divine inspiration. And love.
>
> (*Amores* 1.3.7–12)

Ovid is here claiming for himself a way of rising in the Roman world that is exactly analogous to the way a man, in earlier eras of Roman history, could rise through military valor. By Ovid's day, this was becoming true: Ambition for glory was, in the postwar world, capable of fulfillment in the life of the artist. Ovid is reminding us that it is not just the epic hero's name, but the author's name, that we remember.

However, since he was still a very young man during the years of his marriage, he and his brother were probably still completing the studies in rhetoric and law that would lead to a life of public service in the courts or the Senate. His family, which now included a father-in-law, no doubt still considered his poetry a dubious avocation, despite the encouragement Messalla continued to provide. The theme in the *Amores* that claimed status for the poet's vocation higher than that of military glory would definitely have nettled a father-in-law, had he heard about it. But it was really not a cause for worry, yet.

All things considered, Ovid was, despite his youth, not a bad catch as a husband. Nonetheless, his marriage ended when he was only eighteen years old. In his autobiographical poem in the *Tristia*, written from exile, Ovid wrote exactly two lines about that marriage: "When I was scarce past boyhood I was briefly married / to a wife both worthless and useless" (4.10.69–70). What had happened?

DIVORCE

About one out of six upper-class marriages ended in divorce during the first ten years,[93] and no blame needed to be specified. A divorce was easy to acquire; either husband or wife could initiate it. The husband could say to his wife that she should take her possessions, hand over the keys, and leave.[94] Or the wife could say to the husband that she intended to take her possessions and leave her husband's home; her departure reversed the position of wife that she had assumed when entering his house for the first time. The best evidence for the procedure a couple would follow comes down to us in literature, significantly in the comedies of Plautus: "Take your own things for yourself."

In real life, witnesses from the family had to be present when the words were spoken—or the proceedings might be initiated in a letter or spoken by a messenger. In any case, the divorce was recognized to have taken place the moment the words were spoken. Family members and lawyers would then step in to negotiate the return of the dowry and to settle claims on property that had been jointly acquired during the happier phase of the union.

If Ovid's representations in the *Amores* of the poet's relationship to Corinna resemble Ovid's relationship to his wife, there were obvious internal causes for the fatal phrase to be exchanged: lack of trust, and lack of money. Possibly, the marriage was also pressured from external sources because of Ovid's uncertainty about his fitness for the occupation that his family had chosen for him. And there was also the Roman double standard regarding sex. Roman society told the young man that he could do as he liked—indeed, sexual license was expected of him at that time of life. But "Corinna's" adulteries and abortion would qualify her, in Roman eyes, as a wife who was neither worthy nor useful.

If his wife was useless in bearing heirs, however, she proved immensely useful in launching Ovid's career. At about the same time Ovid and his wife parted, Ovid began reading in public the poems of the *Amores*, to huge acclaim.[95] The first book was published that same year.[96] Suddenly, he was famous. And he was free.

GRAND TOUR AND VOCATION

Like most affluent young men of his time, after completing his rhetorical and legal studies in Rome, Ovid devoted a year or so to travel in the ancient world. A first good guess would have been that Ovid's brother was his companion. But this journey probably took place in 23 BC, and Ovid's brother had died in 24 BC at age twenty. The causes of his death are unknown. In the autobiographical *Tristia*, Ovid does not explain the circumstances. He speaks only of the jolt and of the loss of their close relationship:

> But when he was barely twenty years old, my brother
> died—and from then I lost a part of myself.

> (*Tristia* 4.10.31–2)

The companion Ovid chose for the journey was another poet: Aemilius Macer, one of the other protégés of Messalla. Following a centuries-old itinerary, they would have embarked from Ostia on a ship headed for Greece, whose myth-rich sites they were familiar with through their studies. After a stay in Athens, they would have traveled overland in a jouncing carriage to, probably, Delphi, Corinth, and Epidaurus; perhaps also to Olympia; possibly to Thebes. All of these once-splendid Greek cities had fallen into ruin over the centuries, and hard times had diminished the production of festivals that had made them famous during the era of the great city-states. Nevertheless, in Delphi the Pythian Games continued in honor of the arts, while on the slopes of Mount Parnassus the oracle of Apollo still delivered her prophetic riddles. Some temples and monuments had been restored and rebuilt, and supplied visitors with a number of Roman amenities: aqueducts, sumptuous bathhouses, improved roads. Many years after his journey, Ovid was to set one of the great episodes of the *Metamorphoses* at Delphi, telling the story of how the laurel wreath became the emblem of Apollo's triumph as a lyric poet.

From Greece, a brief sea trip brought travelers to the island of Rhodes, where the Colossus of Rhodes had once stood: an enormous bronze sculpture of Apollo that had collapsed in an earthquake in

228 or 226 BC. The sculpture itself was gone, but Rhodes still held many trophies of its earlier fame. By the first century BC it had become an important center of education for the Romans, renowned for its schools of rhetoric. By the time Ovid could have visited the city, the Roman general Cassius had attacked and devastated Rhodes, where he had earlier been tutored in rhetoric by the famous orator Archelaus. Cassius had been the ringleader of the conspiracy to assassinate Julius Caesar.

But Rhodes was also a convenient stepping-stone to Asia Minor (Anatolia), only eleven miles away. The Anatolian site no traveler would want to miss was Troy. The *Iliad* described the devastation of the city by Greek warriors. The victors had founded a new town on what they believed to be Homer's Troy, in 700 BC. Six hundred years later Julius Caesar, drawing on the myth that affiliated his family with that of Aeneas and thus related him to the goddess Venus, took the city under his protection as a kind of "national shrine."[97] Ovid acknowledges that his own fascination with Troy focused on a famous sculpture of Athena—Minerva—but when he arrived in Troy, he discovered that she had already been smuggled to Rome:

> A heavenly statue of armed Minerva, it's thought,
>   dropped on the hills of Ilium's city.
> (I was curious to see it, and saw the temple and site.
>   That is what remains there; Rome has Pallas.) . . .
> With Priam she was not safe. This was her own wish
>   after she had lost the beauty contest.
> They say she was taken by Adrastus' grandson
>   or thieving Ulysses or Aeneas—
> The culprit is unknown. She is Roman; her guard
>   is Vesta, whose unfailing light views all.

(Fasti 6.421–4, 431–6)

By the first century BC, Romans didn't have to travel to see important works of Greek art. During the formation of the empire, Rome acquired four pieces by Phidias, which were placed in the Temple of Fortune; works by Praxiteles ornamented the Capitoline Hill and the Portico of Octavia.[98] Private mansions and villas and their gardens held tons of what we would consider museum-worthy sculpture: originals, of course, though copies rapidly became available as Romans became even wealthier.

The remainder of the Anatolian coast also had other splendid cities to show: Pergamum, with its famous library and its great altar dedicated to Zeus; Smyrna, where Homer was thought by the ancients to have lived while writing his poetry; Ephesus, which held an important temple to Artemis; Miletus, a center of philosophy and science; Halicarnassus, legendary birthplace of Herodotus, with its gigantic mausoleum, designated as one of the Seven Wonders of the World by the poet Antipater of Sidon in the second century BC. Just beyond Anatolia lay Egypt, which the tourist would enter through the city of "far famed-Alexandria, to sample / the fleshpots of wanton Nile," as Ovid put it (*Tristia* 1.2.79–80).

Of all the days he spent on this these travels, one experience stood out in his memory: the eruption of Etna. Since their vessel would be passing through the Strait of Messina, they would have caught sight of Mount Etna at the very outset of the voyage, knowing they would return for a longer stay. In a letter from exile to the friend who had shared the journey, he recalled that day:

> With you as my guide, we toured all the splendid cities
>   of Asia, with you as my guide saw Sicily plain —
> we watched the sky glow bright with the flames of Etna.

(Epistulae 2.10.21–3)

Its violent eruptions scattered ash as far north as Rome, five hundred miles away. Records of its activity extend back for twenty-four centuries. Romans regarded Etna and other sites of natural magnificence not principally as scenery but as locations where they could experience the haunts of myth.

Etna's formidable presence had long ignited poets, beginning with Pindar. In his *Pythian* Ode 1, Pindar refers to the mythic tradition that hundred-headed Typhon, a Titan quelled by Zeus's thunderbolts, lies beneath the mountain:

> He's pinned beneath
> the pillar of the sky: white-capped Etna, nursing
> all year long her brood of stinging snow.

Within her secret depths
pure springs of unapproachable fire
erupt—her rivers in daytime pour forth
billows of glaring smoke,
while at night the blood-red
rolling blaze whirls boulders crashing
onto the flat plain of the sea.

(Pindar, *Pythian* 1.19–24)[99]

The giant's flailing creates earthquakes, and his enraged roaring from a hundred mouths produces Etna's flames. Other mythic traditions claimed that Etna was the home of Vulcan's forge; this was the explanation preferred by Aeschylus in *Prometheus* and by Vergil in the *Aeneid*.[100] The philosopher Lucretius offered a scientific rationale: The eruptions were the explosive release of forceful winds that had built up deep in the mountain's caverns. But with his reference to Pindar in the *Epistulae ex Ponto*, Ovid seems to recall that moment of his grand tour when he was twenty years old and found his vocation as a poet.

Ovid in His Prime

Even before the sun begins to draw its first bright lines across the temple facades at the summit of the Capitoline Hill, a torch's light falls between the columns of a portico at the back of a handsome family home on a nearby street. In single file, members of the household emerge from under the portico and walk slowly across their garden toward a small altar, dimly visible in the predawn light. At the head of the procession, swathed in white, is the poet Publius Ovidius Naso: a short, slight man who moves with easy dignity in the voluminous toga that he has drawn up over his head to cover his dark hair and shield his eyes from distractions. This is his forty-sixth birthday, March 20 in the year 4 AD.

Behind him, dressed in woolen finery,[101] is the young wife he married a year ago—his third wife—and behind her his stepdaughter, seven years old, cloaked against the chilly damp of early spring. Maintaining a deferential separation from the family group, household slaves carry the equipment for the birthday ritual: a plate of warm cakes covered with a cloth, a pitcher of honey, a small precious box of saffron, a silver libation bowl filled with wine. Well to the rear is one who expertly brandishes a flaming torch, feeding it with air.

Roman citizenship under Augustus has turned many old customs into required religious observances. The birthday of the Roman paterfamilias is one of them, and Ovid's household has made extensive preparation. Much earlier that morning, the slaves had been out clipping long-stemmed blossoms from the garden, by torchlight. They have braided flowers and foliage into fragrant garlands and draped them around the tufa altar that stands before a painted niche in the garden wall. On the altar platform, faggots and scraps of tinder stand ready to be set ablaze.

Arriving at this altar, Ovid gestures for the torch, and as he lights the tinder, the painting in the garden niche springs to life: an image of two dancing youths—the household Lares—flanking the figure of a man togated and veiled like Ovid himself, but accompanied by guardian serpents. This is an artist's rendering of a genius natalis, the god who protects the fertility, the continuity, of the family.

Ovid now reenacts the ritual he learned by watching his father perform it year after year in his rural childhood home. Casting saffron on the fire, he summons and praises the genius in the ceremonial language sanctioned by tradition while the flame fattens and crackles and a rich scent rises from the altar. Then Ovid lifts the god's portion from the warm plate of cake, drizzles it with yet more honey, and lays pieces on the fire. While the flames lick at the offering, he petitions the genius to keep all members of his household at peace with one another and safe from every kind of harm. Now he tilts the libation bowl over the fire, and as the wine hisses, the coiling smoke wavers, hesitates, and finds an updraft; it streams straight toward the morning stars that watch over his forty-sixth birthday. Ovid completes his prayer with a phrase that just might be a joke about the god's nose. The precociously clever little girl laughs, as she was meant to do. Ovid hands around the remaining honey cakes while the first light of dawn streaks the sky overhead.[102]

Once the birthday ritual is finished, Ovid devotes some time to working on new poems. Now a mature man in complete command of his talent, he has conceived of not one but two ambitious works. One is titled Metamorphoses, and its general subject is the transformation of human beings by the will of the gods. The other poem, Fasti, is an exposition of Roman beliefs and religious practices structured on the Roman calendar of festivals.

He returns to his garden, which is his favorite place to write. A wooden couch spread with rugs and cushions has been moved into position between columns of the portico, alongside a table piled with fresh wax tablets.

Before he settles into his morning work, Ovid likes to make a proprietary circuit of this garden. The early morning air is fresh and cool, an aid to deliberation. Ovid makes all the decisions about this garden himself, and has been actively involved in its planning and cultivation from the time he settled in his Roman house.[103] Finding a position in

which the necessary plants can flourish requires an intimate knowledge of every inch of the available ground; unlike the broad acres of
his villa, where an orchard and a vineyard flourish in open fields, the
city garden is a walled and porticoed extension of the house. Sunlight
must be shrewdly deployed within this enclosure, which measures
nine meters at the back end, seven meters on the longer side. The garden must supply food for the table, medicines for everyone who lives
and works in the house, and floral materials for the many domestic
occasions on which garlands and chaplets are required. The challenge
is to create a resource in which the beauty conceals the usefulness.

The most prominent feature in Ovid's garden is the wide circle of
planting at its center, punctuated by a slow-trickling fountain attractive
to birds. The strongly marked circular shape provides emphatic symme-
try to a space surrounded by the somewhat haphazardly shaped rooms
of his house. On this early morning at the vernal equinox, strong light
is just now edging down the columns of the portico; soon its warmth
will release the fragrance of herbs growing in a corner plot that captures the morning light and is shaded from the midday sun.

This is where Ovid begins his inspection. Basil, marjoram, chives,
and mint flourish amid lettuces and bristling leeks and newly bur-
geoning fronds of fennel: The dinner salad will be harvested from
this efficient little triangle of earth. He next turns his attention to the
large glazed earthenware container positioned within sight of honored guests in the dining room that opens onto the portico. Ovid chose
the planting for this ornamental basin himself, months before, with
early blossoming annuals that are now needed for the day's ceremonies. Hyacinths, anemones, and narcissi will capture the light and
rustle in the breeze of late afternoon, their vivid colors drawing the
eyes of the diners, a few of whom will recognize that these blossoms
are literary references too: They are characters in one of Ovid's new
poems, hapless victims of transformation by the callous gods.

From other flower beds, less in sight, more of the same flowers
will be plucked and braided with myrtle into chaplets for the dinner guests. From the shadiest areas of ground, mint and ferns and
verbena will be gathered and strewn on the dining room floor to
be crushed by the diners' feet as they enter, mingling those delicate
scents with the stronger notes of the diners' perfumes.[104]

Ovid steps back under the portico that separates the garden from the house and runs a critical gaze along the newly trimmed box hedge that gives sharp definition to the flower beds flanking the walls. Finally, he lets his eye linger on a shapely tree standing in an antique stone vessel at the tip of the circle, on an axis with the room that houses his library. This is his garden's most recent acquisition: a Laurus nobilis, *its slim trunk as straight and smooth as the columns that form his portico, its crown a dense sphere of glossy leaves. For Ovid, the laurel is both a finishing touch in the garden he has been landscaping with deliberate care for several years and a dramatic character in the* Metamorphoses, *the tale of Phoebus Apollo and Daphne. The young god, who has never been in love, is enflamed by the sight of Daphne and attempts to chase her down. Daphne throws her arms upward, pleading that her father, Peneus, release her from the beauty that has caused Apollo's lust. She changes into a laurel tree just as Apollo's hands reach her breasts.*

Ovid has taken a seat at the table. He finds the wax tablet and goes over the lines with his fingers one more time.

Tree though she was, Apollo still loved her. Caressing the trunk
with his hand, he could feel the heart still fluttering under
        the new bark.
Seizing the branches, as though they were limbs, in his arms'
        embrace,
he pressed his lips to the wood; but the wood still shrank
        from his kisses.
Phoebus then said to her: "Since you cannot be mine in
        wedlock,
you must at least be Apollo's tree. It is you who will always
be twined in my hair, on my tuneful lyre and my quiver of
        arrows.
The generals of Rome shall be wreathed with you, when the
        jubilant paean
of triumph is raised and the long procession ascends the
        Capitol.
On either side of Augustus' gates your trees shall stand sentry,
faithfully guarding the crown of oak-leaves hanging between
        them.

As I, with my hair that is never cut, am eternally youthful,
so you with your evergreen leaves are for glory and praise
    everlasting."
Apollo the Healer had done. With a wave of her new-formed
    branches
the laurel agreed, and seemed to be nodding her head in
    the treetop.

(Metamorphoses 1.553–67)

Ovid remembers the Amores *with nostalgia. It was his first book about the awakening of love, a phenomenal success for him at age twenty. Rereading the poems brings home to him the intensity of the early love, the exciting beginning on the day of the toga ceremony, the wedding night when he felt an overwhelming tenderness toward her.*

He was young, but she was younger—

guileless. Then I loved you, soul and body . . .
Love is a child, and naked. Childhood spells innocence;
    Nakedness, open ways.

(Amores 1.10.13, 15–16)

He smiles as he remembers the lines. But his poem is also about their mutual infidelities, which were part of upper-class Roman life. Recklessly, he had undertaken to educate his young wife in the depravities. He had basked in the admiration of the young men with whom he rode in the Campus Martius, showing off for each other. He would quote his latest poems to them, hinting broadly that the "lessons" the young poet was giving "Corinna" were true to life. His comrades loved to quote his own lines back to him with bawdy laughter, and he had lapped it up.

The end of his first marriage had been bitter and shameful. By the time they separated she was conducting her infidelities in public and flaunting the expensive tokens of admiration she received from these lovers. A husband could not tolerate such affronts to his honor; divorce was the only solution.

It had been followed by a second marriage that had somewhat assuaged his father's wounded pride. That marriage's first child was thriving, a little daughter. His second wife had miscarried their second child and died in the process.[105] The daughter had married young, and now lived abroad with her husband and three children; the continuity of the family had been secured. Unfortunately, she could not attend the birthday celebrations.

At age thirty-four he had decided to publish a revision of Amores in three special volumes. Boldly, he decided he would model the new edition on the erotic elegies by Propertius, his only living competitor in the field of erotic elegy. It should be clear by now that he was on a par with the old masters. As he slowly worked his way through the first scroll, he made a few disquieting discoveries. In particular, he was surprised by the breezy attitude toward adultery. Augustus's legislation aimed at eliminating adultery among members of the upper classes had been passed almost a decade earlier and was of course already a law—an unpopular law, a laughable law! Adultery continued, but writing about erotic liaisons with married women had become politically more and more dangerous.

Ovid remembers what felt embarrassing about his early poems. Revising his book gave him the second chance that life itself never gave. The reader could watch this young man embrace all the follies that lay in wait for a beardless youth. The book now illustrated, by satirizing, the arrogance that permitted the lover to slap and scratch this mistress when he disliked her new hairdo, for example—let the triviality of it stand for all the times a man could slap a woman just because he was man and she wasn't. It now showed the crude enthusiasm for seduction that beardless youth entertained as if by birthright—another male entitlement disallowed to women, who were the property of men. Throughout, it depicted the rash young poet in the act of corrupting the person whose love he took for granted, until the awful knowledge of her deceitfulness could not be ignored. He must—did—eradicate the youthful clumsiness of the poetry. He revised the meter where it was not perfect. The thought now brings a smile to his face.

But now back to work. He has a good reason to press forward with his writing today—he has decided he will read "Apollo and Daphne" to his dinner guests. It will be a surprise for his birthday dinner. It is a fascinating love story, but his friends are going to understand the hidden message: *Even the highest powers are not exempt from transformation.* Ovid's seat has been moved a couple of times during his long morning of work, keeping pace with the gradual incursion of the sun into the walkway of his portico. Late into the morning, a slave carries from the house a wide cloth curtain and hangs it from the pole stretched in the upper space between two columns, for shade. From time to time, a slave brings a cool drink from the kitchen: sometimes water sweetened with honey, sometimes water sharpened with vinegar. Ovid's concentration does not waver. He writes steadily, without needing to consult his notes; like most educated Romans, he has a trained memory and carries much in his head. But in any case, it is wise to stay with the momentum of the meter he has set like a metronome in his body.

Now the piece is finished, and Ovid rises for a stretch. His garden is his clock; the position of the sun tells him it is the sixth hour, time for a stroll to the bathhouse for some exercise and a good soaking. He summons his amanuensis, who will convert the rapidly written cursive on the high-piled stack of wax tablets into neat columns on a papyrus scroll. His dinner guests will begin to assemble in the late afternoon. He must be rested and fresh when they arrive.

By the ninth hour of the day, freshly bathed and shaved, and dressed in a new tunic and short cloak, Ovid is ready to receive his friends. It is never possible to predict the time a guest will arrive for dinner. But someone is bound to arrive at the early end of the conventional gathering hour, so he has given himself plenty of time to inspect the preparations while there is still a possibility of giving additional instructions to the slaves.

Ovid takes pleasure in circumnavigating the private areas of his house. He has overseen the decoration himself and is especially proud of his dining room. Entering the triclinium through the wide portal that separates the diners from the garden, he pauses to enjoy the vivid frescoes. These illustrate the metamorphosis of the girl Arachne into a spider.

The largest wall is segmented into three panels—a large central panel flanked by two narrower ones—dedicated to the goddess Minerva. The central panel shows the contest to which Minerva has challenged Arachne. The female figures are seen in angled profile, and their working posture brings them into equivalency; no longer does the angry goddess tower over the defiant girl. The lower half of each loom shows a slice of the tapestry that each has just begun to weave.

In the tale, Arachne tries to escape by hanging herself, but the goddess intervenes: She shrinks Arachne into the form of a spider. But Ovid did not commission a painting of that episode. In his dining room, the story ends with each of the two glorious "tapestries" occupying a wall of its own. Minerva's painting represents the hierarchy of the gods; Arachne denounces sexual harassment with drastic examples. Nonetheless, a spider motif can be detected in the web-like ornamental traceries on panels surmounting the frescoes in the upper zone of the walls, and in an obscure corner, a small nondescript painted spider seems to hang suspended.

The room's decor never fails to stimulate exactly the kinds of conversation Ovid hopes for: political fulminations, technical disputes and disquisitions, literary gossip, even scholarly footnotes. The three dining couches have been positioned on the diagonal in the room, the better to afford diners a view of the garden, and each couch will afford a different angle on the paintings as well. Empty at this moment, the triclinium has almost the look of a stage set: its black-and-white mosaic floor agleam, the rugs and pillows where the diners will recline a soft tumble of luxuries, the early-spring garden beyond lit to perfection by the declining sun, the shade deepening.

Perhaps because this is a special occasion, the guests arrive promptly, remove their street shoes, put on their decorative slippers, and gather in the garden, where a garlanded table has been set up for pouring mulsum, the honeyed wine always served as an aperitif. The accompanying slaves carry gifts, and these are arranged on the serving table for inspection. The wealthy Fabians' tribute is a heavy silver mixing bowl for wine. Atticus has brought Ovid a small bronze sculpture of a chimera with a lion's head, a goat's body, and a serpent's tail, to bring him good luck in his work on the Metamorphoses. Macer, who lived with Ovid for a year and knows something about his vanity, has commissioned a bronze mirror, while Brutus and Celsus, thinking along the same lines, have commissioned together an encaustic portrait of Ovid—so that later in life he can remember his good looks, they joke. Julius Hyginus has found a rare work of Greek *mythology, on one of his recent voyages to make acquisitions for the library, and has had it copied for Ovid; it is a little-known version of the story of Narcissus.*[106] *Messalla has brought a sundial for the garden, along with verses commemorating their long friendship.*

Before the guests enter the triclinium, *a slave hands each one a freshly prepared chaplet of flowers and arranges it to advantage on each head. Now that the wine has begun to work its way with them, high spirits take over; Ovid has written, in the* Fasti, *"No serious business is conducted by the brow that wears a wreath / and waterdrinkers don't wear flower chains." The wine drinkers make no protest. Then, upon entering the* triclinium, *they remove their slippers and hand them to the slave who accompanies them, and who will wait in attendance crouched at their feet.*

Each of the three long couches in the triclinium *holds three guests, who recline on their left elbows, supported by firm cushions. The couches are placed in the form of a U, with a serving table in the center. As host, Ovid will occupy the far end of the couch on the left as they enter the room; his guest of honor, Messalla, will recline to Ovid's left on the middle couch. The others find their own places, the women next to their husbands.*

Once they are settled, Ovid welcomes them warmly, but briefly. He knows that his guests are hungry; most Romans eat only this one large meal every day. He summons the staff to begin serving. Each diner will hold a plate in the left hand and spoon food onto the plate with the right hand. All the food will have been cut into bite-size pieces, since it is meant to be eaten with the fingers.

Ovid's country villa may have supplied much of the food that evening. Like every Roman, he takes pride in growing his own food for the table. The substantial appetizer course, or gustatio, *includes raw and cooked vegetables, mushrooms, smoked cheese, olives, and an egg dish. The main course, the* mensa prima, *features a roast of young kid, game birds and pullets, and boar and roast pig. The dessert, the* mensa secunda, *consists of nuts and fruit, both dried and fresh. Different wines are served with each course.*[107] *At Ovid's table, conversation is the main attraction, and nothing is permitted to impede it during dinner. But at the end of this particular meal, he announces that he wishes to extend the evening with a recitation from his new* poem. He invites the guests to rise and stretch and refresh themselves while the slaves clear away the last scraps of the mensa secunda and sweep the floor. Then the cellarius will bring a fresh supply of wine, purchased specially for this occasion. The dinner guests will reassemble, with additional guests invited specifically to share this convivium. "Apollo and Daphne" will make its public debut, a milestone in Ovid's life and, he hopes, in the life of his writing.

At age forty-six, he has reached the height of his powers. And now more than ever, he is performing the work he is born to do.

Afterword

Obsessive work, especially when requiring creative immersion, is the best antidote to pain, suffering, and tragedy. I discovered this on my own more than thirty years ago when I had to cope with the suicide of my twenty-eight-year-old daughter. Her death was sudden and unexpected, and the resulting work absorption an automatic response to deep grief. But what if the tragedy is foreseen, yet its ultimate outcome not known? Creative work is then a planned therapy, its underlying motive survival and even hope that the expected tragedy might end on a more positive note. Whatever the cause, Goethe's prescription from *Wilhelm Meisters Wanderjahre* says it all: "*Seelenleiden zu heilen vermag der Verstand nichts, die Vernunft wenig, die Zeit viel, entschlossene Tätigkeit hingegen alles*" ("Healing the soul's pain is never achieved by understanding, rarely by reasoning, more frequently by time, but always through committed activity").

Take Publius Ovidius Naso, arguably one of the greatest poets of all time. Culturally and emotionally, Ovid was a Roman through and through. Exiled at age fifty-one at the height of his fame by Emperor Augustus to Tomis on the Black Sea, at the extreme wild edge of the Roman Empire in what is now Romania, he probably felt sentenced to the severest of all penalties: personal and cultural isolation, to some worse than death. Never allowed to return, he found his only solace in his remaining decade writing poetry—notably his *Tristia*, and later his bitingly sad *Epistulae ex Ponto*, clamoring for pardon. While still in Rome, Ovid had predicted: "My name shall never be forgotten. / Wherever the might of Rome extends in the lands she has conquered, / the people shall read and recite my words." Continuing to write poetry in exile was meant to strengthen that assurance.

And now take the example of Diane Middlebrook, my third wife and great love, to whom I had been married for twenty-two years when she, though sixteen years my junior, died in 2007. She represents another example of the benefits of Goethe's wise advice about coping with tragedies. Many of her obituaries in the United States and the United Kingdom described her as an award-winning poet, biographer, teacher, feminist, and salonnière, all of which was true. Yet if anyone asked her how she would describe herself during the last decade of her life, her answer always was a resounding "I am a biographer!"

Her first biography, *Anne Sexton* (1991), was a huge success—a finalist for the National Book Award and probably the only biography of a poet that ever made it onto the *New York Times* bestseller list. It received enormous press coverage in the United States because in addition to receiving unrestricted access to the extensive archives of Anne Sexton, Diane was allowed to listen to hundreds of hours of that poet's recorded psychoanalytic sessions—at that time a unique event in biographical writings that was both severely criticized for its presumed invasion of a dead person's ultimate privacy as well as applauded as an appropriate and unique example of psychobiography.

Her second biography, *Suits Me: The Double Life of Billy Tipton* (1998), dealt with a female-born jazz musician who passed as a man throughout his adult life, undetected by several spouses and adopted sons. Work on this biography entailed an entirely different—indeed, diametrically opposite—approach from the Sexton book with its enormous archival material, since virtually nothing written was preserved by Billy Tipton, who by necessity led a secretive life. In this instance, the research was journalistic in nature. It involved examining telephone books, real estate records, and newspaper clippings and carrying out numerous personal interviews with friends, acquaintances, and relatives, who all had to be located.

Having honed her biographical skills through two such different projects, she undertook a third biography. *Her Husband* (2003) explored the sensationalized marriage between British poet laureate Ted Hughes and the equally famous American poet Sylvia Plath (a contemporary of Anne Sexton), who, like Anne Sexton, committed suicide. Many American feminists, though not Diane, demonized Hughes as the cause of Plath's suicide, blaming him for his adultery with Assia Wevill, who after marrying Hughes also killed herself. Some of Plath's diaries covering the tumultuous time just before her suicide, though in possession of Hughes, disappeared, and these in turn fueled suspicions about his role.

Diane's interpretation of the Hughes-Plath marriage was so sophisticated and evenhanded that *Publishers Weekly* described it as "the gold standard" by which past and future biographies of these two poets would be judged. The reason for this judgment was not solely the superb prose but also the methodology that Diane employed, claiming that all the missing aspects, complications, conflicts, and synergies were hidden in Hughes's poetry—notably in two collections, *Birthday Letters* (quickly to become a bestseller in the United Kingdom) and *Howls and Whispers* (published only in a private edition of 110 copies, of which she possessed one), that were released shortly before Hughes's death in 1998. Her deconstruction of these poems was the key that enabled her to enter into the Hughes-Plath marriage in a way that had never been done before.

And that brings us to Ovid—not because Hughes worked during the last two years of his life on a new translation of the *Metamorphoses*, but because two years before completing *Her Husband*, Diane Middlebrook had decided to embark on her most ambitious project, a biography of Ovid, whom she had taught in her poetry and poetics classes as an English literature professor at Stanford University for more than thirty years. Having written a biography (*Anne Sexton*) of a poet who had hidden no personal secrets and had left an overabundance of archival material, much of it in her own voice, and having completed one about two poets who left much archival material but hid the most intimate aspects in their poetry, Ted Hughes and Sylvia Plath, she was ready for Publius Ovidius Naso, who died two thousand years ago and left no personal records—not even the name of his mother—but some of the greatest poetry ever written. Diane was convinced that her intimate knowledge of Ovid's poetry and the approach she used in *Her Husband*, combined with a deep immersion into the Rome of Ovid's time, would enable her to write what could, without bragging, be called an Ovidian biography.

Some novelists had already been tempted to do the same, although disguised in fiction. The two most famous are Australian writer David Malouf, with his novel *An Imaginary Life* (1978), and Austrian author Christoph Ramsmayr, with *Die Letzte Welt* (1988). As openly professed novelists who focused mostly on the last years of Ovid's life in exile, they could allow themselves liberties that no biographer could. Diane chose an intriguing compromise. Given the lack of most relevant biographical facts, it clearly was impossible to write a "standard" biography of Ovid, and when asked why she had picked him, she replied semijokingly, "No estates" (referring to the notoriously difficult Ted Hughes estate), "no psychotherapy" (the issue of using Anne Sexton's therapy tapes), "no interviews" (her months-long chase to find Billy Tipton's surviving wives), "no history—I just make it up." Through extensive research and precise citations from an enormous literature on Roman life around that period, coupled with her deeply insightful analysis of Ovid's poetry, she set out to draw a picture of seven crucial days in his life—which nobody would call "making it up." But not long after she immersed herself in the project, fate intervened.

Diane's plans were to complete the Ovid biography in time for publication in 2008, the two thousandth anniversary of the poet's banishment from Rome and the completion of his monumental *Metamorphoses*. When in 2001 she was suddenly diagnosed with a rare form of cancer, a retroperitoneal liposarcoma, a seemingly successful operation gave her confidence that she would be able to complete the project on time. Liposarcomas generally do not metastasize, but they do grow promiscuously unless eliminated completely. Her first surgery had eliminated most of but not the entire tumor, and in 2004 regrowth occurred. This involved a second surgery with a poor prognosis: Not all of the tumor could be removed. The oncologist's frank answer to her direct question "How long have I got?" was "Six months to a couple of years." Her second question, "How will I die?" led to a hardly more assuring response: "You will probably starve to death with not too much pain."

Most people would have given up at this stage, but not Diane, nor I. I helped her search for alternative treatment in 2005—first an experimental immunological approach in Germany that had not yet been approved in the United States, and subsequently finding a superb German surgeon, Dr. Rainer Engemann, in the regional hospital of Aschaffenburg, who was willing to attempt one more operation that the American surgeons had judged to be impossible. The operation in January 2006 lasted over eleven hours. To heap insult on injury, I had broken my hip the preceding month in Oxford and was unable to travel. My stepdaughter, Leah Middlebrook, managed to get leave from her professorial position at the University of Oregon to be with her mother in Aschaffenburg. When we were finally together again in our London home—I on crutches, Diane regaining her energy—both of us decided to follow Goethe's earlier cited advice with a vengeance, becoming total workaholics except for some evening ventures to the theater. Diane now faced a deadline: not only Ovid's two thousandth *Metamorphoses* anniversary but also her life expectancy, because the German operation, though heroic, was not a cure but only a gift of limited life extension. Not all of the liposarcoma could be removed, and even the surgical wizard of Aschaffenburg had to concede that a further operation would be impossible.

In retrospect, I have the impression that Diane was more resigned to her death than I was to losing my much younger spouse. While her focus was to make as much progress as possible on her Ovid biography, I chose a totally new project for my work immersion. During the preceding twenty years, I had turned into an author of fiction and plays, mostly in the genres of "science-in-fiction" and "science-in-theater." I had also written two autobiographies (1992 and 2001), the first Diane's prompting; she wanted to see a record of my life in the fifty-four years before we met. But autobiography and biography are two very different forms of writing, and my chosen subject—biographical sketches of Theodor Adorno, Walter Benjamin, Gershom Scholem, and Arnold Schönberg and their wives—was a dramatic departure from what I had written before. The original motivation was partly autobiographical in that I wanted to address the question of Jewish identity—so differently manifested in a nonreligious way in these four individuals—because it had started to preoccupy me personally late in my own life. But since the resulting book, *Four Jews on Parnassus—A Conversation: Benjamin, Adorno, Scholem, Schönberg,* was also meant as my ultimate homage to Diane, did I subconsciously wish to do it on her turf of pure biography? In any event, I managed to complete the text just before her death. She had read each chapter as I passed it to her for her usual critical scrutiny, an exchange of texts we did throughout our married life.

Diane's work could not be completed. Indeed, as her strength waned, as her blood transfusions had to be repeated with increasing frequency, she faced me one morning upon my return from daily gym exercises associated with my own accident to announce, "There is no purpose in continuing; I will never finish it." This was the lowest of all low points in our joint life, because if true, it meant that we would only wait for her death without the consolation of the only therapy left, Goethe's *entschlossene Tätigkeit*. But the following day, I had a brainstorm:

Since Diane's biography was structured through seven days in Ovid's life and since she had reached at that stage Day 4 (Ovid at twenty), why not rename her book *Young Ovid*, and rewrite the preamble that she had already written in which her seven-day approach was described? Words fail me to describe the nature of my wife's ebullient response, but I myself took it as a spectacular revival of the Diane Middlebrook I had known for the preceding two decades. She resumed her daily writing routine until late October 2007, when she gave the last public lecture of her life at the Centre for Gender Studies at Cambridge University. Diane had been one of the greatest and most popular lecturers I have ever met, the recipient of all major teaching awards at Stanford University, but this lecture brought tears to my eyes as well as to many in the audience. To me because I knew that the Cambridge audience was listening to a dying lecturer, and to the audience because her stunning—almost ethereal—presentation was so moving. A few weeks later, she knew that the end had arrived and flew to San Francisco to die in a hospital on December 15, 2007.

During the last two weeks in the hospital, she was heavily sedated, but during her lucid moments, she continued to think of *Young Ovid*. Diane imagined that an editor from her publisher's office would complete the manuscript, and we even managed to hire two graduate students (Caedmon Haas and Katherine Balsley) from the classics department of Stanford University—financed by the very last grant she received with compassionate speed from the dean of humanities—to check the accuracy of her numerous footnotes and references. As I emailed to Haas and Balsley ("I fully realize that unless a miracle happens with respect to a delay in my wife's expected death, the work will have to be completed posthumously. But I consider it essential for operational reasons and also for my wife's morale that she meet her assistants personally and explain to them in one or two sessions what she would like to have done"), we had very little time. In the event, she still managed to instruct them about details from her hospital bed before her death a few days later.

In spite of diligent efforts on the part of two different writers, it soon became obvious that Diane's uniquely distinct voice—so often mentioned in reviews of her first three biographies—could not be matched and that such a patchwork completion was not acceptable to her daughter or to me. It was simply like an unfinished painting by a master of a unique technique being completed by other and totally different artists. It clearly would have been the wrong "last book" if it appeared as such a literary chimera. There remained only one answer, namely what readers now see: an unfinished posthumous biography—terms that apply with equal force to Ovid as well as to Diane. Call it a spectacular foreplay without ultimate consummation, meaning that an incompletely polished jewel is more precious than any finished pastiche.

Carl Djerassi

Annotated Selections from Ovid's Poetry

FOREWORD

Ovid's first biographer was Ovid. His constant presence in his own texts makes it not only feasible but also rewarding to supplement Diane Middlebrook's unfinished biography with selections from his poetry. The Ovidian corpus is vast and offers an embarrassment of riches. The following selections follow closely on Middlebrook's treatment of Ovid's works. They are included either because she cites them, or because they sound her major themes, or because they round out her portrait of Ovid.

Spatial constraints and copyright issues have necessitated some difficult choices. For example, it is regrettable to omit the *Ars Amatoria* (*The Art of Love*), the poem responsible for Ovid's relegation to the Black Sea. But passing over that work means leaving room for the *Fasti*, which opens up an entirely different window on Ovid and his career.

The following works and translations have been excerpted:

- *Amores* (*Loves*, after ca. 25 BC). From *Ovid: The Erotic Poems*. Penguin Books, 1982. Peter Green, translator.
- *Metamorphoses* (*Transformations*, before AD 8). Penguin Books, 2004. David Raeburn, translator.
- *Fasti* (*Calendar*, before AD 8). Penguin Books, 2004. A. J. Boyle and R. D. Woodard, translators.
- *Tristia* (*Sorrows*, AD 9–12), and *Epistulae ex Ponto* (*Letters from Pontus*, AD 13–16). From *Ovid: The Poems of Exile*. University of California Press, 2005 (orig. Penguin Books, 1994). Peter Green, translator.

Together these works illustrate the diversity of Ovid's poetic output and (despite the difficulties in dating them precisely) represent the three main phases of his career: early Ovid in the *Amores*; middle Ovid in the *Metamorphoses* and *Fasti*; and late Ovid in the *Tristia* and *Epistulae*.

The line numbers accompanying each passage are original to the translations and generally designate the line numbers of the

Latin texts. Wherever possible, the translators' punctuation and formatting (such as italics) have been retained. New titles and brief headnotes have been added in order to lend the selections greater coherency. Whenever Middlebrook has cited or discussed the text, the reader is referred to the relevant pages of her biography.

AMORES

(*Loves*, originally after ca. 25 BC)

From *Ovid: The Erotic Poems*. Penguin Books, 1982. Peter Green, translator.

Ovid's first published work was the *Amores*, a collection of urbane love elegies originally presented in five books, but later condensed into three and reissued ca. AD 1. The collection successfully cemented the playful persona of Ovid, the poet-as-lover, and chronicled his tumultuous relationship with his mistress, Corinna (whose name, if she existed at all, is a learned pseudonym in the spirit of Catullus' Lesbia). On genesis of the *Amores* see pp. 51–62; on their revision, pp. 79–80.

BOOK ONE

1.1: *Cupid's Initiation*

An example of the *recusatio* motif, made famous by the Greek poet Callimachus, in which the singer recuses himself from one kind of song in favor of singing another. See p. 54, and compare Am. 2.18, pp. 14–5.

> Arms, warfare, violence—I was winding up to produce a
>   Regular epic, with verse-form to match—
> Hexameters, naturally. But Cupid (they say) with a snicker
>   Lopped off one foot from each alternate line.
> 5 'Nasty young brat,' I told him, 'who made *you* Inspector of Metres?
>   We poets come under the Muses, we're not in your mob.
> What if Venus took over the weapons of blonde Minerva,
>   While blonde Minerva began fanning passion's flame?
> Who'd stand for Our Lady of Wheatfields looking after rides and forests?
> 10   Who'd trust the Virgin Huntress to safeguard crops?
> Imagine long-haired Apollo on parade with a pikestaff
>   While the War-God fumbled tunes from Apollo's lyre!
> Look, boy, you've got your own empire, and a sight too much influence
>   As it is. Don't get ambitious, quit playing for more.
> 15 Or is your fief universal? Is Helicon yours? Can't even
>   Apollo call his lyre his own these days?
> I'd got off to a flying start, clean paper, one magnificent
>   Opening line. Number two brought me down
> With a bump. I haven't the theme to suit your frivolous metre:
> 20   No boyfriend, no girl with a mane of coiffured hair—'
> When I'd got so far, presto, he opened his quiver, selected
>   An arrow to lay me low,
> Then bent the springy bow in a crescent against his knee, and

Let fly. 'Hey, poet!' he called, 'you want a theme? Take *that!*'
25   His shafts—worse luck for me—never miss their target:
I'm on fire now, Love owns the freehold of my heart.
So let my verse rise with six stresses, drop to five on the downbeat—
Goodbye to martial epic, and epic metre too!
Come on then, my Muse, bind your blonde hair with a wreath of
Sea-myrtle, and lead me off in the six-five groove!

1.3: A Prayer to Venus

See pp. 28, 62–3, 71.

Fair's fair now, Venus. This girl's got me hooked. All I'm asking from her
Is love—or at least some future hope for my own
Eternal devotion. No, even that's too much—hell, just let me love her!
(*Listen*, Venus: I've asked you so often now.)
5   Say yes, pet. I'd be your slave for years, for a lifetime.
Say yes—unswerving fidelity's my strong suit.
I may not have top-drawer connections, I can't produce blue-blooded
Ancestors to impress you, my father's plain middle-class,
And there aren't any squads of ploughmen to deal with my broad
acres—
10   My parents are both pretty thrifty, and need to be.
What *have* I got on my side, then? Poetic genius, sweetheart,
Divine inspiration. And love. I'm yours to command—
Unswerving faithfulness, morals above suspicion,
Naked simplicity, a born-to-the-purple blush.
15   I don't chase thousands of girls, I'm no sexual circus-rider;
Honestly, all I want is to look after you
Till death do us part, have the two of us living together
All my time, and know you'll cry for me when I'm gone.
Besides, when you give me yourself, what you'll be providing
20   Is creative material. My art will rise to the theme
And immortalize *you*. Look, why do you think we remember
The swan-upping of Leda, or Io's life as a cow,
Or poor virgin Europa whisked off overseas, clutching
That so-called bull by the—horn? Through poems, of course.
25   So you and I, love, will enjoy the same world-wide publicity,
And our names will be linked, for ever, with the gods.

1.4: At the Dinner Party (excerpts)

Ovid's instructions to his mistress will remind readers of Ovid's later *Ars Amatoria*. See pp. 67–8.

'So your man's going to be present at this dinner-party?
    I hope he drops down dead before the dessert!
Does this mean no hands, just eyes (any chance guest's privilege) —
    Just to *look* at my darling, while *he*
5   Lies there with you beside him, in licensed embracement
    And paws your bosom or neck as he feels inclined?
I'm no longer surprised at those Centaurs for horsing around over
    Some cute little filly when they were full of wine —
I may not live in the forest, or be semi-equipped as a stallion,
10   But still I can hardly keep my hands to myself
When you're around. Now listen, I've got some instructions for you,
    And don't let the first breeze blow them out of your head!
Arrive before your escort. I don't see what can be managed
    If you do — but anyway, get there first.
15   When he pats the couch, put on your Respectable Wife expression,
    And take your place beside him — but nudge my foot
As you're passing by. Watch out for my nods and eye-talk,
    Pick up my stealthy messages, send replies.
I shall speak whole silent volumes with one raised eyebrow,
20   Words will spring from my fingers, words traced in wine.
When you're thinking about the last time we made love together,
    Touch your rosy cheek with one elegant thumb.
If you're cross with me, and can't say so, then pinch the bottom
    Of your earlobe. But when I do or say
25   Something that gives you especial pleasure, my darling,
    Keep turning the ring on your finger to and fro.
When you yearn for your man to suffer some well-merited misfortune
    Place your hands on the table as though in prayer.
If he mixes wine specially for you, watch out, make him drink it
30   Himself. Ask the waiter for what *you* want
As you hand back the goblet. I'll be the first to seize it
    And drink from the place your lips have touched.
If *he* offers you tit-bits out of some dish he's tasted,
    Refuse what's been near his mouth.
35   Don't let him put his arms round your neck, and oh, don't lay that
    Darling head of yours on his coarse breast.
Don't let his fingers roam down your dress to touch up
    Those responsive nipples. Above all, don't you dare

Kiss him, not once. If you do, I'll proclaim myself your lover,
40   Lay hand upon you, claim those kisses as mine.
So much for what I can see. But there's plenty goes on under
        A long evening wrap. The mere thought worries me stiff.
Don't start rubbing your thigh against his, don't go playing
        Footsy under the table, keep smooth from rough...
51 Keep pressing fresh drinks—but no kisses—on your husband,
        Slip neat wine in his glass if you get the chance.
If he passes out comfortably, drowned in sleep and liquor,
        We must improvise as occasion dictates.
55 When we all (you too) get up and leave, remember
        To stick in the middle of the crowd—
That's where you'll find me, or I you: whenever
        There's a chance to touch me, please do...
61 At nightfall he'll lock you inside, and I'll be left weeping
        On that cold front doorstep...
65 What you *can* do is show unwilling, behave as though you're frigid,
        Begrudge him endearments, make sex a dead loss.
69 But whatever the outcome tonight, when you see me tomorrow
        Just swear, through thick and thin, that you told him No.'

1.5: Corinna in the Afternoon

The first poem in the *Amores* to mention Corinna by name. See pp. 59, 62.

A hot afternoon: siesta-time. Exhausted,
        I lay sprawled across my bed.
One window-shutter was closed, the other stood half-open,
        And the light came sifting through
As it does in a wood. It recalled that crepuscular glow at sunset
        Or the trembling moment between darkness and dawn,
Just right for a modest girl whose delicate bashfulness
        Needs some camouflage. And then—
In stole Corinna, long hair tumbled about her
10   Soft white throat, a rustle of summer skirts,
Like some fabulous Eastern queen *en route* to her bridal-chamber—
        Or a top-line city call-girl, out on the job.
I tore the dress off her—not that it really hid much,
        But all the same she struggled to keep it on:
15 Yet her efforts were unconvincing, she seemed half-hearted—
        Inner self-betrayal made her give up.
When at last she stood naked before me, not a stitch of clothing,
        I couldn't fault her body at any point.
Smooth shoulders, delectable arms (I saw, I touched them),

20   Nipples inviting caresses, the flat
Belly outlined beneath that flawless bosom,
      Exquisite curve of a hip, firm youthful thighs.
But why catalogue details? Nothing came short of perfection,
      And I clasped her naked body close to mine.
25   Fill in the rest for yourselves! Tired at last, we lay sleeping.
      May my siestas often turn out that way!

1.9: A Lover Is a Fighter

A poem justifiably famous for its conflation of amorous pursuits and military service. See p. 65.

Every lover's on active service, my friend, active service, believe me,
      And Cupid has his headquarters in the field.
Fighting and love-making belong to the same age-group—
      In bed as in war, old men are out of place.
5   A commander looks to his troops for gallant conduct,
      A mistress expects no less.
Soldier and lover both keep night-long vigil,
      Lying rough outside their captain's (or lady's) door.
The military life brings long route-marches—but just let his mistress
10   Be somewhere ahead, and the lover too
Will trudge on for ever, scale mountains, ford swollen rivers,
      Thrust his way through deep snow.
Come embarkation-time *he* won't talk of 'strong north-easters',
      Or say it's 'too late in the season' to put to sea.
15   Who but a soldier or lover would put up with freezing
      Nights—rain, snow, sleet? The first
Goes out on patrol to observe the enemy's movements,
      The other watches his rival, an equal foe.
A soldier lays siege to cities, a lover to girls' houses,
20   The one assaults city gates, the other front doors.
Night attacks are a great thing. Catch your opponents sleeping
      And unarmed. Just slaughter them where they lie.
That's how the Greeks dealt with Rhesus and his wild Thracians
      While rustling those famous mares.
25   Lovers, too, will take advantage of slumber (her husband's),
      Strike home while the enemy sleeps: getting past
Night patrols and eluding sentries are games both soldiers
      And lovers need to learn.
Love, like war, is a toss-up. The defeated can recover,
30   While some you might think invincible collapse;
So if you've got love written off as an easy option

You'd better think twice. Love calls
    For guts and initiative. Great Achilles sulks for Briseis—
        Quick, Trojans, smash through the Argive wall!
35   Hector went into battle from Andromache's embraces
        Helmeted by his wife.
    Agamemnon himself, the Supremo, was struck into raptures
        At the sight of Cassandra's tumbled hair;
    Even Mars was caught on the job, felt the blacksmith's meshes—
40   Heaven's best scandal in years. Then take
    My own case. I was idle, born to leisure *en déshabillé,*
        Mind softened by lazy scribbling in the shade.
    But love for a pretty girl soon drove the sluggard
        To action, made him join up.
45   And just look at me now—fighting fit, dead keen on night exercises:
        If you want a cure for slackness, fall in love!

1.14: A Bad Hair Day

See pp. 66-7, 69.

I *told* you to stop using rinses—and now just look at you!
    No hair worth mentioning left to dye.
Why couldn't you let well alone? It grew so luxuriantly,
    Right down to below your hips,
5   And fine—so fine you were scared to set it, like silken
        Threads in a vivid Chinese screen,
Or the filament spun by a spider, the subtle creation
    That she hangs beneath some deserted beam.
It was neither dark nor blonde, but a brindled auburn,
10   A mixture of both, like some tall cedar when
The outer bark's stripped off, in a dew-wet precipitous
    Valley of Ida. Not to mention the fact
That it was so tractable, could be dressed in a hundred styles, and
    Never made you get cross. With no pins
15   Or curlers to make it go brittle, no bristling side-combs,
        Your maid could relax. I've been there
Often enough while she fixed it, but never once saw you
    Pick up a hairpin and stick it in her arm.
If it was early morning, you'd be propped up among lilac
20   Pillows and coverlets, your hair
Not yet combed out. Yet even in tangled disorder
    It still became you. You looked like a wild
Exhausted Maenad, *al fresco.*
    Poor down-fine tresses,

What torture they had to endure!
25 You decided on corkscrew ringlets. The irons were heated,
    Your poor hair crimped and racked
Into spiralling curls. 'It's a crime,' I told you, 'a downright
    Crime to singe it like that. Why on earth
Can't you leave well alone? You'll *wreck* it, you obstinate creature,
30   It's *not for burning*. Why, in its natural state
It'd make the best perm look silly—' No good. Her crowning
    Glory, that any mod god might well
Have envied, sleek tresses like those that sea-wet naked
    Dione holds up in the picture—gone, all gone.
35 Why complain of the loss? You silly girl, you detested
    That waist-length tangle, so stop
Making sad *moves* in your mirror. You must get accustomed
    To your own New Look, and forget
Yourself if you aim to attract. No rival's incantations
40   Or tisanes have harmed you, no witch
Has hexed your rinse, you haven't—touch wood—had an illness;
    If your hair's fallen out, it's not
Any envious tongue that's to blame. You applied that concoction
    Yourself. It was you that did it. *All your fault.*
45 Still, after our German conquests a wig is easily come by—
    A captive Mädchen's tresses will see you through.
You'll blush, it's true, when your borrowed plumage elicits
    Admiration galore. You'll feel that the praise (like the hair)
Has been bought. Once you really deserved it. Now each compliment
50   Belongs to some Rhine maiden, not to you.
Poor sweet—she's shielding her face to hide those ladylike
    Blushes, and making a brave effort not to cry
As she stares at the ruined hair in her lap, a keepsake
    Unhappily out of place. Don't worry, love,
55 Just put on your make-up. This loss is by no means irreparable—
    Give it time, and your hair will grow back as good as new.

BOOK TWO

2.13: *Corinna's Abortion*
See p. 67.

Corinna got pregnant—and rashly tried an abortion.
    Now she's lying in danger of her life.
She said not a word. That risk, and she never told me!
    I ought to be furious, but I'm only scared.

5   It was me by whom she conceived—or at least, I assume so:
          I often jump to conclusions. Ilithyia, Queen
     Of the Afric shore, whose presence broods over alluvial
          Canopus, Memphis, palmy Pharos and that
     Broad delta where swift Nile discharges seaward

10   In seven meandering streams:
     By your sistrum I beg you, by the holy head of Anubis
          (So may Osiris evermore love your rites,
     The slow snake writhe through your sanctuary, the horned bull
          Apis grace your processions!), ah look down

15   In mercy, Goddess: through one spare both of us; in your
          Hands her life lies—and mine in hers.
     She has kept your holy days, a regular worshipper,
          Asperged by the eunuch priests
     With dripping laurel-switches—and your compassion

20   For girls in labour is well-known.
     Ilithyia, Goddess of Childbirth, hear my entreaties, save her—
          She's worth it, truly. Just say the word,
     And I'll robe myself in white, burn incense on your smoking
          Altar, lay at your feet the gifts I vowed,

25   With a label reading 'From Ovid, in grateful thanks for Corinna's
          Recovery'—ah, please make it all come true!
     Look, sweetheart, I know how you're feeling, I know it's no time for
          Recriminations—but *never* try that again!

2.16: Ovid at Sulmona

See pp. 26–7, 63.

     I am here in Sulmona, my own Pelignian riding,
          A small place, but lush with streams:
     Though the ground parch and crack under a blazing summer
          Sun, though the Dog Star glares

5   Like brass, clear rills still wander through these fertile meadows,
          The grass remains fresh and green.
     Wheat yields well in this soil, the vine still better; in places
          You can glimpse an olive grove,
     And along the slow river-bank, by knee-deep pastures,

10   The turf grows rank and moist.
     But my flame isn't here—or rather, to change the image,
          Though my heart's on fire, the kindling spark is away.
     Offered a place in the sky between Castor and Pollux, I'd still say
          No. What's heaven worth minus you?

15   May those who have scored the world with endless highways

Lie uneasy in dank clay graves!
If they had to cut trunk-roads, they should have made it a rule that
    Girls were obliged to travel with their beaux.
Suppose I was crossing the Alps in a blizzard, all goose-pimples—
20   With my girl along I'd take the trip in my stride.
With her, I'd cheerfully sail through sand-shoals, or put to sea when
    A gale was blowing full blast;
I'd baulk at nothing—the monsters yelping from Scylla's
    Virgin groin, the reefs of Cape Malea,
25 Those maelstrom waters that wreck-glutted Charybdis
    Spews up and sucks down by turns—
Even suppose a typhoon took charge of us, and towering
    Waves washed our guardian gods away,
You could wind your white arms about my shoulders—so lissom
30   A weight would be easy borne:
Think of the times young Leander swam over to Hero, till that
    Last night when the lamp blew out
And he was lost. But without you, my sweet, even this, my favourite
    Landscape—these water-meadows, the rows
35 Of teeming vines, a cool breeze stirring the treetops, some peasant
    Singing away as he waters his patch of land—
Looks barren and strange, un-Pelignian, somewhere else, quite different
    From the farm on which I was born:
More like Scythia, or the bloody rock of Prometheus,
40   With such neighbours as Britons in woad
Or wild Cilician pirates. Elm loves vine, vine sticks with elm—then
    Why must my mistress and I
Be parted so often? You swore you'd stay with me always,
    On my life you swore it, by
45 Your eyes, those stars of my heart; but a girl's oath is lighter
    Than leaves in autumn, whirled
Away by wind or wave. Yet if you've a glimmer of feeling
    Left for me, then make your promises deeds,
Get out the trap, harness your quick-stepping ponies,
50   Shake up the reins, and away,
Wild manes flying! May all winding roads and valleys
    Be straight where you pass, and the high hills lie down for you!

2.18: An Update on Ovid's Career

Poem 2.18 probably belongs, wholly or partly, to the second edition of the *Amores*. Ovid ostensibly refers to the *Ars Amatoria* (1 BC or after) at vv. 19–20, and to the *Heroides* (published sometime before the *Ars*) at vv. 21–6. Furthermore, he mentions a tragic play, quite possibly his lost *Medea* (ca. 13 BC), at vv.

13–16. The *Medea* factors into *Am.* 3.1 (pp. 15-7) and 3.15 (p. 19), where Ovid seems not yet to have written the play. If this state of affairs is correct, poem 2.18 documents the poet's recusatio of tragedy and his return to love elegy for his reading public.

> While you are taking your poem up to the wrath of Achilles
>   And arming your oath-bound heroes for the fray,
> Love-in-idleness, Macer, and the shades of dalliance
>   Preoccupy *me*. That tender erotic urge
> 5 Shatters my high-flown intentions. The times I've ejected
>   My mistress, only to have her nestle back
> In my lap. I'm ashamed, I told her. Weeping, she whispered:
>   'Ashamed of loving poor me?' and wound her arms
> Tight round my neck, sabotaged me with unending
> 10   Kisses. So, I'm surrendering, have recalled
> My imagination from military active service, to cope with
>   A sex-war on the domestic front.
> Still, I *did* assume the sceptre, began writing a tragic opus —
>   Tragedy suited my style, I was going well,
> 15 But Love guffawed at my costume: that cloak, those crimson buskins,
>   The sceptre I'd grabbed in my plebeian paw.
> Once again the will of my obstinate mistress checked me,
>   And passion has triumphed over the tragic bard.
> Now I stick to my proper last — verse-lectures on seduction
> 20   (I tend to be wrong-footed by my own advice!),
> Or love-lorn heroines' letters — Penelope to Ulysses,
>   Phyllis' tearful complaint on being ditched;
> Appeals to Paris, Macareus, ungrateful Jason; something
>   Calculated to stir Hippolytus *and*
> 25 His father; or the Final Message Department — Dido clutching
>   A naked sword, and Sappho her Lesbian lyre.
> My friend Sabinus has played international postman
>   With uncommon speed — replies
> From all over the world are now in: Penelope remembers
> 30   Ulysses' hand, Phaedra has read the note
> Hippolytus penned; Aeneas (turned pious) has answered
>   Poor Dido's appeal; there's even a *billet-doux*
> For Phyllis, if she's alive still; for Hypsipyle an unpleasant
>   Comeback from Jason; Sappho, whose love is returned,
> 35 Gives the lyre she vowed to Apollo. Even you, friend Macer,
>   – Insofar as it's safe for a martial poet — lace
> Your warfare with 'Love the Golden': Paris, adulterous Helen
>   (Noble but Naughty), Laodameia (True

40 Unto Death). If I know you, you'll get more pleasure from that lot
        Than from warfare—so why not give up and join my camp?

BOOK THREE

3.1: A Contest of Elegy and Tragedy

See p. 63. Poem 3.1 might have belonged to the fifth book of *Amores* edition one, relocated to book three for the collection's second edition. Ovid's poetic ambition has grown, and he is seriously tempted to work within the genre of tragedy, a higher form than love elegy. The "masterpiece" mentioned in v. 70 could well be the nascent *Medea*.

There's this ancient wood—no axe has thinned it for ages,
    It might well be some spirit's home.
At its centre, a sacred spring, an arched limestone grotto,
    And sweet birdsong all around.
5   While I was strolling here, through an overwoven
    Dapple of shade, and wondering just what task
My Muse should embark on next, there appeared before me
    Elegy, perfumed hair caught up in a knot,
And short—I think—in one foot: good figure, nice dress, a loving
10   Expression. Even her lameness looked chic.
Behind her stalked barnstorming Tragedy, fraught brow hidden
    By flowing hair, mantle a trail in the dust,
Left hand waving a royal sceptre, high Lydian
    Boots encasing her calves.
15 'Won't you *ever*,' she asked me, 'have done with love as a subject?
    Why get stuck in the same old poetic rut?
Your efforts to shock make gossip for drunken parties, a buzz at
    Every street-corner. As you walk by
Fingers point, people whisper: 'Look, there goes that poet
20   With the ultra-combustible heart.'
All this shameless parade of your sexual activities makes you
    The talk of the whole town—and what do you care?
It's high time your inspiration chose a loftier model:
    You've idled enough. Start on some major work.
25 Your present theme cramps your style. Try the deeds of heroes—
    A subject (you'll find) more worthy of your art.
You've been playing at poetry—ballads for girl-adolescents,
    Juvenile stuff, the eternal *enfant terrible*.
Now why not turn *my* way, make Roman tragedy famous,
30   Give me the inspiration that I need?'

With that she nodded three or four times, her scarlet buskins
    Holding her upright against the weight of her hair.
At this point, or so I recall, a mischievous expression
    Crept over Elegy's face. (Had she got
35 A myrtle-wand in her hand? I think so.) 'You posturing
    Windbag,' she cried, 'do you *have* to be such a bore?
Can't you *ever* stop your pomposity? At least you condescended
    To attack me in elegiacs, you turned my own
Metre against me—not that I'd ever dream of comparing
40   Your high palatial vein with my own
Minuscule talent. Besides, I'm frivolous, like my subject,
    And equally unheroic. All the same,
Without me Our Lady of Passion would be plain vulgar—
    She needs my help as adviser and go-between.
45 The door your tough buskin can't break down flies open
    At one flattering word of mine;
Corinna took lessons from me, how to hoodwink porters
    Or spring the most foolproof lock,
How to slip out of bed in her nightdress and move with unerring
50   Feet, like a cat, through the night.
Yet I've earned my advantage. I've beaten you by submitting
    To indignities which your pride
Would recoil from in horror. The times I've been nailed to indifferent
    Front doors, for any passer-by to read!
55 Why, I even remember lying snug in a maid's bosom
    Till some crusty chaperone took off—
Not to mention the time I was sent as a birthday present
    To that frightful girl who just tore me into shreds
And flushed me away. It was I who awakened your dormant
60   Poetic genius. If *she's* after you now
It's me you should thank for it.' 'Ladies, please listen,' I told them
    Nervously, 'don't take offence—
One of you honours me with sceptre and buskins: high-flown
    Utterance springs to my lips at her touch.
65 But the other offers my passions undying glory: come then,
    Short foot and limping metre, it's you I choose!
I'm sorry, Tragedy. Just be patient awhile. Your service
    Demands a lifetime. *Her* needs are quickly met.'
The goddess forgave me. I'd better get on with this little volume
70   While I may—my subconscious is hatching a masterpiece.

3.7: A Case of Impotence

See pp. 62–3.

I can't fault the girl on looks, or style, or sophistication—
    And I'd tried for her often enough. *But*
There we lay, in bed, embracing, and all to no purpose:
    I was limp, disgusting, dead.
5   Heaven knows I wanted it badly, and so did my partner,
    But still I failed to measure up.
She tried every trick—wound her arms (whiter than snow or
    Ivory) around me, pressed
Her thighs up snug under mine, plied me with sexy kisses,
10   Tongue exploring like mad,
Whispered endearments, called me her master, tried me
    With nice four-letter words—they often help.
No good. My member hung slack, as though frozen by hemlock,
    A dead loss for the sort of game I'd planned.
15   There I lay, a sham, a deadweight, a trunk of inert matter,
    Not even sure if I was alive, or a ghost.
What sort of old age shall I have (if I ever reach it)
    When I can't make out as a youth?
I'm ashamed, at my age. Little good in being young and virile
20   If as far as *she* could tell
I was neither. She left my bed with sisterly decorum,
    Pure as a Vestal off to tend
The sacred flame. But it's not all that long since I made it
    Twice with that smart Greek blonde, three times
25   With a couple of other beauties—and as for Corinna,
    In one short night, I remember, she made me perform
Nine times, no less. Perhaps some Thessalian hell-brew has ruined
    My physical urges, maybe I'm a victim of spells
And herbal concoctions. Perhaps some witch is busy transfixing
30   My image, and name, in red wax,
Sticking pins through my liver. Magic spells can transform wheatfields
    Into barren tares, can dry up springs at source,
Charm acorns off oaks, grapes from vines, strip orchards bare of
    Their fruit without human aid—so what's to stop
35   Some magician giving my member a local anaesthetic?
    Maybe *that* was the trouble, made worse
By embarrassment when I couldn't, the final humiliating
    Blow to my masculine pride.
Such a marvellous girl—her own dress couldn't cling closer

40   Than I did to her: I eyed her, touched her, but that
        Was as far as it went. Put Nestor in my position,
                Tithonus even, and despite their decrepitude
        They'd rise to the test like boys. I'd the chance to possess her,
                But she got no deal. What can I pray for now?
45   I'm sure the gods must regret the gift with which they endowed me—
                Just look at the way I've messed it up! I got
        Everything that I hoped for, an enthusiastic welcome,
                Kisses, the girl on her own: yet where
        Did all my good fortune take me? What's ownership minus
50   Possession? To leave such wealth intact
        Was a trick fit for misers. I lay there like Tantalus, parching
                Because of his indiscretion, eyes on the fruit
        That always hung just out of reach. I mean, one just *doesn't*
                Get up simon-pure after a night with a girl—
55   And it's not that she wasn't seductive, just think of those marvellous
                Kisses she wasted on me, the tricks she tried!
        She could have shifted an oak-tree, broken hard adamant,
                Worked up unfeeling stones:
        A living, virile partner, for her, was a pushover—but just then
60   I lacked both virility and life.
        What joy can a blind man get from a painted picture?
                What's the use of a singer performing for the deaf?
        I imagined every variety of erotic pleasure, invented
                No end of positions—in my head—
65   But still my member lay there, an embarrassing case of
                Premature death, and limper than yesterday's rose.
        Yet *now*—what perverse timing!—just look at it, stiff and urgent,
                Eager to go campaigning, get on the job.
        (Oh why can't you lie down? I'm ashamed of you, you bastard—
70   I've been caught by your promises before.
        You let me down, it was *your* fault I landed weaponless
                In this embarrassing and expensive fix.)
        My girl tried everything, even some gentle massage
                Of the offending part—
75   Yet *still* it wouldn't come up. All her varied resources
                (She saw) left it quite unmoved.
        Then she really got mad. 'You're sick,' she told me. 'Stop wasting
                My time. Who sent you along
        To gatecrash my bed? Look, either some witch has hexed you
80   Or you've just been making love with another girl.'
        That did it. She jumped out of bed, her nightdress flying, with a
                Delectable flash of bare feet,

And to stop her maids from guessing nothing had happened
  Splashed around with some water—as though it had.

3.15: Farewell to Elegy

See pp. 26, 61. A sphragis-type poem, in which the poet leaves his "seal" on the *Amores*. Here he takes leave of love elegy and moves upward and onward to tragedy (vv. 17–20). Like *Am.* 3.1, 3.15 seems to be a holdover from book five of edition one, possibly the last poem in the original collection.

Mother of tender loves, you must find another poet:
  My elegies are homing on their final lap.
Postscript concerning the author: of Paelignian extraction,
  A man whose delights have never let him down,
5 Heir—for what that's worth—to an ancient family,
  No brand-new knight jumped up
Through the maelstrom fortunes of war. Mantua boasts her Virgil,
  The Veronese their Catullus. *I* shall become the pride
Of my fellow-Paelignians—a race who fought for freedom,
10 Freedom with honour, in the Italian wars
That scared Rome witless. I can see some visitor to Sulmona
  Taking in its tiny scale, the streams and walls,
And saying: 'Any township, however small, that could breed so
  Splendid a poet, I call great.' Boy-god,
15 And you, Cyprian goddess, his mother, remove your golden
  Standards from my terrain—
Horned Bacchus is goading me on to weightier efforts, bigger
  Horses, a really ambitious trip.
So farewell, congenial Muse, unheroic elegiacs—
20 Work born to live on when its maker's dead!

METAMORPHOSES

(*Transformations*, before AD 8)

From *Ovid: Metamorphoses*. Penguin Books, 2004. David Raeburn, translator.

The *Metamorphoses*, an epic poem about supernatural transformations, is Ovid's most famous and most influential achievement. His only surviving work composed in pure dactylic hexameter (the traditional epic meter) rather than elegiac couplets, the poem spans from the creation of the world down to the poet's own era.

The *Metamorphoses* is also Ovid's longest work. Although lacking final form at the time of his relegation, the epic nevertheless comprises fifteen books worth of transformations. The selections below are essential to Middlebrook's discussion, but only scratch the poem's surface. The following stories are recommended in addition:

- The Creation and Ages of Mankind (1.5–150; see p. 12)
- Lycaeon (1.163–243)
- Io (1.568–747)
- Callisto (2.401–530; see pp. 27-8)
- Europa (2.833–75)
- Actaeon (3.138–272; see p. 27)
- Narcissus and Echo (3.339–510)
- Minerva and the Muses, and their sub-narratives, including the rape of Proserpina (5.250–678; see pp. 27, 35-7).
- Niobe (6.146–312)
- Tereus, Procne, and Philomela (6.424–674; see p. 40)
- Medea (7.1–403)
- Daedalus and Icarus (8.183–235)
- Meleager (8.260–546)
- Philemon and Baucis (8.611–724)
- Byblis (9.454–665)
- Myrrha (10.298–502)
- Atalanta and Hippomenes (10.560–707)
- Midas (11.85–193)
- Ceyx and Alcyone (11.410–748)
- Hecuba (13.429–575)
- Glaucus and Scylla (13.898–14.74)

BOOK ONE

Author's Prologue (1.1–4)

Changes of shape, new forms, are the theme which my spirit impels me
now to recite. Inspire me, O gods (it is you who have even
transformed my art), and spin me a thread from the world's beginning
4   down to my own lifetime, in one continuous poem.

Apollo and Daphne (1.452–567)

See pp. 29–30, 73, 78–9

Apollo's first love was Daphne, the child of the river Penéüs.
Blind chance was not to be blamed but Cupid's spiteful resentment.
Phoebus, still in the flush of his victory over the serpent,
455   had noticed the love-god bending his bow and drawing the string
to his shoulder, and asked him: 'What are you doing with grown-up
        weapons,
you mischievous boy? That bow would better be carried by me.
When I fire my shafts at my foes or beasts, they're unfailingly
        wounded.
My numberless arrows have just destroyed the venomous Python,
460   which filled whole acres of mountainside with its belly's infections.
You be content with your torch and use it to kindle some passion
or other; but don't usurp any honours belonging to me!'
The son of Venus replied: 'Your arrows, Apollo, can shoot
whatever you choose, but I'll shoot you. As mortal creatures
465   must yield to a god, your glory will likewise prove to be subject
to mine.' Then he beat his wings and cut a path through the
        atmosphere,
nimbly alighting upon the heights of shady Parnassus.
Once there he drew from his quiver two arrows of contrary purpose:
one is for rousing passion, the other is meant to repel it.
470   The former is made of gold, and its head has a sharp, bright point,
while the latter is blunt and weighted with lead one side of the reed
        shaft.
That was the arrow which Cupid implanted in Daphne's bosom;

the other was aimed at Apollo and smote to the core of his being.
Phoebus at once was filled with desire, but Daphne fled
475   from the very thought of a lover. She joyed in the forest lairs
and in spoils of captive beasts, like the virgin goddess Diana,
binding her carelessly flowing locks in a simple headband.
Courted by suitors in droves, Peneüs' daughter rejected them.
Stubbornly single, she'd roam through the woodland thickets, without
480   concern for the meaning of marriage or love or physical union.
Often her father remarked, 'You owe me a son, my daughter,'
or else he would say, 'Now when, my child, will you give me a
        grandson?'
Marriage torches to Daphne were nothing less than anathema.
Blushes of shame would spread all over her beautiful cheeks,
485   she would lovingly cling to her father's neck in a coaxing appeal
and say to him, 'Darling Father, I want to remain a virgin
for ever. Please let me. Diana's father allowed her that.'
Peneüs granted her wish; but Daphne's peculiar beauty
and personal charm were powerful bars to her prayer's fulfilment.
490   Phoebus caught sight of her, fell in love and longed to possess her.
Wishes were hopes, for even his powers of prophecy failed him.
Think of the flimsy stubble which burns in a harvested cornfield;
and think of a blazing hedgerow fired by a torch which a traveller
has carelessly brought too close or dropped behind him at daybreak.
495   So was the god as his heart caught fire and the flames spread through
to the depths of his soul, and passion was fuelled with empty hope.
He eyes the hair hanging loosely over her neck, and murmurs,
'What if that hair were neatly arranged!' He looks at her bright eyes
burning and twinkling like stars; he studies her lips, so teasingly
500   tempting; he fondly admires her hands with their delicate fingers;
he dotes on the shapely arms, so nearly bare to the shoulder;
what's hidden he thinks must be even better. But swift as the light
        breeze,
Daphne is gone, with never a pause as he calls out after her:
'Stop, dear Daphne, I beg you to stop! This isn't an enemy
505   chasing you. Stop! You would think I'm a wolf pursuing a lamb,
a lion hunting a deer or an eagle pouncing on fluttering
doves in mid-air, but I'm not! It is love that impels me to follow you.
Have pity! How frightened I am that you'll fall and scratch those
        innocent
legs in the brambles. You mustn't be hurt on account of me!
510   The ground where you're rushing away is so rough. Slow down, my
        beloved,
I beg you. Don't run so fast and I promise to slow down too.

Now ask who it is that desires you. I'm not a wild mountain-dweller;
this isn't an uncouth shepherd, minding the flocks and the herds
round here. Impetuous girl, you have no idea who you're running
> from.
515 That's why you're running so fast. Listen! I am the master of Delphi,
Claros and Ténedos, Pátara's temple too. My father
is Jupiter. I can reveal the past, the present and future
to all who seek them. I am the lord of the lyre and song.
My arrows are deadly, but one is even more deadly than they are,
520 the shaft which has smitten a heart that has never been wounded
> before.
Healing is my invention, the world invokes me as Helper,
and I am the one who dispenses the herbs with the power to cure.
Alas! No herbs have the power to cure the disease of my love.
Those arts which comfort the whole of mankind cannot comfort their
> master!'

525 Apollo wanted to say much more, but the terrified Daphne
ran all the faster; she left him behind with his speech unfinished.
Her beauty was visible still, as her limbs were exposed by the wind;
the breezes which blew in her face managed also to flutter her dress;
and the currents of air succeeded in blowing her tresses behind her.
530 Flight made her all the more lovely; but now the god in his youthful
ardour was ready no longer to squander his breath on wheedling
pleas. Spurred on by desire, he followed the trail with new vigour.
Imagine a greyhound, imagine a hare it has sighted in open
country: one running to capture his prey, the other for safety.
535 The hound is about to close in with his jaws; he believes he is almost
there; he is grazing the back of her heels with the tip of his muzzle.
The hare isn't sure if her hunter has caught her, but leaps into freedom,
clear of the menacing jaws and the mouth which keeps brushing
> against her.
So with Apollo and Daphne, the one of them racing in hope
540 and the other in fear. But the god had the pinions of love to encourage
> him.
Faster than she, he allowed her no rest; his hands were now close
to the fugitive's shoulders; his breath was ruffling the hair on her neck.
Her strength exhausted, the girl grew pale; then overcome
by the effort of running, she saw Peneüs' waters before her:
545 'Help me, Father!' she pleaded. 'If rivers have power over nature,
mar the beauty which made me admired too well, by changing
my form!' She had hardly ended her prayer when a heavy numbness
came over her body; her soft white bosom was ringed in a layer

550   of bark, her hair was turned into foliage, her arms into branches.
The feet that had run so nimbly were sunk into sluggish roots;
her head was confined in a treetop; and all that remained was her beauty.

Tree though she was, Apollo still loved her. Caressing the trunk
with his hand, he could feel the heart still fluttering under the new bark.
555   Seizing the branches, as though they were limbs, in his arms' embrace,
he pressed his lips to the wood; but the wood still shrank from his kisses.
Phoebus then said to her: 'Since you cannot be mine in wedlock,
you must at least be Apollo's tree. It is you who will always
be twined in my hair, on my tuneful lyre and my quiver of arrows.
560   The generals of Rome shall be wreathed with you, when the jubilant
            paean
of triumph is raised and the long procession ascends the Capitol.
On either side of Augustus' gates your trees shall stand sentry,
faithfully guarding the crown of oak-leaves hanging between them.
As I, with my hair that is never cut, am eternally youthful,
565   so you with your evergreen leaves are for glory and praise everlasting.'
Apollo the Healer had done. With a wave of her new-formed branches
the laurel agreed, and seemed to be nodding her head in the treetop.

BOOK TWO

Phaëthon and the Chariot of the Sun (2.1–328) (excerpts)

Phaëthon has grown up believing the claim of his mother, Clymene, that
his father is Phoebus, the sun-god. However, after a peer scoffs at this claim,
Phaëthon makes his way to the palace of Phoebus, far off in the east, in order
to confirm his heritage. See pp. 29–30, 55–6.

Picture the Sun's royal seat, an imposing building with towering
columns, resplendent in glittering gold and blazing bronze;
its pediment proudly surmounted by figures in burnished ivory;
the double doors at the entrance a sheen of shimmering silver.
5   More wonderful yet is the workmanship which Vulcan displayed
on the portals' reliefs: the ocean encircling the central earth
on a detailed map of the world, with the Sun's great canopy over it.
There in the waves are the sea-gods: Triton holding his conch-horn,
Próteus who constantly changes his shape, and the giant Aegaéon,
10   gripping the monstrous backs of the whales with his hundred arms;
Doris along with her daughters, some of them shown to be swimming,
while others are resting upon the rocks and drying their green hair
or riding along on a fish. The nymphs have different features,

but show the family likeness that might be expected in sisters.

15 Embossed on earth are the men in their cities and beasts in their forests;
the water-nymphs next to their streams and the other rural divinities.
Crowning these pictures the heavens, brightly portrayed, with the signs
of the zodiac, six on the right-hand door and six on the left.

Pháëthon quickly mounted the steep approach to the palace,
20 and entered the house of the god whom he wished to be sure was his
father.
Marching boldly towards the face of his sire, he halted
a little way off, as it hurt his eyes to come any closer.
Garbed in a robe of royal purple, radiant Phoebus
was sitting there on a throne which was glowing with brilliant emeralds.
25 Standing close on his right and his left were the Spirits of Day,
of Month and of Year, the Centuries and Hours at their equal intervals.
Also in waiting were youthful Spring with her wreath of flowers,
Summer naked but for her garland of ripening corn ears,
Autumn stained with the juice of trodden clusters of grapes,
30 And icy Winter, whose aged locks were hoary and tangled.

Then from his place in the centre the Sun, with his all-seeing eyes,
caught sight of the young man trembling in awe of his strange
surroundings.
'Why have you come?' he enquired. 'And what do you seek in this
stronghold,
Phaëthon, offspring of mine, whom his father could never disown?'
35 'O Phoebus, my father, light that illumines the infinite universe,'
answered the youth, 'if you will allow me to call you my father,
if Clýmene is not trying to cloak some guilty secret,
grant me a sign, my father, whereby all men must believe
that I am truly your son, and banish this doubt from my own mind.'
40 Then, in response, his father removed the circlet of sparkling
rays which adorned his head, commanded the youth to come nearer,
and folded him close in his arms. 'You are truly mine,' he assured him.
'Denial would do you injustice, and Clymene did not deceive you.
Away with your doubts! Now ask me whatever favour you will,
45 and I shall bestow it. To witness my promise, I call on the Stygian
marsh which the gods must swear by, though I have never set eyes on it.'
Phaëthon answered at once. He asked for his father's chariot,
with leave to control the wing-footed horses, for just one day.

His father at once regretted his oath. Repeatedly shaking
50 his lustrous head, he exclaimed: 'Your request has proved my promise

too rash. How I wish I could break it! Dear son, I confess to you freely,
this is the only wish I could ever be moved to refuse you.
Still, I can argue against it. Believe me, you're looking for danger!
The favour you ask is great, my Phaëthon, far too great

55   for the strength that you have. You are only a boy, too young to
        attempt it.
Your destiny's mortal; your wishes transcend your mortal limits.
Indeed your ignorant heart is pursuing what even immortals
can never attain. We all may flatter ourselves as we will,
yet none save I has the strength to stand in the fiery chariot

60   and hold his footing. Even the ruler of vast Olympus,
who hurls the deadly thunderbolts forth from his awesome hand,
shall never control this car; and what have we greater than Jove?

88   …Oh listen, my son! Don't force me to make you a gift that can only
prove fatal. Be warned and amend your prayer before it's too late.

90   I can understand that you need some indisputable proof
that my own blood runs in your veins. So here you have it: my fatherly
fears and misgivings prove me to be your father. Look, boy,
look at my face. How I wish your eyes were able to pierce
deep down to my heart and catch a glimpse of your father's anxiety.

95   Finally, look all round you: survey whatever the wealthy
cosmos contains, and make your choice of the bountiful riches
of earth and sea and sky. Be sure I'll refuse you nothing.
This one thing only I beg you not to demand. It's a sentence,
not honour you're asking for; punishment, Phaëthon, never a present.

100   Why are your fingers caressing my neck, you ignorant boy?
Never fear, I have sworn by the Stygian marsh, and I'll surely give you
whatever you choose to ask for. But choose more wisely, I beg you!'

His warnings were finished, but Phaëthon still resisted the sun god's
pleas and pressed his request in his burning desire for the chariot.

105   And so, delaying as long as he could, his father conducted
the young man down to the lofty conveyance which Vulcan had made
        him.
The axle and pole were constructed of gold, and golden too
was the rim encircling the wheels, which were fitted with spokes of silver.
Chrysolites, jewels arranged in a pattern along the yoke,

110   reflected their brilliant splendour on shining Phoebus himself.
And while self-confident Phaëthon studied the car in amazement
at such fine workmanship, Dawn was awake to open her purple
gates in the glimmering east and bathe her forecourt in roseate
glory; the stars were routed, and Lucifer brought up the rear,

115   as last of all he abandoned his watch in the brightening sky.

When Titan saw that the morning star was inclining earthward,
the sky growing pink and the horns of the waning moon disappearing,
he gave the command to the fleet-footed Hours to harness his steeds.
The goddesses quickly performed his bidding. Forth from the lofty
120 stables they led the fire-breathing stallions, fully refreshed
with ambrosia juice, and carefully fastened the jingling bridles.
Next the father anointed the face of his son with a holy
balsam, to offer protection against the scorching flames,
and placed his radiant crown on the young man's head. Then heaving
125 sighs from his troubled heart in gloomy foreboding, he said:
'If you are still able to take one piece of advice from your father,
spare the goad, my son, and put more strength in the reins.
My horses will speed unencouraged; the task is to curb their impatience.
Don't follow a route directly across the sky's five zones:
130 the path is cut at a slanting angle and runs in a wide arc,
well inside the three middle zones and carefully avoiding
the southern pole and the zone to the ·north with its biting winds.
You must keep to that road—the ruts from my wheels will be clearly
      visible;
then, to give earth and sky an equal share of your warmth,
135 don't drive the chariot down or scale the top of the ether.
Venture to climb too high, and you'll burn the ceiling of heaven,
the earth if you sink too low; for safety remain in the middle.
Swerving too far to the right, you'll be caught in the coils of the Serpent;
too far to the left, you'll collide with the Altar near the horizon.
140 Hold to a course in between. The rest I resign to Fortune;
I pray her to help and take care of you better than you take care
of yourself. As I speak, the dewy night has reached its appointed
goal on the shores of the west. The time for delaying is over.
The summons has come, for the darkness has fled and Auróra is glowing.
145 Now grasp the reins in your hands—or if your ambitious purpose
can yet be altered, take my advice and not my chariot.
Allow me to give my light to the earth, and watch me in safety
While still you can, while still you are standing on solid earth,
Before you have blindly mounted the car you so foolishly asked for.'

150 Phaëthon nimbly jumped into place on the light-framed chariot.
Standing aloft, he excitedly seized the featherweight reins
and shouted his thanks from the car to his worried and anxious father.
Meanwhile the sun god's team of winged horses—Fiery, Dawnsteed,
Scorcher and Blaze—were impatiently filling the air with their whinnies,
155 snorting out flames and kicking the bolted gates with their hooves.
As soon as Tethys, blind to the fate which awaited her grandson,

had shot the bolts back and the limitless sky was open before them,
at once they were off; and galloping forward into the air,
they cut through the mists which stood in their way; then rose on their
        wings
160 and quickly outdistanced the winds which had sprung up too in the east.
But the load that they carried was light, not one that the Sun's strong
        horses
could easily feel, and the yoke seemed far less heavy than usual.
As ships with inadequate ballast will toss and roll on the billows,
swept along through the ocean, too light to be firmly stable,
165 so Phoebus' chariot, robbed of its normal weight, leapt high
in the air, tossed up from below, as though it were empty.

As soon as they sensed this, the four-horse team ran wild, and leaving
the well-worn track, they continued galloping helter-skelter.
Phaëthon panicked. He lacked both the skill to manage the reins
entrusted to him and all idea of the line of his route;
170 and if he had known it, the horses would still have been out of control.
It was then that the stars of the Northern Plough, which are known as
        the Oxen,
lost their chill in the rays and, growing too hot, for the first time
vainly attempted to bathe in the sea which had always been barred
        to them.
Likewise the Serpent, whose home is close to the polar icecaps,
sluggishly cold before and dangerous to none, for the first time
175 started to swelter and sweat and seethed with a new-found fury.
Even Boötes who guards the Bear is said to have fled
in confusion, slow though he was and heavily tied to his wain.

But when the unhappy Phaëthon looked from the top of the firmament
down on the earth and saw it lying so far, far deep beneath him,
180 terror suddenly struck him: his face turned pale and his knees shook;
his vision grew darkly blurred in the dazzling, glaring brightness.
He dearly wished that he'd never set hands on his father's steeds;
he regretted the quest for his birthright and winning the favour he'd
        asked for.
Longing now to be known as Merops' son, he was swept
185 along like a ship at the north wind's mercy, whose pilot abandons
the tiller as useless and trusts the craft to the gods and to prayers.
But what could he do? Long miles of sky lay behind him, more
were ahead. He measured his route both ways, as he first looked forward
out to the west, which fate never meant him to reach, and then
190 looked back to the east. Bewildered and dazed, he could neither let go

of the reins nor cling on; and he couldn't remember the names of the
    horses.
To add to his terror, dispersed all over the patterned sky,
he spied some phenomenal shapes in the likeness of huge wild beasts.
195 Right there, a creature was curving its pincers out into two great
arcs — the Scorpion, with menacing tail and its claws flexed round
each way to encompass the space of two whole signs of the zodiac.
When youthful Phaëthon sighted it, soaked in a sweat of black venom,
curving its spear-point tail towards him and threatening to sting,
200 he was frozen with fear and, completely unnerved, let go of the reins.

When the steeds were aware of the reins lying loosely over their backs,
they broke from their course and, with no one to check them, they
    wildly bolted
through unknown regions of air, wherever their instinct led them.
They galloped at random, charging the stars in their fixed positions
205 high in the heavenly vault, and forcing the chariot along
through the trackless sky, now scaling the topmost heights, now
    hurtling
down in a headlong dive through space more close to the earth.
The moon was astonished to see her brother's horses careering
below her own; and smoke rose up from the smouldering clouds.

Phaëthon loses control of the chariot, careening wildly through the heavens
and scorching the earth in his wake. The great Earth Mother, in agony from the
flames, prays to Jupiter to intervene. Reluctantly, Jupiter agrees.

Now the Father omnipotent called on the gods to witness,
305 especially Phoebus who'd lent his chariot: failing his own help,
all of the world would be doomed, he said. Then he made for the heights
from where he normally veils the earth in a mantle of cloud
and also awakens the thunder and launches his lightning bolts.
But now the clouds that he needed to cover the whole wide earth
310 and the rain to pour from the sky were lacking. So what was the answer?
A thunderclap! Next a bolt was carefully poised by his right ear.
Jupiter hurled it at Phaëthon, flinging both driver from chariot
and life from body at once. He quenched one fire with another.
The horses stampeded. Rearing up in different directions,
315 they slipped the yoke from their necks and tore the reins as they broke
    loose.
Here the bridle was tossed, and there the pole with the ripped-off
axle, there the spokes of the shattered wheels and, scattered
all over the ether, the fragments of metal which once were a chariot.

Phaëthon's corpse spun down head first, with the fire of the thunderbolt
320   scorching his flame-red hair. He fell through the sky in a long trail,
blazing away like a comet which sometimes appears in a clear sky,
never to land upon earth, but looking as if it is falling.
Far from his home, in a distant part of the world, the Erídanus,
longest of rivers, received him and washed the smoke from his charred
        face.
325   The Hespérian naiads found his body, perceptibly showing
the three-forked lightning's effects, and buried it there in a tomb.
They also inscribed the stone of his grave with the following epitaph:

> HERE LIES PHAËTHON, CHARIOTEER OF
> HIS FATHER'S HORSES.
> THEY BOLTED AND BROUGHT HIM LOW;
> BUT HIGH WERE HIS SPIRIT AND DARING.

BOOK FOUR

The Daughters of Minyas and Their Stories (4.1–388) (excerpts)

After Bacchus takes dominion over his birthplace, Thebes, all the women of the
city join in his ecstatic revels—except for the Minyades, or daughters of Minyas, who remain indoors and busy themselves with the domestic tasks of spinning and weaving. To fill the hours they tell each other stories, whose themes
of human passion and divine vengeance are as Ovidian as their culminating
metamorphoses. See pp. 32–3.

Only a handful of women rejected the revels of Bacchus.
One was Alcíthoë, Minyas' daughter, foolhardy enough
to deny that the god was Jupiter's son; and her impious sisters
shared this wicked belief. Now orders had come from the priest
5   for a solemn festival: ladies and serving-women were therefore
excused from their household duties; all were to wear the fawnskin,
take off their headbands, garland their hair and carry the leaf-tipped
thyrsus; the wrath of the god would be dire against any who slighted him.
So the seer proclaimed. Obediently mothers and young wives
10   left their looms and baskets of wool with their tasks unfinished.
Burning incense, they called on the god by his different titles...
31   'Lord, in your gentle mercy be with us!' the Theban women
prayed as they duly worshipped; only the daughters of Minyas
stayed indoors and marred the feast with their untoward housecraft,
drawing the wool into thread and twisting the strands with their thumbs,

35   or moving close to the loom and keeping their servants occupied.
      One of the daughters, while deftly spinning, advanced a suggestion:
      'While others are idle and fondly observing their so-called festival,
      we are detained by Minerva, who better deserves our attention.
      But why don't we also relieve the toil of our hands by telling
40   stories of different kinds and take it in turns to speak,
      while the rest of us quietly listen? The time will go by more quickly.'
      Her sisters approved the idea and asked her to tell the first story.
      Then she pondered which of the many tales that she knew
      was the best one to choose: perhaps the story of Babylonian
45   Dércetis, goddess whose body was changed to a scale-covered fish,
      now swimming about in a lake, as the people of Palestine think?
      Or ought she to tell how Dercetis' daughter acquired her wings
      and passed her declining years perched up in a white-painted dovecote?
      Or how a naiad made use of her spells and exceedingly potent
50   herbs to turn the bodies of youths into voiceless fishes,
      until she was changed to a fish herself? Or should she relate
      the tale of the mulberry tree, which used to produce white fruit
      but was stained with blood and came to burgeon with dark red berries?
      This was the story she chose, because it was less familiar;
      and thus she began, as the thread whirled round on the twisting spindle.

Pyramus and Thisbe (4.55–166)

The tale of Pyramus and Thisbe, a template for Shakespeare's *Romeo and Juliet*,
is arguably the best known of the Minyades' stories.

55   'The tale of Pýramus, known as a youth of exceptional beauty,
      and Thisbe, by far the loveliest maiden in all the East.
      They lived on adjoining estates in the lofty city of Babylon,
      ringed, as they tell, with its walls of brick by Queen Semíramis.
      Neighbourhood made for acquaintance and planted the seeds of
           friendship
60   which time matured into love. They'd have been united in marriage,
      had not their fathers opposed it. But feelings may not be forbidden;
      their hearts belonged to each other and burned with an equal passion.
      No one was in their confidence; nods and gestures the only
      means of conversing; the closer their secret, the stronger the flame.

65   'The walls that divided the two estates had a tiny hole,
      a cranny formed long ago at the time the partition was built.
      In the course of the years, this imperfection had never been noticed;
      but what is not sensed by love? The lovesick pair were the first

70   to find it, and used it to channel their whispered endearments in safety.
      Often, when both had taken their places, Pyramus this side,
      Thisbe on that, and caught the sound of the other's breathing,
      "You spiteful wall!" they would cry. "Why stand in the way of poor
          lovers?
76   You mustn't think we're ungrateful; we grant that we owe it to you
77   that our words have been able to find their way to the ears of our loved
          ones.
74   If you would only allow us to lie in each other's arms!
75   If that is too much, could you open your cranny enough for a kiss?"
      Exchanges like these were useless, with such an impassable barrier.
      Night came on and they said goodbye, each printing a kiss
80   their side of the wall with lips that never could feel a response.

      'Dawn on the following day had extinguished the stars of night,
      and the sun's bright rays had melted the frost and dried the fields
      when the lovers came to their usual tryst. This time, after sighing
      their tale of woe, they made a decision: when all was quiet
85   that night, they would try to elude their guards and steal out of doors;
      then once they'd escaped from their homes, they'd abandon the city
          as well.
      In case they got lost on their journey out in the open country,
      their rendezvous would be Ninus' tomb, where they'd hide in the shade
      of a certain tree—a tree which was tall and heavily laden
90   with snow-white berries, a mulberry—close to a cooling fountain.
      The plan was agreed. Though the day passed all too slowly, at last
      the sun plunged into the waves and night invaded the heavens.

      'Craftily, using the darkness, Thisbe manoeuvred the doors
      on their hinges and crept from the house unseen. With her face well
          covered,
95   she came to the tomb and sat down under the mulberry tree.
      Love made her brave; when all of a sudden a lioness also
      arrived to slake her thirst in the nearby fountain, her foaming
      jaws besmeared with the blood of the cattle she'd newly slaughtered.
      The moonlight allowed Babylonian Thisbe to sight this beast
100   some distance away and scuttle in fear to a murky cave.
      In her flight the cloak she was wearing fell to the ground behind her.
      When the savage creature had quenched her thirst with a long, cool drink
      and was padding back to the woods, she chanced on the flimsy mantle
      without its owner and mauled it inside her gory mouth.
105   Pyramus stole out later and came on the scene to observe
      the unmistakable tracks of a wild beast, there in the deep dust.

At once he grew deadly pale; but when he had also discovered
the blood-drenched cloak, he exclaimed: "One night shall ruin two
      lovers!
Thisbe deserved far better to live to a ripe old age.
110   Mine is the guilty soul. Poor girl, it is I who've destroyed you
by making you find your way at night to this frightening place,
without being there to meet you. I call upon all of the lions
whose lairs are under this cliff to tear my body apart,
not my innocent love's, and devour my flesh in their merciless jaws!
115   Yet merely to pray for death is a coward's part." Then he picked up
Thisbe's mantle and carried it into the shade of the mulberry.
Bitterly weeping, he kissed the garment he knew so well,
and cried to it: "Now be soaked in the blood of Pyramus too!"
As he spoke, he plunged the sword he was wearing into his side
120   and at once, in his death-throes, pulled it out of the seething wound.
As he lay stretched out on the earth, his blood leapt up in a long jet,
just as a spurt from a waterpipe, bursting because of its faulty
leadwork, gushes out through a tiny crack to create
a hissing fountain of water and cuts the air with its impact.
125   Splashed by the blood, the fruit on the mulberry tree was dyed
to a red-black colour; the roots were likewise sodden below
and tinged the hanging berries above with a purplish hue.

'Thisbe now returned to the scene, still afraid, but reluctant
to fail her lover, anxiously looking this way and that,
130   and longing to tell him what terrible danger she'd lately avoided.
The spot she could recognize, also the shape of the tree that she saw,
but the fruit's strange colour was puzzling. Could she have come to the
      wrong place?
While she wondered, she noticed some blood, then quivering limbs
pulsating upon the ground. She stepped back, paler than boxwood,
135   shivering like the sea when a light breeze ruffles the surface;
but after a little while she realized this was her lover,
and hammered resounding blows of grief on her innocent shoulders.
Tearing her hair and flinging her arms round Pyramus' body,
140   weeping over his wounds and mingling her tears with his blood,
she covered his death-cold face again and again with her kisses.
"Pyramus! What dread chance has taken you from me?" she wailed,
"Pyramus, answer! It's Thisbe, your dearest beloved, calling
your dear name. Listen, please, and raise your head from the ground!"
145   Pyramus' eyes were heavy with death, but they flickered at Thisbe's
name. He looked once more at his love, then closed them for ever.

'Recognizing her cloak and his ivory scabbard lying
empty, Thisbe exclaimed: "Poor Pyramus, killed by your own hand,
aided by love! I also can boast a hand with the courage
150   to brave such a deed, and my love will lend me the strength to strike.
I'll follow you down to the shades and be known as the ill-starred
          maiden
who caused and shared in your fate. Though nothing but death, alas,
could tear you away, not even death shall be able to part us.
You sad, unhappy fathers of Thisbe and Pyramus, hear us!
155   We both implore you to grant this prayer: as our hearts were truly
united in love, and death has at last united our bodies,
lay us to rest in a single tomb. Begrudge us not that!
And you, O tree, whose branches already are casting their shadows
on one poor body and soon will be overshadowing two,
160   preserve the marks of our death; let your fruit forever be dark
as a token of mourning, a monument marking the blood of two lovers."
She spoke, then placing the tip of the sword close under her breast,
she fell on the steely weapon, still warm with her Pyramus' blood.
Those prayers, however, had touched the hearts of the gods and the
          parents:
165   the fruit of the mulberry tree, when it ripens, is now dark red;
and the ashes surviving the funeral pyres are at rest in the same urn.'

The Minyades continue to spin their stories, including the tryst of Mars and
Venus (167–89, already famous from book 8 of the *Odyssey*) and Salmacis and
Hermaphroditus, who were merged into a single entity, the first hermaphro-
dite (274–388).

The Daughters of Minyas Transformed (4.389–415)

Alcithoë's story was ended, and still the daughters of Minyas
390   kept at their weaving in scorn of Bacchus, profaning his feast day.
Suddenly, out of nowhere, their ears were harshly assaulted
by clattering drums, the fearful skirling of Phrygian pipes
and the strident clashing of cymbals. The perfume of myrrh and of
          saffron
pervaded the air. Then, hard to believe, the looms began
395   to grow green and the weaving to change into leafy curtains of ivy.
Part of it turned into vines, with the threads transformed into tendrils.
Fronds shot out of the warp, and the purple dye in the tapestry
lent its brilliant hue to clusters of deep-coloured grapes.
By now the day had completed its course, and the time was approaching

400 which couldn't be firmly established as either darkness or light
but a kind of disputed no man's land between night and day,
when the building suddenly seemed to be shaken and flames to leap
from the oil-rich lamps; the room was aglow with flickers of fiery
red and filled with howling spectres of savage beasts.

405 The sisters already were hiding in different corners around
the smoky house, to escape from the flames and the flickering lights;
and while they were searching for darkness, their limbs shrivelled up
and a membrane
stretched across them to trap their arms in gossamer bat-wings.
How they had come to lose their former appearance they could not

410 tell for the gloom. They lacked any feathers to lift them upwards,
but simply hovered in air, sustained by their filmy, transparent
wings. When they tried to speak, their minuscule bodies would only
allow them to sigh for their lot in the thinnest and shrillest of squeaks.
Their haunts are covered spaces, not trees; as they loathe the daylight,

415 they fly in the night and take their Latin name from the evening.

BOOK SIX

Arachne and Minerva (6.1–145)

Ovid's most famous narrative about Minerva, the goddess of war and domestic
arts. The poet's apparent fascination with the goddess is a major thread of Middlebrook's biography. On this episode see pp. 37–9, 81.

Minerva, who'd lent an attentive ear to the Muses' narration,
Commended their song and their justified anger against the Piérides.
Then she said to herself: 'Is praising enough? I also
need to be praised in turn. No mortal shall scoff at my power

5 unpunished.' She therefore considered how best to dispose of a Lydian
girl, called Aráchne, who claimed (so she'd heard) to equal herself
in working with wool. Arachne's distinction lay not in her birth
or the place that she hailed from but solely her art. Her father, Idmon
of Cólophon, practised the trade of dyeing wool in Phocaéan

10 purple; her mother was dead but, like her husband, had come
from the people. Their daughter, however, had gained a high reputation
throughout the Lydian towns for her work with wool, although
she'd been born in a humble home and lived in a village, Hypaépa.

15 The nymphs used often to leave their haunts, Mount Tmolus' vines
or the banks of the river Pactólus, to gaze on Arachne's amazing
artistry, equally eager to watch her handwork in progress
(her skill was so graceful) as much as to look at the finished article.

Perhaps she was forming the first round clumps from the wool in its
        crude state,
20   shaping the stuff in her fingers and steadily teasing the cloud-like
fleece into long soft threads. She might have been deftly applying
her thumb to the polished spindle. Or else they would watch her
        embroider
a picture. Whatever she did, you would know Minerva had
taught her. Arachne herself, in indignant pride, denied such a debt.
25   'Let us hold a contest,' she said. 'If I'm beaten, I'll pay any forfeit.'

Minerva disguised herself as a hag with hoary locks
and hobbled along with a stick to support her tottering frame.
She spoke at once to Arachne. 'Not all old age's effects',
she said, 'are to be despised; experience comes with the years.
30   So take a little advice from me: you should aim to be known
as the best among humankind in the arts of working with wool;
but yield the palm to Minerva, and humbly crave her forgiveness
for boasting so rashly. The goddess will surely forgive if you ask her.'
Arachne looked at her sullenly, left the threads she was spinning
35   and almost hit her rebuker. With anger written all over
her face, she made her response to the goddess she'd failed to recognize:
'Leave me alone, you stupid old woman! The trouble with you
is you've lived too long. You can give your advice to what daughters
        you have
40   or the wives of your sons. I'm clever enough to advise myself.
Don't think your warnings have done any good. I'm set on my course.
Why doesn't Minerva arrive in person? She's shirking this contest!'
'She's here!' the goddess exclaimed, as she dropped her disguise as
        a crone
and appeared as Minerva. At once the nymphs and the Lydian women
45   paid suitable homage. Only Arachne remained unafraid,
but she did turn red and her cheeks were suffused with a sudden,
        involuntary
blush which soon disappeared, as the sky glows crimson at early
dawn and rapidly whitens again in the rays of the sunrise.
50   She still refused to withdraw. In her crass determination
to win, she fell to her ruin. Minerva accepted her challenge
and offered no further warnings; the contest could start at once.

Straightaway they both set up their looms in different places.
Each loom was carefully strung with the slender threads of the warp.
55   The warp was attached to the crossbeam, a stick separated the threads,
and the weft could then be inserted between them by pointed shuttles,

drawn over and under by hand, and tapped into place as the wooden
comb with its notches between the teeth was sharply lowered.
The two contestants made haste; with robes hitched up to the girdle,
60   they moved their experienced arms, the labour lightened by pleasure.
Webs were woven in threads of Tyrian purple dye
and of lighter, more delicate, imperceptibly merging shades.
Think how a tract of the sky, when the sun breaks suddenly through
at the end of a rain shower, is steeped in the long, great curve of a
            rainbow;
65   the bow is agleam with a range of a thousand various hues,
but the eye cannot tell where one fades into another; adjacent
tones are so much the same, though the difference is clear at the edges.
Such were the colours the two contestants used in the fabric.
Their patterns were also shot with flexible threads of gold,
as they each spun out an old tale in the weft of their separate looms.

70   Minerva depicted the rock of Mars on the heights of Cecrops
and wove the ancient dispute concerning the name of the land.
The twelve Olympians, Jove in their midst, with august dignity
sat upon lofty thrones. Each of the gods was denoted
by typical features. The image of Jove was proud and majestic.
75   Neptune, the god of the ocean, was shown on his feet and striking
the rugged crag with his great long trident, while sea-water gushed forth
out of the cleft in the rock, to establish his claim to the city.
Minerva characterized herself by her helmeted head,
her sharp-pointed spear, her shield and the aegis guarding her breast.
80   The picture suggested the earth had been struck by the goddess's spear
to produce the olive tree covered with berries and grey-green foliage.
The gods looked on in amazement, and victory crowned her endeavour.

So that Minerva's rival could have some clear indication
of what reward to expect for such crazily reckless defiance,
85   four contests were added, one in each of the web's four corners,
all in their own bright colours, with smaller designs for the detail.
One corner was filled by Thracian Haemus and Rhódope, snow-clad
mountains today but formerly mortals, a brother and sister
who'd claimed the titles of Jove and Juno. The second corner
90   contained the pitiful fate of a mother, the queen of the Pygmies,
who'd fought against Juno and lost; the goddess transformed her into
a crane and made her declare perpetual war on her own tribe.
Antígone featured third, one more who had dared to compete
with great Jove's consort but later been punished by queenly Juno
95   and changed to a kind of bird. It sadly counted for nothing

that she was the Trojan king Laómedon's daughter.
Instead she applauds herself with the clattering bill of a white-feathered
    stork.
The fourth and remaining design showed Cínyras in his bereavement,
embracing the temple steps which had once been the limbs of his
    beautiful
100   daughters, and seeming to weep as he lay prostrate on the marble.
Minerva finally added a border of olive branches,
symbol of peace, so using her tree to complete the tapestry.

Arachne's picture presented Európa seduced by Jove
in the guise of a bull; the bull and the sea were convincingly real.
105   The girl appeared to be looking back to the shore behind her,
calling out to the friends she was leaving, afraid of the surging
waves which threatened to touch her and nervously lifting her feet.
Astérië also was shown, in the grip of a struggling eagle;
Leda, meekly reclining under the wings of the swan.
110   And there was Jove once again, but now in the form of a satyr,
taking the lovely Antíope, sowing the seeds of her twins.
You could see how he caught Alcména disguised as her husband
    Amphítryon,
then how he stole fair Dánaë's love in a shower of gold;
how he cheated Aegína as fire; Mnemósyne, dressed as a shepherd;
Prosérpina, Ceres' child and his own, as a speckled serpent.

115   Neptune's affairs were also revealed in Arachne's tapestry.
He changed to a menacing bull to possess the daughter of Aéolus;
taking the shape of the river Enípeus, he fathered the giant
son of Alóeus; he posed as a ram to confuse Theóphane.
Ceres, the bountiful mother of crops, with her golden tresses,
knew the god as a horse; snake-haired Medúsa, who bore
120   the winged horse Pégasus, knew a winged bird; and Melántho a dolphin.
All these scenes were given authentic settings, the persons
their natural likeness. There was Apollo, dressed as a farmer,
shown as wearing the wings of a hawk or the skin of a lion,
and fooling the daughter of Mácareus, Isse, disguised as a shepherd.
125   Bacchus, appearing as counterfeit grapes to deceive Erígone;
Saturn, as one more horse who fathered Chiron the centaur.
The outer edge of the tapestry, fringed by a narrow border,
was filled with flowers all interwoven with tendrils of ivy.

Not Pallas, not even the goddess of Envy could criticize weaving
130   like that. The fair-haired warrior goddess resented Arachne's

success and ripped up the picture betraying the gods' misdemeanours.
She was still holding her shuttle of hard Cytórian boxwood
and used it to strike Arachne a number of times on the forehead.
The wretched girl was too proud to endure it, and fastened a halter
135   around her neck. She was hanging in air when the goddess took pity
and lifted her up. 'You may live, you presumptuous creature,' she said,
'but you'll hang suspended forever. Don't count on a happier future:
my sentence applies to the whole of your kind, and to all your
        descendants!'
With that she departed, sprinkling the girl with the magical juice
140   of a baleful herb. As soon as the poison had touched Arachne,
her hair fell away, and so did the ears and the nose. The head
now changed to a tiny ball and her whole frame shrunk in proportion.
Instead of her legs there are spindly fingers attached to her sides.
The rest is merely abdomen, from which she continues to spin
145   her thread and practise her former art in the web of a spider.

BOOK FIFTEEN

Author's Epilogue (15.871–9)

See p. 10.

Now I have finished my work, which nothing can ever destroy—
not Jupiter's wrath, nor fire or sword, nor devouring time.
That day which has power over nothing except this body of mine
may come when it will and end the uncertain span of my life.
875   But the finer part of myself shall sweep me into eternity,
higher than all the stars. My name shall be never forgotten.
Wherever the might of Rome extends in the lands she has conquered,
the people shall read and recite my words. Throughout all ages,
if poets have vision to prophesy truth, I shall live in my fame.

FASTI

(*Calendar*, before AD 8)

From *Ovid: Fasti*. Penguin Books, 2004. A. J. Boyle and R. D. Woodard, translators.

The *Fasti* find Ovid pushing elegiac poetry in a different direction, away from the erotic variety of his youth and into etiology—inquiry into the causes of or reasons for cultural institutions, in this case the religious practices and festivals inscribed in the Roman calendar. Originally slated for twelve books, one for each month of the year, Ovid's banishment from Rome interrupted the poem's composition after book six (June). Although Middlebrook's unfinished biography addresses little of the *Fasti*, the excerpts below resonate with her approach, particularly her interest in fertility and the feminine. The excerpts also elucidate the often enigmatic mindset of Ovid's poetry, especially the Romans' scrupulous attitude toward religion.

BOOK ONE

Author's Prologue (1.1–62)

     Times and their causes, arranged through the Latin year,
          Stars sunk beneath earth and risen, I'll sing.
     View this work peacefully, Caesar Germanicus,
          And direct the course of my timid ship.
5   Do not refuse a trifling honour. Be present
          To support service vowed to your godhead.
     You will recognize sacred rites unearthed from ancient
          Annals and how each day deserved its mark.
     You will discover here the feast-days of your house,
10   And often read of your grandfather and father.
     The glories they have stamped on the painted Fasti
          You, too, will win with Drusus, your brother.
     Let others sing of Caesar's arms, me of Caesar's altars
          And all the days he added to our rites.
15   Sanction with a nod my effort to laud your kin,
          And drive from my heart this dreadful terror.
     Look kindly upon me and empower my song;
          Genius stands and declines with your gaze.
     My page shakes at the judgement of a learned *princeps*,
20   As if sent to be read by the Claros god.
     We witnessed the eloquence of your refined voice
          Helping fearful victims with civil arms.
     We know, too, when passion impels you to our art,

How mightily your flood of talent rolls.
25 If it's allowed and lawful, poet, guide a poet's reins;
  Gladden the whole year with your auspices.
Times were being arranged by the city's founder,
  When he established ten months for his year.
Clearly, Romulus, you studied arms more than stars,
30   The conquest of neighbours was your main care.
Yet reason, too, Caesar, may have prompted him,
  And he has grounds to defend his error.
He decreed the time an infant needs to quit
  Its mother's womb sufficient for a year.
35 The same number of months after her husband's death
  Witness a wife's grief in the widowed home.
Purple-gowned Quirinus was mindful of these things
  When he gave simple folk the year's rules.
The month of Mars was first, that of Venus second;
40   She was his line's *princeps*, Mars was his father.
The third was named for the old, the fourth for the young,
  The bunch following were marked by number.
Numa did not pass Janus or our ancestral dead,
  And prefixed two months to the ancient ten.

45 In case you do not know the rules of different days,
  Lucifer's duties are not all the same.
The day is *nefastus* when the three words are mute;
  Fastus when legal action is allowed.
Do not think the rules remain fixed for the whole day:
50   What's *fastus* now, was *nefastus* this morning.
After the god gets his sacrifice, all speech is allowed
  And the distinguished praetor's words are freed.
A day exists, too, when law locks people in booths;
  One, too, which recurs in cycles of nine.
55 Ausonia's Kalends are claimed for Juno's cult;
  A great white lamb falls for Jove on the Ides.
No god protects the Nones. The day after these three
  (Take care you are not deceived) will be black.
The curse is from history. On those days Rome suffered
60   Tearful losses beneath the frown of Mars.
I have stated once what applies to the whole *Fasti*,
  Lest I am forced to cut the cord of events.

BOOK THREE

March 17: Liberalia (3.713–90)

March 17, the festal day devoted to Bacchus or Liber, was the day upon which
Roman boys received the toga of manhood (*toga virilis*). See p. 42.

> The third day after the Ides celebrates Bacchus:
>> Bacchus, favour this poet singing your feast.
> 715 I will omit Semele (if Jove had not crammed her
>> With lightning, you'd have been a puny runt),
> And how your father's body filled the mother's task
>> For your birth in due time as a boy.
> The Sithonian and Scythian triumphs need an epic,
> 720   And your tribes' defeat, spicy India.
> A Theban mother's vile trophy will meet silence
>> And you, Lycurgus, who stormed at your son.
> Look, I would love to tell of sudden fish and Tyrrhene
>> Monsters, but it is not this section's theme.
> 725 This section's theme is to expound the causes why
>> The Vine-Planter calls people to his cakes.
>
> Before your birth altars lacked suitable respect,
>> Liber, and grass could be found on cold hearths.
> When Ganges and the whole East were crushed, they record,
> 730   You reserved the first fruits for great Jove.
> You first offered cinnamon and captive incense
>> And the roasted flesh of triumphal bulls.
> The inventor's name gives 'libations' and *liba*,
>> The 'cakes' partly offered to sacred hearths.
> 735 The god receives cakes because he loves sweet juices,
>> And honey was found by Bacchus, they say.
> He was leaving sandy Hebrus attended by satyrs
>> (Our tale is not displeasingly playful),
> And had reached Rhodope and blooming Pangaea;
> 740   The hand-held cymbals of his companions clashed.
> Look, the ringing gathers strange aerial things, bees,
>> Who trail the sounds of the tinkling brass.
> Liber collects the swarm, shuts it in a hollow tree
>> And is rewarded by finding honey.
> 745 When the satyrs and the bald old man tasted it,
>> They ransacked every grove for yellow combs.
> The old man hears the swarm buzzing in a rotted elm;
>> He spots the wax and pretends otherwise.
> Sitting lazily on his donkey's sunken back,

750 He guides it to the elm's hollow bark.
He stood on the donkey, assisted by branches,
     And probed hotly for honey stored in the trunk.
Thousands of hornets swarm. They jab his bald head
     With stingers and freckle his pug-nosed face.
755 He falls headlong and is kicked by the donkey's heel.
     He shouts to his friends and implores their help.
The satyrs come running and laugh at their father's
     Bloated face; he limps from an injured knee.
The god also laughs and shows him how to smear mud;
760   He obeys and spreads dirt over his face.

Father Liber enjoys honey, and we rightly give
     The finder bright honey poured on hot cakes.
Why a woman has charge of this is not obscure:
     He incites bands of women with his wand.
765 Why an old woman, you ask? That age is more prone
     To wine and it loves the teeming vine's gift.
Why an ivy wreath? Bacchus loves the ivy most.
     Why this, too, is so, takes no time to learn.
They say that, when his stepmother hunted for the boy,
770   Nymphs from Nysa screened the crib with its leaves.

I still have to find why boys receive the toga
     Of liberty, bright Bacchus, on your day:
Either because you always look like a boy or youth,
     And your age seems to lie between the two.
775 Or, because you are a father, fathers entrust
     Their dear sons to your care and divinity.
Or, because you are Liber, the robe of *liberty*
     And life's *liberal* journey start with you.
Or because, when earlier men worked fields harder
780   And a senator tilled his father's land,
And a consul received his rods at the curved plough
     And it was no crime to have calloused hands,
Country folk visited the city then for the shows
     (The gods were honoured, not people's pastimes:
785 The grape's inventor conducted on his own day
     The shows now held with the torch-goddess).
Was it to surround the newcomer with a crowd
     That it seemed the right day to give the toga?
Father, turn here your gentle head with horns appeased,
790   And grant my genius billowing sails.

March 19: Quinquatrus (3.809–48)

As Middlebrook notes, Ovid's birthday, March 20, fell on the second day of
Quinquatrus, a festival of Minerva. See pp. 33–5.

One day intervenes and there is Minerva's feast,
810   Titled from the conjunction of five days.
The first day lacks blood, no sword-fights are lawful.
    The cause: Minerva was born on this day.
The next four days are celebrated on raked sand;
    The war-hungry goddess loves the drawn sword.
815 Now make your prayers to Pallas, boys and gentle girls:
    Skill depends on placating Pallas well.
After placating Pallas let the girls learn
    To card wool and unload the full distaffs.
Pallas, too, teaches how to shuttle the standing warp
820   And to pack the straggling work with combs.
Worship her, cleaners of stained and damaged garments,
    Worship her, workers of the bronze dye-vats.
No one will make good sandals against Pallas' wish,
    Though he outrank Tychius in skill.
825 Even if a craftsman surpass ancient Epeüs,
    The anger of Pallas will maim him.
You, too, who remove sickness with Phoebus' art,
    Reserve the goddess a few of your fees.
And teachers, a class often cheated of your pay,
830   No rebuff (she attracts new pupils),
Nor from you engravers and encaustic painters
    And sensualist masters of stone.
Hers are a thousand tasks: she must be goddess of song.
    If I'm worthy, may she be my work's friend.
835 Where the Caelian Hill descends from its summit
    To the plain and the street is almost level,
You can see the small shrine of Minerva Capta,
    Which the goddess received on her birthday.
The name's cause is in doubt. We call shrewd genius
840   'Capital', and the goddess has genius.
Or is it because they say she sprang motherless,
    Shield and all, from her father's caput, 'head'?
Or because she was a 'captive' from crushed Falerii?
    (An early inscription signifies this.)
845 Or because she has a law prescribing 'capital'
    Punishment for goods stolen from the place?
Whatever the reason for your tide, Pallas,
    Always guard our leaders with your aegis.

BOOK FOUR

April 21: Parilia (4.721–862)

Ovid conflates the rites of the *Parilia*, which honor Pales, the god of sheep and shepherds, with the birthday of Rome and the fraternal strife between Romulus and Remus. The *Parilia* eventually became synonymous with the birthday of Rome.

Night is gone, dawn lifts. The *Parilia* calls me,
    Not vainly—with gentle Pales' favour.
Gentle Pales, favour my song of pastoral rites,
    If I honour your deeds with my service.
725 Truly I have often brought handfuls of calf ash
    And bean stalks burned for purification.
Truly I have jumped the triple row of flames
    And felt sodden laurel's dripping water.
The goddess is moved and favours the work. The ship
730   Leaves dock, my sails already have their winds.

Go, folk, seek fumigant from the virginal altar;
    Vesta will give it, Vesta's gift will cleanse.
The fumigant will be horse's blood and calf ash;
    The third thing is a hard bean's empty stalk.
735 Shepherd, purify the sheep full-fed at early dusk.
    First water the ground and sweep it with twigs,
Fix leaves and boughs to the sheep-pens for adornment,
    And cover and deck the doors with long wreaths.
Make your pure sulphur emit its sky-blue smoke
740   And smoking sulphur sting the bleating sheep.
Burn rosemary and pine and the Sabine plants,
    Let the torched laurel crackle in mid-hearth.
Have a basket of millet follow millet cakes:
    The rural goddess enjoys this food best.
745 Bring her special food and milk-pail; cut up the food
    And pray to woodland Pales with warm milk.
Say: 'Take care alike of sheep and masters of sheep.
    Let all harm be averted from my stalls.
If I used sacred pasture, sat by a sacred tree,
750   And my ignorant sheep browsed on graves;
If I entered a forbidden wood, and the nymphs
    And half-goat god bolted from my sight;
If my knife has robbed a grove of a shady bough
    To give ailing sheep a basket of leaves:
755 Forgive my offence. Do not fault me for sheltering

My flock from the hail in a rustic shrine,
Nor harm me for disturbing the pools. Pardon, nymphs,
    Trampling hooves for muddying your stream.
Goddess, placate for us the springs and fountain spirits,
760   Placate the gods dispersed through every grove.
Keep from our sight the Dryads and Diana's bath
    And Faunus lying in the fields at noon.
Drive diseases away. Health to men and to herds,
    Health to the guard dogs, that vigilant pack!
765 May I never drive home less than the morning's count,
    Or groan at wolf-torn fleeces in my hands.
Banish hateful hunger. May grass and leaves abound,
    Water to wash the body and to drink.
May I milk full udders, my cheeses make money,
770   My wicker sieves pass the watery whey.
May the ram be lustful, his pregnant mate return
    The seed, and lambs aplenty fill my pens.
May wool be produced, unabrasive to girls,
    Soft and fit for the most dainty hands.
775 May my prayers be fulfilled, and let us make each year
    Great cakes for Pales, the shepherds' mistress.'

Placate the goddess with this. Utter this four times
    Facing east and wash your hands with fresh dew.
It is then allowed to set a bowl for mixing
780   And drink snow-white milk and the purple must;
And later to hurl mighty limbs and speeding feet
    Over fiery heaps of crackling straw.

I have explained the custom but not its origin.
    Confusion casts doubt and baulks my efforts.
785 Consuming fire cleanses all and melts flaws in metal.
    Is that why it purifies sheep and shepherd?
Or, because the contrary seeds of the universe
    Are fire and ocean, two discordant gods,
Did our fathers join these elements and think it fit
790   To touch bodies with flames and splashing water?
Or, since they contain life's cause, are lost by exiles,
    Turn bride to wife, are these two thought important?
I hardly believe that some think Phaëthon's referred to
    And Deucalion's excessive waters.
795 One group also says that sparks suddenly leapt out
    When shepherds were pounding rock with rock.

The first of course died, the second was caught in straw.
    Is the Parilia flame based on this?
Or did Aeneas' piety cause this custom,
800   When fire offered safe passage in defeat?
Is it nearer the truth that, when Rome was founded,
    They ordered the Lares to move house,
And, as the farmers changed their homes, they fired
    Their rustic sheds and abandoned hovels,
805 And both flock and farmer vaulted through the flames?
    Which happens now, too, on your birthday, Rome.

Chance gives the poet scope. The city's birth has come.
    Be present for your deeds, great Quirinus.
Already Numitor's brother had been punished,
810   All the shepherd crowd were led by the twins.
The two agree to unite the peasants and build walls.
    Who should construct the walls is disputed.
'There is no need for any fight,' said Romulus;
    'Birds are greatly trusted, let us try birds.'
815 They agree. One ascends the wooded Palatine's cliff,
    The other at dawn climbs Aventine's peak.
Remus sees six birds, the other twelve in sequence.
    The pact holds: Romulus controls the city.
A suitable day is picked to mark walls with a plough.
820   Pales' rites approached. The work began then.
A ditch is dug to solid rock, earth's fruits are thrown
    To the bottom and soil fetched from nearby.
The ditch is refilled with dirt, an altar tops the fill,
    And the new hearth enjoys its kindled fire.
825 The king grips the plough and marks the walls with a furrow;
    A white cow and snowy bull bore the yoke.
The king said: 'As I found the city, be present, Jove,
    And Father Mavors and Mother Vesta.
Attend all gods whom it is pious to summon:
830   Let this work of mine rise with your auspices.
Grant it long years, dominion over mistress earth,
    And the lordship of the East and the West.'
He prayed. Jove furnished omens with thunder on the left
    And hurtled lightning from heaven's left.

835 The augury is cheered. The citizens throw down
    Foundations and soon a new wall stood.
Celer urges on the work, whom Romulus had called,

Saying, 'Celer, your job is to prevent
Anyone from crossing the walls or the ploughed ditch.
840   Execute whoever dares to do this.'
Remus, unaware of this, mocked the lowly walls
And said, 'Will these make a people secure?'
No delay; he leapt. Celer hits the fool with a spade;
He drops on to the hard ground, gushing blood.
845   When the king learnt this, he swallows the sobs welling
Inside and coffins the wound in his breast.
He rebuffs open tears and keeps his brave example,
Saying: 'So may enemies cross my walls.'
Yet he grants funeral rites and no longer suspends
850   His weeping. Cloaked piety is patent.
He pressed last kisses on the lowered bier and said:
'Farewell brother, removed against my will.'
He anointed the body for cremation; Faustulus
And Acca did the same, hair loosed in grief.
855   Then the (not yet named) Quirites wept for the youth;
Finally the lamented pyre was torched.

A city rises (who could then have believed it?)
To set its victor's foot upon the earth.
Rule all things and ever subject to great Caesar,
860   And often possess many of that name;
And when you stand sublime within a mastered globe,
May your shoulders tower over everything.

BOOK SIX

June 9: Vestalia (6.249–460)

Vesta was the goddess of the hearth, in whose temple in the Roman Forum
burned the city's sacred flame. In Ovid's hands her cult practices become a narrative of Roman nationhood, whose frontiers extend as far as Troy and the *Pal-
ladium*, the renowned Trojan statue of Minerva. See pp. 73–4.

Vesta, favour me. Our lips open in your service,
250   If we are allowed to approach your rites.
I was lost in prayer. I felt a divine presence
And the joyful ground glowed with purple light.
Indeed I did not see you (farewell poetic lies!);
No man may have gazed upon you, goddess.
255   My areas of ignorance and crippling mistakes
Became known to me without instruction.

Rome, they say, had held its fortieth *Parilia*,
    When the flame's guardian goddess was enshrined.
It was the kindly king's work, whose god-fearing mind
260   Surpassed any the Sabine land has bred.
The roofs of bronze you see today were then of straw,
    And walls were woven from pliant wicker.
This little spot which contains the Hall of Vesta
    Was unshaven Numa's mighty court.
265 But the temple's present shape existed before,
    They say. A sound cause underlies its form.
Vesta equals Earth. Sleepless fire underlies both;
    Earth and hearth denote their own fixity.
Earth is like a ball resting on no support,
270   A great weight hanging in the air beneath.
Its very rotation keeps the globe balanced;
    There are no comers to press any part.
And, since it's located in the centre of the world,
    So that it touches no side more or less,
275 If it weren't convex, it would be nearer to one part,
    And the world would lack earth's central weight.
Syracusan art has hung a globe in enclosed air,
    A tiny model of the boundless world,
And there the earth is equidistant from the top
280   And bottom. This is caused by its round shape.
The temple looks the same. No comer protrudes in it,
    And the dome protects it from rain showers.

Why, you ask, do virgin attendants serve the goddess?
    I shall find the correct causes here, too.
285 Juno and Ceres, they recount, were born from Ops
    By Saturnus' seed. Vesta was the third.
The first two married, both gave birth, it's reported;
    One of the three stayed ignorant of men.
What is strange, if a virgin likes virgin attendants
290   And allows only chaste hands at her rites?
Understand Vesta as nothing but living flame;
    You see no substances born from flame.
She is a virgin *de iure*, giving and taking
    No seed, and loves virginity's escorts.

295 For long I stupidly thought Vesta had statues;
    I soon learned that the rotunda has none.
That temple encloses an undying fire
    But no image of Vesta or of fire.

Earth stands by vital force. Vesta is named from *vital*
300   *Standing*; her Greek name may have the same cause.
The hearth is named from flames and since it *heartens* all;
      But it was once at the front of the house.
Hence, too, I think, our word '*vestibule*', and we preface
      Prayers with Vesta, who holds the first place.

305 It was once the custom to sit on long benches
      By the hearth and think the gods dined with you.
Today, too, when ancient Vacuna's rites are held,
      Men stand and sit before Vacuna's hearths.
There survives to this time a piece of ancient custom:
310   A clean platter offers Vesta food.
Look, loaves of bread hang from garlanded donkeys,
      And chains of flowers veil rough millstones.
Farmers formerly roasted only spelt in ovens
      (Oven Goddess, Fornax, has her own rites).
315 The hearth baked the bread which was buried in its ash;
      A chipped tile was laid on the warm floor.
Hence the baker respects the hearth and the hearth's mistress
      And the donkey turning the pumice millstones.

Should I omit or recount your shame, red Priapus?
320   It is a very playful, tiny tale.
Coroneted Cybele, with her crown of turrets,
      Invites the eternal gods to her feast.
She invites, too, satyrs and nymphs, rural spirits;
      Silenus is present, uninvited.
325 It's not allowed and too long to narrate the gods'
      Banquet: night was consumed with much wine.
Some blindly stroll shadowy Ida's dells, or lie down
      And rest their bodies in the soft grass.
Others play or are clasped by sleep; or link their arms
330   And thump the green earth in triple quick step.
Vesta lies down and takes a quiet, carefree nap,
      Just as she was, her head pillowed by turf.
But the red saviour of gardens prowls for nymphs
      And goddesses, and wander back and forth.
335 He spots Vesta. It's unclear if he thought she was a nymph
      Or knew it was Vesta. He claims ignorance.
He conceives a vile hope and tries to steal upon her,
      Walking on tiptoe, as his heart flutters.
By chance old Silenus had left the donkey

340 He came on by a gently burbling stream.
The long Hellespont's god was getting started,
    When it bellowed an untimely bray.
The goddess starts up, frightened by the noise. The whole crowd
    Fly to her; the god flees through hostile hands.
345 Lampsacus slays this beast for Priapus, chanting:
    'We rightly give flames the informant's guts.'
You remember, goddess, and necklace it with bread.
    Work ceases; the idle mills are silent.

I'll tell what Jupiter Pistor's altar on Thunderer's Hill
350   Means, more renowned for its name than cost.
The Capitol was squeezed by a ring of fierce Gauls;
    The long siege had already brought famine.
Jupiter summoned the gods to his royal throne,
    And tells Mars. 'Begin!' He reports at once:
355 'No one, I suppose, knows the state of their suffering
    And my heartache must voice its complaint.
But, if you require a brief account of their pain
    And shame: *Rome lies beneath Alpine foe.*
Is this to whom you promised world dominion,
360   Jove? To whom you would subject the earth?
When Rome pounded her neighbours and Etruscan arms,
    Hope quickened. Now she's exiled from her *Lar.*
We have seen aged, triumphal generals drop
    In halls of bronze, draped in the *toga picta.*
365 We have seen the tokens of Ilian Vesta removed.
    Clearly Romans believe some gods exist.
But, if they gazed back at the hill you inhabit
    And your many homes clamped by the siege,
They would know that divine worship is futile
370   And anxious gifts of incense stillborn.
If only they had the chance to fight! Let them arm—
    And let them tumble, if they cannot win.
Now they are shut on their hill, starving and afraid
    Of the coward's fate, besieged by barbarians.'
375 Then Venus, fair Quirinus with crook and purple robe,
    And Vesta spoke up for their Latium.
Jove replied: 'Concern for those walls is universal.
    Gaul will pay the penalty with defeat.
Now make their dwindling corn appear plentiful,
380   Vesta, and do not desert your site.
Have the hollow mill grind all their uncrushed grain,

   Hands soften it and hearth fires bake it.'
  He ordered. The Saturnian virgin nodded
    At her brother's orders. It was midnight.
385 Toil had made the generals sleep. Jupiter scolds them
    And delivers his will with holy lips:
  'Get up, and from the stronghold's height into the foe
    Hurl the resource you least desire to hurl.'
  Sleep departs, and the strange riddle prods them to ask
390   What resource to release against their wish.
  It seemed to be Ceres. They throw down Ceres' gifts,
    Which clatter on the helmets and long shields.
  Hope of defeat by famine dies. The foe is routed
    And a white altar built to Pistor Jove.

395 I happened to come back from Vesta's feast by the path
    Where Via Nova joins the Roman Forum:
  I saw a barefoot lady come down toward me.
    I was stunned to silence and I halted.
  An old woman nearby saw me. She tells me to sit,
400   And says, in trembling tones, her head shaking:
  'Soaking swamps occupied this ground, where the forums
    Are now. The stream's overflow drenched the ditch.
  Lake Curtius over there with its dry altars
    Is now solid ground, but was first a lake.
405 Where the Velabrum ushers parades to the Circus
    Was nothing but willows and hollow reed.
  Often revellers, returning on the city's waters,
    Sang and attacked boatmen with drunken words.
  The god who's defined by different shapes had not yet
410   Been named for averting the river.
  Here also was a grove thick with rushes and reeds,
    And a marsh none would approach in shoes.
  The pools have receded, the banks confine their waters,
    The land is now dry; but the custom stays.'
415 She had explained the cause. 'Farewell, dear old lady,'
    I said; 'May the rest of your life be gentle.'

  I learned the rest long ago in my childhood years,
    But should not pass it by because of that.
  Dardanus' descendant, Ilus, had just built new walls
420   (Ilus, still rich, had the wealth of Asia);
  A heavenly statue of armed Minerva, it's thought,
    Dropped on the hills of Ilium's city.

(I was curious to see it, and saw the temple and site.
    That is what remains there; Rome has Pallas.)
425 They consult Smintheus. Darkly in his shady grove
    He uttered these sounds with unlying lips:
'Keep heaven's goddess safe; you will keep the city safe.
    She will take with her the seat of power.'
Ilus keeps her safely locked high on the citadel;
430   The charge passes to his heir Laomedon.
With Priam she was not safe. This was her own wish
    After she had lost the beauty contest.
They say she was taken by Adrastus' grandson
    Or thieving Ulysses or Aeneas—
435 The culprit is unknown. She is Roman; her guard
    Is Vesta, whose unfailing light views all.

Ah, how terrified the Fathers were when Vesta
    Burned and was almost buried by her roof.
The holy fires were blazing with the fires of sin,
440   Flame mingled with flame, pious with profane.
Her dumbstruck attendants untied their hair and wept;
    Fear itself had removed their bodies' strength.
Metellus flies into their midst and in a great voice
    Cries, 'To the rescue! Tears are no help.
445 Take the tokens of fate in your virgin palms:
    You require hands, not prayers, to grasp them.
O pity! Do you waver?' He saw them waver
    And collapse on to their knees in panic.
He scoops water and lifts his hands: 'Forgive this man,
450   Holiness: I'll go where no man may enter.
If this is a crime, let me be punished for the act
    And Rome be absolved by my life's forfeit.'
He spoke, and burst in. The abducted goddess approved,
    And was saved by the service of her priest.
455 Now, under Caesar, you shine brightly, holy flames;
    Now there will be—and is—fire on Ilian hearths.
No priestess will be said to profane her headband
    While he leads, none will be buried alive.
So the unchaste die, interred in what they have defiled:
460   Tellus and Vesta are the same god.

TRISTIA

(*Sorrows*, AD 9–12)

From *Ovid: The Poems of Exile*. University of California Press, 2005 (orig. Penguin Books, 1994). Peter Green, translator.

On Ovid's dismissal from Rome see p. 11. If we are to believe the first book of the collection, Ovid began work on the *Tristia* during the voyage to Tomis, where he would serve out his life-long sentence of *relegatio*. Relegation, although it mandated Ovid's deportation from the city, was a less harsh punishment than exile, *exsilium*, which would have stripped him of his property and his Roman citizenship. It is customary, however, to refer to the poet's banishment generally as exile and to the works of this period as his exile poetry.

With this five-volume work Ovid launches the final phase of his elegiac career: elegy as the poetry of lament, born of missing both his loved ones and the urbane delights of Rome. The following excerpts reflect bitter experience and contrast sharply with Middlebrook's portrayal of Ovid's triumphs.

BOOK ONE

1.1: *Ovid at Sea*

> Little book—no, I don't begrudge it you—you're off to the City
>   without me, going where your only begetter is banned!
> On your way, then—but penny-plain, as befits an exile's
>   sad offering, and my present life.
> 5   For you no purple slip-case (that's a colour
>   goes ill with grief), no title-line picked out
> in vermilion, no cedar-oiled backing, no white bosses
>   to set off those black
> edges: leave luckier books to be dressed with such trimmings:
> 10   never forget my sad estate.
> No smoothing off your ends with friable pumice—appear for
>   inspection bristly, unkempt.
> And don't be embarrassed by blots. Anyone who sees them
>   will sense they were due to my tears.
> 15   Go, book, and bring to the places I loved my greeting—
>   let me reach them with what 'feet' I may!—
> And if, in the throng, there's one by whom I'm not forgotten,
>   who should chance to ask how I am,
> tell him I live (*not* 'he's well'!), but emphasize I only
> 20   survive by courtesy of a god.

For the rest, keep silent. If people demand more details
    take care not to blab out
any state secrets: a reader, once reminded, will remember
    the charges against me, I'll be condemned
25   in public, by popular vote. Though such accusations may wound you,
    make no defense. A good (for nothing) case
stands beyond any advocacy. Find one who sighs at my exile,
    who can't read *those poems* dry-eyed,
and who prays (but in silence, lest the malicious hear him)
30   that Caesar's wrath may abate,
my sentence be lightened. Anyone gets my prayers
    for happiness, who prays the gods to bestow
a benison on the unhappy. May his hopes be fulfilled, may ebbing
    Imperial anger give me the chance to die
35   on my native soil! Yet, book, though you follow
    all my instructions, you may still be dismissed
as falling short of my genius. Any judge must unravel
    not the act alone, but also its context—if
context is what's stressed, then you're in the clear. But poems
40   come spun from serenity; my heart
is clouded with sudden troubles. Poems demand for the writer
    leisure and solitude: *I'm* tossed by sea and wind,
savaged by winter. Terror chokes off creation. My hapless
    throat cringes every moment in fear
45   of a sword's edge slicing through it. Your fair-minded critic
    will be amazed that I achieve even this much,
will peruse my work with indulgence. Put even Homer
    amid dangers like mine, his genius would fail
when faced with such troubles. Lastly, remember to go unbothered
50   by public opinion: if you leave a reader cold
don't worry—I'm not favoured enough by Fortune
    for you to keep tally on your praise!
While I walked safe still, I yearned for recognition,
    was on fire to make myself a name;
55   but now, let it suffice me not to detest the poems,
    the pursuit that undid me: it was my own wit
brought me to exile. So go in my stead, you have licence,
    be my eyes in Rome (dear God, how I wish I could be
my book!)—but don't assume just because you've reached the Big City
60   from abroad you'll be incognito. You may
lack a title: no matter, your style will still betray you;
    dissimulate all you like, it's clear you're mine.
Slip in unnoticed, then: I wouldn't want my poems

to do you harm. They're not

65   so popular as they were. If you meet someone who refuses
        to read you because you're mine, who thrusts you away,
'Look at the title,' tell him, '*I'm* not Love's Preceptor;
        that work has already paid
the penalty it deserved.' Perhaps you thought I'd send you

70   up the Palatine, bid you climb
to Caesar's home? Too *august.* The site—and its incumbent
        gods—must excuse me, but the bolt that struck my head
came from that Citadel. The Beings up there are forgiving
        (Shall I ever forget it?), but I still fear the gods

75   who did me harm. A dove, once raked, hawk, by your talons
        takes fright at the faintest whirr of wings.
A ewe lamb that's been dragged from the fangs of a hungry
        wolf won't dare to stray far from the fold.
Had Phaëthon lived, he'd have steered clear of those horses

80   he once was crazy about, kept out of the sky.
What scares *me* is Jove's weaponry, I've been its target:
        whenever there's thunder I'm sure
the lightning's for me. Any Greek who's avoided shipwreck
        off the rocks of Euboea steers clear

85   of those waters thereafter; my small skiff, once beam-ended
        by a fierce hurricane, shudders at sailing back
into the eye of the storm. So be watchful, unassuming:
        seek no readers beyond the common sort.
Look at Icarus: flew too high with that rickety plumage,

90   gave his name to the Icarian Sea.
Should you row, or hoist sail to the breeze? It's hard at this distance,
        to decide: you must improvise as occasion dictates.
Catch him when he's at leisure, when his mood's all mellow,
        when his temper has lost its edge;

95   find someone to murmur a few words of introduction
        and present you (hesitant still, still scared
to approach him): *then* make your bid. On a good morning
        and with better luck than your master's, you might just
get in there and ease my suffering. None but the person

100   who himself inflicted my wounds
can, like Achilles, heal them. Only take care your helpful
        efforts don't hurt me instead—in my heart
hope runs well behind fear—or rewake that quiescent
        fury, make *you*

105   an extra occasion of punishment. When you've won admission
        to my inner sanctum, and reached your proper domain

the book-bins, there you'll find your brethren, all in order,
    all worked through and through with the same
vigilant care. Most of these will display their titles
110   openly, have a label for all to read;
but three you'll find skulking in an obscure corner;
    even so, they teach, something everyone knows,
how to go about loving. Avoid them, or, if you have the courage,
    berate them as parricides! At least if you still feel
115 respect for your father, don't treat any one of this trio
    (though it teach you the way itself) with love.
There are also fifteen books of *Metamorphoses*, worksheets
    lately saved from my exequies:
To them I bid you say that the new face of my fortunes
120   may now be reckoned one more
among their bodily changes: by sudden transformation
    what was joyful once is made fit matter for tears.
I meant (if you're curious) to give you still further instructions,
    but I fear I've been holding you up—
125 besides, little book, if you took all my afterthoughts with you
    your bearer would find you a heavy load.
It's a long trek: make haste. Meanwhile my habitation
    remains the world's end, a land from my land remote.

1.3: Last Night in Rome

Nagging reminders: the black ghost-melancholy vision
    of my final night in Rome,
the night I abandoned so much I dearly treasured—
    to think of it, even now, starts tears.

5   That day was near dawning on which, by Caesar's fiat,
    I must leave the frontiers of Italy behind.
I'd lacked time—and inclination—to get things ready,
    long procrastination had numbed my will:
Too listless to bother with choosing slaves, attendants,
10   the wardrobe, the outfit an exile needs,
I was dazed, like someone struck by Jove's own lightning
    (had I not been?), who survives, yet remains unsure
whether he's dead or alive. Sheer force of grief unclouded
    my mind in the end. When my poor wits revived
15 I had one last word with my friends before departure—
    those few friends, out of many, who'd stood firm.

My wife, my lover, embraced me, outwept my weeping,
    her undeserving cheeks
rivered with tears. Far away in north Africa, my daughter
20   could know nothing of my fate. From every side,
wherever you looked, came the sounds of grief and lamentation,
    just like a noisy funeral. The whole house
mourned at my obsequies—men, women, even children,
    every nook and corner had its tears.
25   If I may gloss the trite with a lofty comparison,
    such was Troy's state when it fell.
By now all was still, no voices, no barking watchdogs,
    just the Moon on her course aloft in the night sky.
Gazing at her, and the Capitol—clear now by moonlight,
30   close (but what use?) to my home,
I cried: 'All you powers who dwell in that neighbour citadel,
    you temples, never more to be viewed
by me, you high gods of Rome, whom I must now abandon,
    accept my salutation for all time!
35   And although I assume my shield so late, after being wounded,
    yet free this my exile from the burden of hate,
and tell that heavenly man what error beguiled me, let him
    not think my remissness a crime—so that what you know
may likewise be discerned by the author of my expulsion:
40   with godhead appeased, I cannot be downcast.'
Such my prayer to the powers above; my wife's were countless,
    sobs choked each half-spoken word;
she flung herself down, hair loose, before our familial
    shrine, touched the dead-cold hearth with trembling lips,
45   poured out torrential appeals on behalf of the husband
    she mourned in vain. Our little household gods
turned a deaf ear, the Bear wheeled round the Pole Star,
    and ebbing dark left no room
for further delay. What to do? Seductive love of country
50   held me back—but this night was decreed my last,
tomorrow came exile. The times friends said 'Hurry!' 'Why?' I'd
    ask them,
        'Think to what place you're rushing me—and from where!'
The times I lied, swearing I'd set up an appropriate
    departure-time for my journey! Thrice I tripped
55   on the threshold, thrice turned back, dragging lethargic
    feet, their pace matched to my mood.
Often I'd make my farewells—and then go on talking,
    kiss everyone goodbye all over again,
unconsciously repeat identical instructions, eyes yearning

60   back to my loved ones. In the end—
'Why make haste?' I exclaimed, 'it's Scythia I'm being sent to,
        it's Rome I must leave: each one a prime excuse
for postponement: my living wife is denied her living
        husband for evermore: dear family, home,
65 loyal and much-loved companions, bonded in brotherhood
        that Theseus might have envied—all
now lost to me. This may well be my final chance to embrace them—
        let me make the most of one last extra hour.'
With that I broke off, leaving my speech unfinished,
70   and hugged all my dear ones in turn—
but while I'd been speaking, and amid their tears, the morning
        star (so baneful to me) had risen high
and bright in the heavens. I felt myself ripped asunder
        as though I'd lost a limb; a part of me
75 seemed wrenched from my body. So Mettus must have suffered
        when the horses avenging his treachery tore him in two.
Now my family's clamorous weeping reached its climax,
        sad hands beat naked breasts,
and my wife clung to me at the moment of my departure,
80   making one last agonized tearful plea:
'They can't tear you from me—together,' she cried, 'we'll voyage
        together, I'll follow you into exile, be
an exile's wife. Mine, too, the journey; that frontier station
        has room for me as well: I'll make little weight
85 on the vessel of banishment! While your expulsion's caused by
        the wrath of Caesar, mine springs from loyal love:
this love will be Caesar for me.' Her argument was familiar,
        she'd tried it before and she only gave it up—
still reluctant—on practical grounds. So I made my exit,
90   dirty, unshaven, hair anyhow—like a corpse
minus the funeral. Grief-stricken, mind whirling-black, she fainted
        (they tell me), fell down half-dead,
and when she came round, hair foul with dust, and staggered
        back to her feet from the cold floor,
95 wept now for herself, and now for hearth and household
        bereft of their lord, cried her lost husband's name
again and again, groaning as though she'd witnessed
        her daughter's corpse, or mine, on the high-stacked pyre;
longed to expunge, by dying, all sense of hardship,
100   yet through her regard for me could not succumb.
Let her live, then, ever to support her absent husband's
        living lot, since this is what fate has willed.

1.6: To My Devoted Wife

One of several exile poems addressed to Ovid's unnamed third wife. See p. 76.

> Not so dear was Lyde to the Clarian poet, not so truly
>   loved was Bittis by her singer from Cos
> as you are deeply entwined, wife, in my heart: you merit
>   a less wretched if not a better man.
> 5   You are the underthrust beam shoring up my ruin:
>   if I am anything still, it's all due to you.
>   You're my guard against stripping and despoliation
>   by those who went for the timbers of my wreck.
>   Just as the ravening wolf, bloodthirsty and famine-driven,
> 10   prowls in search of unguarded sheepfolds, just as
>   a hungry vulture will scan the wide horizon
>   for corpses still above ground, just so
>   that nobody, bad faith battening on our bitter troubles,
>   would (if you'd let him) have seized
> 15   my remaining goods. Your courage, those influential
>   friends — I can never thank them enough — put paid
>   to his tricks. So accept this tribute from a poor but honest
>   witness — if such a witness carries weight:
>   In probity neither Hector's wife excelled you,
> 20   nor Laodameia, who clove
> 21   to her husband even in death. If you'd had Homer
> 22   to sing your praises, Penelope's renown
> 33   would be second to yours, you'd stand first in the honoured roll-call
> 34   of heroines, pre-eminent for courage and faith —
>   whether this quality's inborn, produced by your own nature,
>   devotion that owes nothing to a master's words,
> 25   or whether that princely lady, for years your honoured patron,
>   has trained you to be a model wife by long
>   inurement, assimilation to her own example (if great things
>   may properly be compared with small).
>   Alas, my verses possess but scanty strength, your virtues
> 30   are more than my tongue can proclaim,
>   and the spark of creative vigour I once commanded
> 32   is extinct, killed off by my long
> 35   misfortunes. Yet in so far as our words of praise have power
>   you shall live through these verses for all time.

1.10: *A Ship Named* Minerva

Another key text in Middlebrook's correlation of Ovid with Minerva. See p. 35.

I have (may I always keep!) Minerva's protection: my vessel
 bears her painted casque, borrows her name.
Under sail she runs well with the slightest breeze; her rowers
 speed her along when there's need for oars.
5 Not content with outstripping any companion vessel
 she'll somehow contrive to overhaul any craft
that's set out before her: no storms will spring her timbers,
 she'll ride tall waves like a flat calm;
first met at Cenchreae, harbour of Corinth; since then
10 the faithful guide and companion of my flight,
kept safe by the power of Pallas through countless hazards,
 across endless gale-swept seas. Safe still—
I pray!—may she thread vast Pontus's entrance-channel
 and enter the waters of the Getic shore.
15 But as soon as she'd brought me into Aeolian Helle's seaway,
 setting course for the long haul through the narrows, then
we swung away westward, leaving Hector's city,
 and made harbour at Imbros. Thence
with a light following breeze our wearied vessel
20 rode over to Samothrace,
from where it's a short haul to Tempýra on the Thracian
 coast, and a parting of the ways between
master and ship: I planned an overland journey
 through Thrace, while she was to sail back
25 into Hellespontine waters, coasting along the Troad,
 past Lampsacus, home of the country god
Priapus, through the straits between Sestos and Abydos—
 scene of not-quite-virgin Helle's fatal flight—
to Cyzicus in the Propontis, barely linked to the mainland,
30 Cyzicus, Thracian colony of renown,
and so to Byzantium, guarding the jaws of Pontus,
 great gateway between twin seas.
May she win past all these, I pray, and with a strong following
 south wind wing her way through the Clashing Rocks,
35 skirt Thynias' bay, set course by Apollo's city
 under Anchialus' lofty walls, and thence
sail on past the ports of Mesémbria and Odéson,
 and that citadel named
for the wine-god, and the hilltop where Megarian exiles
40 (we're told) made their home from home;

cruising thence may she safely reach the Milesian foundation
    to which I'm consigned by the wrath
of an injured god. If she makes it, I'll sacrifice to Minerva
    a lamb for services rendered: I can't afford
45   anything larger. You too, twin brother-gods of this island,
    sons of Tyndareus, watch over our separate paths
with propitious power (one craft is to thread the Symplégadés,
    the other's for Thracian waters). Make the winds,
though we're bound for diverse destinations, favour
50   this vessel and that alike!

1.11: *Landfall*

Every word you've read in this whole book was written
    during the anxious days
of my journey: scribbling lines in mid-Adriatic
    while December froze the blood,
5   or after we'd passed the twin gulfs of the Isthmus
    and transferred to another ship,
still verse-making amid the Aegean's savage clamour
    (a sight, I fancy, that shook the Cyclades).
In fact, I'm surprised myself that in all that upheaval
10   of spirit and sea inspiration never flagged.
How to label such an obsession? Shocked stupor? Madness?
    No matter: by this one care all cares are relieved.
Time and again I was tossed by wintry tempests
    and darkly menacing seas;
15   time and again the day grew black with storm-clouds,
    torrents of wind-lashed rain;
time and again we shipped water; yet my shaky
    hand still kept writing verses—of a sort.
Now winds whistle once more through the taut rigging,
20   and massy-high rears up each hollow wave:
the very steersman, hands raised high to heaven,
    his art forgotten, turns to prayer for aid.
Wherever I look, there's nothing but death's image—
    death, that my split mind fears
25   and, fearing, prays for. Should I come safe to harbour
    terror lurks there too: more hazards on dry land
than from the cruel sea. Both men and deep entrap me,
    sword and wave twin my fear:
sword, I'm afraid, hopes to let my blood for booty,

30   wave wants the title of my death. Away
          on our left lies a barbarous coast, inured to rapine,
              stalked ever by bloodshed, murder, war—
          the agitation of these wintry waves is nothing
              to the turbulence in my breast.
35   All the more cause for indulgence, generous reader,
              if these lines fall short—as they do—
          of your hopes: they were not written, as formerly, in my garden,
              while I lounged on a favourite day-bed, but at sea
          in wintry light, rough-tossed by filthy weather, spindrift
40   spattering the paper as I write.
          Rough winter battles me, indignant at my presumption
              in ignoring its fierce threats, still scribbling away.
          Let the storm have its will of the man—but let storm and poem
              reach their end, I pray, each at the same time!

BOOK TWO

The entirety of *Tristia* book two consists of a single poem to the emperor Augustus, in which Ovid apologizes for his offenses. According to the poet, they were twofold: "a poem and an error" (v. 207). The former was the *Ars Amatoria* (*The Art of Love*), a three-book instruction manual on committing adultery in Augustan Rome. The latter offense is uncertain, though Ovid implies (vv. 103–10) that he had discovered something intolerably embarrassing to Augustus. In addition to pleading for mercy, Ovid makes some ingenious excuses for his prior work—too ingenious by half, perhaps, and doomed to fall on deaf ears.

2: A Plea to Augustus (excerpts)

      Books, my unlucky obsession, why do I stay with you
          when it was my own talent brought me down?
      Why go back to those fresh-condemned Muses, my nemesis? Isn't
          one well-earned punishment enough?
5   Poetry made men and women eager to know me—
          that was my bad luck;
      poetry made Caesar condemn me and my life-style
          because of my *Art*, put out
      years before: take away my pursuit, you remove my offences—
10   I credit my guilt to my verses. Here's the reward
      I've had for my care and all my sleepless labour:

a penalty set on talent. If I'd had sense
I'd have hated the Learned Sisters, and with good reason,
    divinities fatal to their own
15   adherents. But now, such madness attends my disorder,
      I'm bringing my bruised foot back
to the rock I stubbed my toes on, exactly as a defeated
    fighter returns to the lists, or a wrecked ship
sails out again into rough seas. Perhaps the same object
20   may (as with Telephus) cure the wound it caused,
and the Muse, having stirred that wrath, may now assuage it:
    poetry often moves the gods on high.
Caesar himself bade Italy's mothers and married daughters
    to hymn Ops, goddess of plenty, with her turret crown,
25   just as he'd done for Apollo at the celebration
    of those Games that are viewed but once
in any lifetime. On such precedents, merciful Caesar,
    let my poetic skills now soften your wrath—
just wrath indeed, I'll not deny I deserved it:
30   I haven't become *that* shameless—yet unless
I'd sinned, what could you have forgiven? My plight afforded
    you the chance to show mercy. If each time
a mortal erred, great Jupiter fired off his thunderous
    batteries, he'd soon be out of bolts...

I've prayed to delay your assumption to starry heaven, one more
    voice among many all offering up the same
petition; I've burnt loyal incense, I've supported
60   all public prayers on your behalf. And need
I say that my books—even those that form the charge against me—
    are crammed with countless allusions to your name?
Inspect that major work, which I've still left uncompleted,
    on fabulous bodily changes, and you'll find
65   much trumpeting of your name there, manifest pledges
    of my loyal devotion. Not
that your glory's enhanced by verses, or possesses scope for
    even further inflation: Jove has renown
in abundance—yet still derives pleasure from the recital
70   of his deeds, from providing a theme
for poets, and when they recount his battles with the Giants
    it may well be that he purrs at praise of himself.
Others may celebrate you in loftier, more appropriate
    language, and sing your praises with more wealth
75   of talent; and yet a god's not *only* won by the slaughter

of a hundred bulls: a pinch of incense will do.
A brute, and most cruel of all to me, was that unnamed person
   who read you frivolous extracts from my work
when passages that offer you reverent homage
80   are there to elicit a kinder verdict! Yet
who could have been my friend, when *you* were angered?...

Why did I see what I saw? Why render my eyes guilty?
   Why unwittingly take cognizance of a crime?
105 Actaeon never intended to see Diana naked,
   but still was torn to bits by his own hounds.
Among the high gods even accidents call for atonement:
   when deity's outraged, mischance is no excuse.
On the day that my fatal error misled me, disaster
110   struck my modest yet blameless house:
modest perhaps, but (it's said) of lofty ancestral
   lineage, second to none
in distinction, notable neither for poverty nor for riches,
   breeding knights of the middle road,
115 and however lowly a house (judged by means or derivation),
   still raised to prominence through my renown.
They may say I misused my talent with youthful indiscretion—
   but my name's still known world-wide;
the world of culture's well acquainted with Ovid, regards him
120   as a writer not to be despised.
So this house that was dear to the Muses now has fallen under
   a single (though far from exiguous) charge;
yet its fall is such that it can recover, if only
   time mellow affronted Caesar's wrath,
125 whose leniency in the punishment that he assigned me
   has undercut all my fears!
My life you gave me, your wrath stopped short of execution—
   that, sire, was to use your power with true restraint!
In addition, as though mere life were too small a present,
130   I kept my inherited wealth: this you did not
confiscate, nor condemn my deeds by decree of the Senate,
   nor order my exile through a special court.
No—as a sovereign should, yourself, with stern invective,
   avenged your own wrongs. What's more,
135 your edict, however severe and threatening, showed mercy
   when, naming my punishment, it described
me not as 'exiled' but as 'relegated', with sparing
   treatment of my fortune. Indeed,

there's no punishment worse for anyone in his right senses
140   than the displeasure of so great a man...

Show mercy, I beg you, shelve your cruel weapons,
180   the bolts that—to my loss—I know too well:
Show mercy, our fatherland's father, remember that title,
      don't kill my hopes of one day placating you.
I do not ask for return—though common observation
      shows the high gods have often granted such
185 petitions, and more—: a milder, less distant exile
      would remit the worst of my sentence. *Here*
is the ultimate torture for me, exposed amid foes—what banished
      person lives more remote from home?
I alone have been dispatched to the Danube's sevenfold outflow,
190   to shiver beneath the dead weight of northern skies:
only the river (scant barrier!) lies between me and countless
      barbarian hordes. Although
other men have been exiled by you for graver offences
      none was packed further off:
195 beyond here lies nothing but chillness, hostility, frozen
      waves of an ice-hard sea.
Here, on the Black Sea's bend sinister, stands Rome's bridgehead,
      facing out against Scyths and Celts,
her latest, shakiest bastion of law and order, only
200   marginally adhesive to the empire's rim.
So I beg you, as a suppliant, withdraw me to safety, do not
      rob me of peace of mind as well
as of my country—do not leave me to risk tribal incursions
      across the Danube, don't let me be exposed,
205 your citizen, to capture—no man of Latin blood should ever
      wear barbarous shackles while Caesar's line survives.
It was two offences undid me, a poem and an error:
      on the second, my lips are sealed—
my case does not merit the reopening of your ancient
210   wounds, Caesar: bad enough to have hurt you once.
But the first charge stands: that through an improper poem
      I falsely professed foul adultery. If so,
Divine minds, it's clear, must be sometimes prone to error;
      besides, there are many trifles lie beneath
215 your notice. Just as Jupiter, watching both gods and high heaven,
      lacks leisure to care for lesser things,
so while you gaze around on your dependent empire
      some minor matters will escape your eye.

Should you, the Imperial Princeps, desert your station
220   to peruse my limping verse?
The weight of Rome's name is not so casual, your shoulders
      do not sustain so light a load that you
can direct your godhead to my inept frivolities
      and examine, in person, my leisure work...

Yet it's no crime in itself to tum out wanton verses:
      the chaste can read much they mustn't do.
Very often your eyebrow-arching matron sees street-girls,
310   undressed, game for every kind of sex—
the very Vestal's eye observes prostitutes' bodies,
      yet incurs no penalty as a result.
But why, it's asked, is my Muse so excessively wanton, why does
      my book encourage everyone to make love?
315 Now *that*, I confess, was all wrong: error manifest, culpable:
      the choice, the perverted skill—I regret them both.
Why didn't I rather churn out yet another epic poem
      on how Troy fell to the Greeks?
Why not write about Thebes, and her fratricidal brothers,
320   and the champions at each of her seven gates?
No lack of material, either, from warlike Rome—and a worthy
      labour, to chronicle her patriots' deeds!
Finally, since you've filled the world with your meritorious
      achievements, Caesar, couldn't I find one theme
325 out of such plenty? Your deeds should have attracted my talents
      as the sun's radiance attracts the eye—
An unfair reproof: the field I plough is scrannel,
      whereas *that* task called for the richest soil.
Pleasure boats may be fine on small lakes—but that's no reason
330   for their braving the open sea.
I might—should I doubt even this?—have a knack for lighter
      measures, be up to minor verse; but if
you bid me tell of the Giants blasted by Jupiter's firebolts,
      my efforts are bound to wilt under such a load.
335 It would call for a rich talent to wrap up Caesar's fearsome
      acts, to prevent the subject eclipsing the work—
still, I made the attempt. No good. I seemed to belittle
      and (oh, abominable!) actually to harm
your prowess. So I turned back to my lightweight youthful poems,
340   stirred my heart with a false love—
Would I had not! but my fate was drawing me onward, my very
      brilliance worked to my own hurt.

Ah, why did I ever study? Why did my parents give me
      an education? Why did I learn so much
345 as the A B C? It was my *Art's* wantonness turned you
      against me, because you were convinced
it encouraged illicit sex. But no brides have become intriguers
      through me: no one can teach what he doesn't know.
Yes, I've written frivolous verses, erotic poems — but never
350   has a breath of scandal touched my name. There's no
husband, even among the lower classes, who questions
      his paternity through any fault of mine!
My morals, believe me, are quite distinct from my verses —
      a respectable life-style, a flirtatious Muse —
355 and the larger part of my writings is mendacious, fictive,
      assumes the licence its author denies himself.
A book is no index of character, but, a harmless pleasure,
      will offer much matter to delight the ear...

Yet even the fortunate author of your own *Aeneid* brought his
      Arms-and-the-Man into a Tyrian bed —
Indeed, no part of the whole work's read more often
535   than this union of illicit love. When young,
Virgil also depicted the passions of Amaryllis
      and Phyllis in pastoral eclogues. I too
gave offence, though long ago, with this kind of composition —
      now my old fault incurs a new punishment.
540 Yet I'd already issued these poems when with my fellow
      knights I passed in review before your stern
tribunal unfaulted. So the writings I thought harmless
      in my wild youth harm me now
in my old age. Retribution comes late and heavy
545   for that early squib, the penalty's remote
from the time of the sin. But don't think all my work so lightweight —
      I've often put out under full sail:
I wrote six books of the *Fasti*, had six more rough-drafted,
550   each covering one month of the year;
but this work, complete with its opening dedication,
      Caesar, to you, was cut short
by my fate. I presented the tragic stage with a royal drama,
      in language befitting the high tragic style;
555 I also described — though this work lacks final revision —
      the transformation of bodies into novel shapes.
If only you would, briefly, revoke your anger
      and read, at your leisure, those few lines —

really a few—in which, beginning with the Creation,
560   I bring the work down
to your own times, Caesar, you'll learn what guidance, what inspiration
      you've given me, with what warmth I treat you and yours.
I never flayed any victim with a mordant poem,
      my verse levels charges at none.
565 Guileless, I've always avoided embittered wit: not a single
      letter has been imbued with poisonous jests.
After writing so much, I'm the only one out of thousands
      done down by my own Muse.
So no Roman, I'd guess, rejoices at my misfortunes:
570   many, indeed, have grieved. Nor, if there exists
any gratitude for my kindness, can I really believe that
      someone would kick me when I'm down.
O father, O guardian and salvation of our country,
      may your godhead be moved by these and other pleas!
575 I don't ask for repatriation—or only perhaps when you're softened
      at last by the weary length
of my punishment—all I crave now is a safer, more tranquil
      place of exile, one chosen to match my offence.

BOOK THREE

3.7: To Perilla, a Poet

The identity of Perilla is much disputed. Some believe she was Ovid's step-daughter by his third wife (see p. 76), or perhaps his protégé. Others believe she is a literary construct, a *scripta puella*, as Corinna herself might have been in the *Amores*.

Go quickly, scribbled letter, my loyal mouthpiece,
      and greet Perilla for me. Her you'll find
either sitting in the company of her sweet mother
      or among her books and poems. When she hears
5   of your arrival, she'll drop whatever she's doing, and ask you,
      right away, why you've come—and how I am.
Tell her I live, but a life I'd rather not be living,
      that time has not eased my ills—and yet
that despite all I've gone back to the Muses who undid me,
10   and am, once again, writing elegiac verse.
Say to her: 'Are you too still attached to our common studies,
      making elegant poems in a non-Roman style?
For nature gave you, besides your modesty and beauty,

true talent, rarest of gifts—which I
15   was the first to direct to the Muses' spring, lest your fecund
        vein of pure water run dry; I was the first
to see this in your early girlhood, when, as father to daughter,
        I became your companion and your guide.
So if the same fire still burns in your bosom, the Lesbian
20   singer alone will surpass your work. Yet I fear
lest my present misfortune prove an obstacle to you,
        lest my sufferings leave your mind a blank.
While we could, we often read our poems to each other,
        and I was often your teacher, often your judge:
25   now I'd lend an ear to the verses you'd just written,
        now draw a blush from you when you ran dry.
Perhaps, since my books harmed me, you too may be made anxious
        by the example of my punishment?
Don't worry, Perilla: just ensure that no man—or woman—
30   can learn from *your* writings how to deal with love!
So, my accomplished young lady, reject all those excuses
        for sloth, go back to the literary arts
and your sacred calling. Long years will mar those classic features,
        senility's wrinkles furrow your ancient brow:
35   age, ruinous age, advancing with silent footsteps
        will lay a cold hand on your beauty. When they say
"She was lovely once" you'll grieve, complain that your mirror
        lies, lies, lies. You possess
a modest fortune (true, you well deserve a great one),
40   yet even supposing you had unlimited wealth,
Fortune gives one man a bonus, bankrupts his neighbour,
        and yesterday's millionaire is a beggar today.
In brief, there's nothing we own that isn't mortal
        save talent, the spark in the mind.
45   Look at me—I've lost my home, the two of you, my country,
        they've stripped me of all they could take,
yet my talent remains my joy, my constant companion:
        over *this*, Caesar could have no rights. What if
some savage's sword should cut short my existence?
50   When I'm gone, my fame will endure,
and while from her seven hills Mars' Rome in triumph
        still surveys a conquered world, *I shall be read.*
You too—may your work and art find better fortune!—
        evade, by all means you can, those coming flames!'

3.13: A Birthday in Exile

Compare this poem to Middlebrook's depiction of Ovid's festive birthday in
Rome, pp. 80–3.

> My birthday god's here again, on time—and superfluous:
>   what good did I get from being born?
> Cruel spirit, why come to increase this wretch's years of exile?
>   You should rather have cut them short.
> 5   If you cared for me at all, if you felt the slightest
>   shame, you wouldn't be hounding me thus beyond
> my native land: no, you should have done your best to sever
>   the bond between us when first you recognized
> the ill-starred child that I was, and at parting, like my comrades,
> 10   you too should have bid me a sad farewell
> in the Rome I'd be forced to leave. What's Pontus to you? Has Caesar's
>   wrath dispatched you, like me, to the world's
> icy extremity? You expect, I assume, the usual honours—
>   that I should wear a white robe,
> 15   a smoking altar wreathed with floral garlands, the crackle
>   of incense in that holy fire, myself
> to offer the cakes that mark my birthday, to utter
>   fine and propitious prayers?
> I am not so circumstanced, my life's not such that I'm able
> 20   to rejoice at your advent. For me an altar of death
> hung round with funereal cypress would be better suited,
>   a tall pyre to burn my corpse.
> It's no pleasure to offer up incense when gods are indifferent,
>   and in such misfortunes no propitious words
> 25   come to mind. Still, if today I must pray for something,
>   return no more, I beg you, to such a land
> so long as I'm still detained in this next-to-the-world's-limit
>   wilderness. They call it *hospitable*. They lie.

BOOK FOUR

4.10: Ovid's Autobiography

Of all the exile poetry, 4.10 is indispensable to a biography of Ovid. See pp. 10,
17, 46, 51–2, 66, 71–2, 79.

> Who was this I you read, this trifler in tender passions?
>   You want to know, posterity? Then attend:—
> Sulmo is my homeland, where ice-cold mountain torrents

make lush our pastures, and Rome is ninety miles off.
5   Here I was born, in the year both consuls perished
        at Antony's hands; heir (for what that's worth)
to an ancient family, no brand-new knight promoted
        just yesterday for his wealth.
I was not the eldest child: I came after a brother
10   born a twelvemonth before me, to the day
so that we shared a birthday, celebrated one occasion
        with two cakes, in March, at the time
of that festival sacred to armed Minerva — the first day in it
        stained by the blood of combat. We began
15   our education young: our father sent us to study
        with Rome's best teachers in the liberal arts.
My brother from his green years had the gift of eloquence,
        was born for the dash of words in a public court;
but I, even in boyhood, held out for higher matters,
20   and the Muse was seducing me subtly to her work.
My father kept saying: 'Why study such useless subjects?
        Even Homer left no inheritance.' Convinced
by his argument, I abandoned Helicon completely,
        struggled to write without poetic form;
25   but a poem, spontaneously, would shape itself to metre —
        whatever I tried to write turned into verse.
The years sped silently by: we arrived at manhood,
        my brother and I, dressed for a freer life,
with the broad stripe and the purple draped from our shoulders,
30   each still obsessed by his own early pursuits.
But when he was barely twenty years old, my brother
        died — and from then I lost a part of myself.
I did take the first step up the governmental ladder,
        became a member of the Board of Three;
35   the Senate awaited me; but I chose to narrow my purple
        stripe: there lay a burden beyond my strength.
For such a career I lacked both endurance and inclination:
        the stress of ambition left me cold,
while the Muse, the creative spirit, was forever urging on me
40   that haven of leisure to which I'd always leaned.
The poets of those days I cultivated and cherished:
        for me, bards were so many gods.
Often the ageing Macer would read me what he'd written
        on birds or poisonous snakes or healing herbs;
45   often Propertius, by virtue of that close-binding
        comradeship between us, would recite

his burning verses. Ponticus, noted for epic, and Bassus,
    pre-eminent in iambics, both belonged
to my circle; Horace, that metrical wizard, held us
50   spellbound with songs to the lyre.
Virgil I only saw, while greedy fate left Tibullus
    scant time for our friendship. He
came after Gallus, then Propertius followed:
    I was next, the fourth in line.
55 And as I looked up to my elders, so a younger generation
    looked up to me: my reputation soon spread.
When first I recited my earliest poems in public
    my beard had only been shaved once or twice:
she fired my genius, who now is a Roman byword
60   because of those verses, the girl to whom I gave
the pseudonym of 'Corinna'. My writing was prolific,
    but what I thought defective, I myself
let the flames claim for revision. On the brink of exile,
    raging against my vocation, my poems, I burnt work
65 that could have found favour. My heart was soft, no stronghold
    against Cupid's assaults, prey to the lightest pang.
Yet, despite my nature, though the smallest spark would
    ignite me, no scandal ever smeared my name.
When I was scarce past boyhood I was briefly married
70   to a wife both worthless and useless; next
came a bride you could not find fault with, yet not destined
    to warm my bed for long; third and last
there's the partner who's grown old with me, who's learnt to shoulder
    the burden of living as an exile's wife.
75 My daughter, twice pregnant (but by different husbands) made me
    a grandfather early on, while she was still
just a slip of a girl. By then my father had completed
    his lifespan of ninety years. For him I wept
just as he would have done had I been the one taken.
80   Then, next, I saw my mother to her grave.
Ah, lucky the pair of them, so timely dead and buried,
    before the black day of my disgrace!
And lucky for me, that they are not still living
    to witness my misery, that they felt no grief
85 on my account. Yet if there survives from a life's extinction
    something more than a name, if an insubstantial wraith
does escape the pyre, if some word, my parental spirits,
    has reached you about me, if charges stand to my name
in the Stygian court, then understand, I implore you

90   —and you I may not deceive—that my exile's cause
was not a crime, but an error. So much for the dead. I return now
        to you, my devoted readers, who would know
the events of my life. Already my best years were behind me—
        age had brindled my hair, and ten times since my birth,
95   head wreathed with Pisan olive, the victorious Olympic
        charioteer had carried off the prize
when the wrath of an injured prince compelled me to make my way to
        Tomis, on the left shore of the Black Sea.
The cause (though too familiar to everyone) of my ruin
100   must not be revealed through testimony of mine.
Why rake up associates' meannesses, harm done me by house-slaves,
        and much further suffering, not a whit less harsh
than the exile itself? Yet my mind disdained to yield to trouble,
        showed itself invincible, drew on its strength,
105 till I, forgetting myself and my old leisured existence,
        took arms on occasion with unpractised hand;
by sea and land I suffered as many misfortunes
        as the stars between the unseen and the visible poles.
Through long wanderings driven, I at length made landfall
110   on this coast, where native bowmen roam; and here
though the din of neighbouring arms surrounds me, I still lighten
        my sad fate as best I can
with the composition of verse: though there is none to listen
        this is how I spend, and beguile, my days.
115 So the fact that I live still, to grapple with such grim hardships,
        unwearied, yet, of the light and all it brings,
I owe, my Muse, to you: it's you who afford me solace,
        who come as rest, as medicine to my cares;
you my guide and comrade, who spirit me from the Danube
120   to an honoured seat on Helicon; who have
offered me that rare benefit, fame while still living,
        a title rarely granted till after death.
Nor has Envy, belittler of all that's present, sunk her
        malignant fangs into any work of mine:
125 for although our age has produced some classic poets,
        Fame has not grudged my gifts renown.
There are many I'd rank above me: yet I am no less quoted
        than they are, and most read throughout the world.
So if there's any truth in poetic predictions, even
130   should I die tomorrow, I'll not be wholly earth's.
Which I was it triumphed? True poet or fashion's pander?
        Either way, generous reader, it is you I must thank.

BOOK FIVE

5.10: *Backwater Life*

Ovid's description of daily life in Tomis stands in sharp contrast to the idylls
of Sulmona (*Am.* 2.16, pp. 13–14) or to the urbanity of Rome (see pp. 45–8,
55, 76–8).

Since I've been here in Pontus, three times the Danube
    has frozen; three times the offshore sea's iced up.
Yet I feel I've been absent as many years from my country
    as Troy was besieged by its Greek foes.
5   You'd think time stood still, so slowly does it travel,
    with such dragging steps does the year complete its course.
For me the summer solstice never shortens
    the nights, midwinter never shrinks my days:
for me, I'll swear, nature has been made over
10   and draws out everything commensurate
with my wearisome troubles. Or is it that time in general
    goes on as before, and it's just *my* time that drags
now I'm stuck by the ill-named 'Euxine' (kind to strangers
    it's not) and the Scythian coastal bend
15   sinister (yes indeed). Countless threatening tribes surround us,
    who think living except by pillage a disgrace.
Nothing's safe outside: our hill-settlement's protected
    only by low walls and a good defensive site.
The horde descends, like birds, when you least expect it,
20   and, barely glimpsed, is away again with its spoils.
Often inside the walls, gates shut, their poisoned arrows
    still reach us: we collect them off the streets.
Few dare to farm: the wretches that plough their holdings
    must do it one-handed (the other grasps a sword);
25   the piping shepherd is helmeted, while his timorous
    ewes dread not wolves but war.
Our fortress barely defends us: even inside it
    that native mob mixed with the Greeks
is scary—barbarians form over half the population
30   and live here without distinction. Even if you don't
fear them, the sight of their chest-long hair, their sheepskins,
    is enough to fill you with loathing—even those
who are held to be descended from the first Greek settlers
    have exchanged their ancestral dress for Persian trews.
35   They have commerce with one another through their common language,
    while I must use signs to indicate my needs.

Here *I'm* the barbarian, understood by no one,
      and these stupid peasants mock my Latin speech,
slander me to my face with impunity, on occasion
40   (I suspect) laugh at my exile. When I reply
to their talk with a nod or a shake of the head, they find me
      silly, absurd. On top of this, unjust
justice is meted out here with the sword-blade, very often
      wounds are inflicted in open court. Harsh Fate,
45   to give me, when my star is so unlucky, no shorter
      a thread of life! That I'm deprived of the sight
of my country, of you, my friends, that I'm consigned to this Scythian
      outback—such things, yes, I resent: each one
is a heavy penalty. It was right I should be severed
50   from Rome—but not to rot in such a place.
What am I saying? I'm mad—for offending Caesar's godhead
      I deserved to lose my very life as well!

5.14: A Monument of Sorrows

How great a monument I've built you in my writings,
      wife dearer to me than myself, you yourself can see.
Though Fortune strip much from their author, yet my talent
      shall make you illustrious; as long
5   as I'm read, your legend and mine will be read together—
      not all of you will burn up in that sad pyre.
and though through your husband's misfortunes you may provoke pity,
      you'll find some women who want to be what you are,
who, because you share *my* sorrows, will call you lucky,
10   envy you. I couldn't have given you more
by giving you riches: the rich man's shade brings nothing
      of his own to the shades below.
I endowed you with a name that's immortal, you enjoy the advantage
      of the greatest boon I could bestow.
15   Besides, as the sole guardian of my possessions,
      no small honour is yours,
for my voice is never silent concerning you, you should be
      proud of your husband's testimony. That none
may be able to call it excessive, show your persistence,
20   preserve me and your loyalty at once—
since while I stood secure, no charges were levelled
      against your probity, true; but (at best) it was free
from reproach, no more. Now my fortune's demolition

has cleared *you* a space in which to build
25   a structure that all may see. To be good—that's easy
          with all snags removed, when there's nothing to stop a wife
fulfilling her duty. But not to avoid the storm-cloud
          when a god thunders—*that* is true married love,
that's loyalty indeed. Too rare, the virtue ungoverned
30   by Fortune, that never wavers when Fortune flees!
Yet when Virtue's her own reward, and holds herself upright
          in far from cheerful condition, then even if
you encompass all space and time, there's no era will pass her over
          in silence, she'll be admired to the world's end.
35   Do you see how Penelope's faith wins praise down the ages,
          how her name never dies? Do you perceive
how the wives of Admetus and Hector still figure in poems—
          Evadne too, who burnt herself on her husband's pyre;
how Laodameia, whose husband Protesilaüs
40   was first man ashore at Troy, still lives
on men's lips? I don't need your death, only your devotion,
          your love; you aren't required to seek renown
the hard way. And don't feel I'm making this admonition
          because of non-action by you: I'm just providing sails
45   for a boat that's being rowed. A reminder of what you're already doing
          is praise, and exhortation approves your deeds.

EPISTULAE EX PONTO

(*Letters from Pontus*, AD 13–16)

From *Ovid: The Poems of Exile*. University of California Press, 2005 (orig. Penguin Books, 1994). Peter Green, translator.

Ovid followed the *Tristia* with another collection of exile poetry, this one in four books. Whereas the former volume is despairing yet hopeful, the latter is marked more by a sense of resignation: The poet has settled into the role of a displaced person. Ovid also names more names, as the political risk of being his friend seems to have lessened with time.

BOOK ONE

1.4: *To My Wife, from Her Old Man*

Now, already, white hairs have brindled my waning
    age, the lines of senility score my face;
now strength and vigour abate in my broken body,
    the games that delighted my youth no longer please.
5   If you came upon me now, you'd no longer recognize me,
    such ruin's been wrought on my looks.
I admit the years are responsible — yet there's a second
    cause: unremitting hardship, distress of mind.
Spread out my misfortunes to match the year's long tally
10   and I'd be older than Nestor, believe you me.
You see how oxen, working iron-hard ploughland
    (and what's more tough than an ox?) are broken, worn down
by toil; the earth that's never allowed to lie fallow
    is exhausted through overcropping, decays.
15   Run a horse in every race, without intermission,
    and it's bound, eventually, to collapse.
A ship, however strong, that's never dried out will founder
    during some deep-sea voyage: so I too
am debilitated by an unmeasured load of troubles,
20   made an old man before my time.
Leisure sustains the body, the mind too feeds upon it,
    but excessive toil wears both
to nothing. Observe what praise later ages heaped on Jason
    for venturing into these parts!
25   Yet his effort, compared to mine, was lightweight, unimportant
    (let's hope those 'great names' don't suppress the truth!):
He set out for Pontus at the bidding of Pelias,

whose rule scarce reached the borders of Thessaly;
 but it was the wrath of Caesar that wrought *my* downfall—Caesar
30 whose name strikes awe from dawnlands to furthest west!
Thessaly's nearer Pontus than Rome to the Danube delta—
 his voyage was briefer than mine.
He had as his companions the flower of Achaean manhood,
 but in my exile I was abandoned by all;
35 I ploughed the vasty deep in fragile timbers—but solid
 the hull that bore Aeson's son.
I had no Tiphys as helmsman, no Phineus to teach me
 which routes to follow, which to shun;
Queen Juno and Pallas offered *him* protection,
40 no gods safeguarded *my* life; he obtained
assistance from Cupid's clandestine arts—far better
 had Love never learnt them from me!
He came back home, but I shall die in this land, if the heavy
 wrath of that injured deity persists.
45 So, most faithful of wives, my task is surely harder
 than that which Jason endured.
You too, who were young when I left the City, doubtless
 have been aged by my troubles: may the gods
let me see you as now you are, bestow fond kisses
50 on your brindling hair, fold my arms
round your far-from-plump body, assure you that 'It's worry
 on my account that's thinned you down so much—',
tell, amid mingled tears, the full tale of my sufferings,
 enjoy an unhoped-for colloquy, offer those
55 true gods the Caesars—also the wife who's worthy of Caesar—
 due debt of incense from my grateful hand.
May the Prince be appeased, may Memnon's mother Aurora
 with rosy lips call forth this day—soon, soon!

BOOK TWO

2.3: To Cotta Maximus

Maximus was the son of Marcus Valerius Messalla Corvinus, the patron of the
Ovidii. See pp. 44–5, 49–58.

Maximus, you whose great name is matched by shining virtues,
 who refuse to let your true nature be eclipsed
by your high birth, my idol till my life's last moments
 (for how does my status here differ from death?)—the thing

5   you're doing in not disowning an afflicted comrade
           is the rarest of gestures for your age:
       shameful to say, yet true (did we but admit it), approval
           of friendship among the common run of men
       is dictated by profit. Expedience crowds out honour,
10   and loyalty stands or falls pat on success.
       You couldn't find one man in a thousand who supposes
           virtue really to be its own reward:
       a fine action's intrinsic merit, if there's no pay-off,
           leaves people cold, they resent being good for free.
15   Nothing but profit's prized: go take from the grasping
           mind its hope of reward, and who'll seek a friend?
       Income's the passion today, every investor's busy
           totting up on anxious fingers just what he's made.
       The once-revered goddess of friendship is on the market,
20   has her pitch like a whore, ready to trade for cash.
       So I admire you the more for not yielding to the torrent,
           not going with this outflow of common vice.
       Nobody's loved who hasn't Fortune's support: one threatening
           noise from her, and all in sight take off.
25   Look at me—once fortified with friends by the dozen,
           so long as a following breeze bellied my sails;
       but now winds and clouds have whipped up a stormy ocean
           I'm abandoned in mid-sea on a leaking craft.
       When I was cast forth, and the rest wouldn't even know me,
30   there were two or three of you only who gave me aid,
       and amongst these you stood out: no follower, but a leader,
           more fit to set than seek an example; when all
       you'll concede, on the facts, is that I committed an error
           it's your sense of duty and probity that helps.
35   Virtue, in your judgement, needs no rewarding,
           should always be sought for herself
       unencumbered with alien lucre. You consider it shameful
           to stand off a friend who needs pity, or withdraw
       your friendship because he's unlucky. When a swimmer's exhausted,
40   to support his chin with a finger shows more warmth
       than letting him drown. Just think what Achilles did for Patroclus
           dead—and this life (believe me) is like a death.
       Theseus escorted Pirithoüs to the Stygian river:
           how distant my death from Styx?
45   Pylades was on hand to succour crazy Orestes:
           my fault has no little madness in it too.
       Do you too—as you are doing—share the praise proper

to such great heroes, bring the fallen what help you can.
   If I know you well, if you're still the man you once were
50   today, if your courage hasn't failed, the more
that Fortune rages, the more you'll resist her, taking
   care, as is right, that *she* doesn't conquer *you*.
To fight well, you need a foe who's a good fighter:
   thus I'm helped and hurt by the same cause.
55 Doubtless, my dear young friend, you find it beneath you
   to join forces with the goddess perched on her globe;
you're steadfast, and since the sails of my damaged vessel
   are not as you'd wish, you must handle them as they are.
This ruin, so shaken men think to see it falling
60   each moment, survives, propped up
on your shoulders. At first you were angry, and with good reason,
   as relentless as he whom my offence
had justly pricked: the distress which touched great Caesar,
   that, you declared forthwith, was yours as well.
65 But when you learnt the origins of my disaster,
   they say you groaned aloud over my mistake.
Your letter, then, was the first to bring me comfort, give me
   hope that the injured god could be appeased;
then, too, the constancy of that long friendship moved you,
70   assumed by me before your birth, so that
though you *became* friends with others, to my friendship
   you were born: it was in your cradle that I kissed you first.
This fact—don t forget that your house has had my devoted service
   since my own childhood—makes *me* a charge on *you*,
75 and one of long standing. Your father, whose eloquence in Latin
   was no whit inferior to his noble birth
first urged me to commit my verse to public judgment,
   was my talent's mentor and guide.
Nor, I maintain, can your brother so much as remember
80   my earliest service to him. But it was you
whom I cherished above all others, so that whatever
   befell, you alone won my friendship and my thanks.
Elba was where we spent our last sad hours together,
   tears running down our cheeks,
85 and when you asked, was the news true that these rumours
   had spread about my offence, I stuck
between half-hearted confession, half-hearted denial,
   choking with classic fright,
and like snow melted by a damp south wind, the tears welled
90   up in distress, flowed free. Remembering this,

and because you see that my 'crime' can lie forgotten
    once that first error wins pardon, you take thought
for your old friend in these sorry circumstances,
    apply your healing poultices to my wounds.
95   In return for all this, should free choice be allowed me,
    I'd call a thousand well-earned blessings down
upon you, but if I'm restricted to *your* vows, then my prayers
    will be for your mother's—after Caesar's—health,
since this, I remember, when you were fattening altars
100   with incense, was always your first plea to the gods.

2.4: To Atticus, My First Reader

A retrospective on a friendship from Ovid's glory days as a poet.

Accept this discourse of Ovid's from the ice-bound Danube,
    Atticus—friend whom my judgement must not doubt!
Do you still retain memories of your ill-fated companion,
    or has your concern now wearied of its role?
5   The gods are not so hard on me that I'd find it credible,
    justifiable for you to forget me so soon.
Before my eyes your image always lingers, your features
    are printed by memory on my mind.
I recall all those serious talks that we had together,
10   and not a few hours of fun—
Often the time seemed too short for our long discussions,
    often the day was done before my words,
often you'd listen to a poem freshly drafted,
    sit in judgment on some new work.
15   What you had praised, I would figure had pleased the public,
18   and more than once I erased on your advice;
17   to have my book rasped smooth by a friend's file—this was
16   the sweet reward your admonitions brought.
We were always together, in porticoes, on street-corners,
20   side by side at the theatre, in the public squares—
in short, my dearest friend, our affection ever rivalled
    the love Achilles felt for Nestor's son.
Though you drank deep draughts of Lethe's deadening water
    I cannot believe these things could fade from your mind:
25   sooner shall long summer days attend the winter solstice,
    with summer nights slower than those at the year's turn,
or Babylon have no heat, no cold year's turn grip Pontus,
    or the rank lily outscent the Paestan rose,

than you shall be touched by oblivion of our friendship—
30   no part of my fate could ever be *that* unbright!
But take care lest this trust of mine be termed fallacious
        and foolish credulity on my part: keep faith,
be constant, protect your old comrade—just so long as
        I'm not a burden—in any way you can.

BOOK FOUR

4.4: A Hopeful Rumor

Even in the latter days of exile Ovid found occasion to hope for his return to Rome.

No day is ever so sodden with southern rain-clouds
        that the water pelts down without a break;
no place is so barren that among the clinging brambles
        there's no useful plant to be found.
5   Grave misfortune has made nothing quite so wretched
        that no scintilla of pleasure offsets its ills.
See me then, stripped of home, country, friendly contacts,
        tossed up as flotsam on the Black Sea coast,
still finding ways to brighten my sad features,
10   not to remember my fate.
For while I strolled, alone, on the golden sands, behind me
        there came (it seemed to me) a rustle of wings,
and when I looked back, I could see no physical presence,
        but my ears picked up these words:
15   'I am Rumour, I've flown here a measureless distance to bring you
        good news: the coming year
will be radiant and happy—the consul will be Pompeius,
        your dearest friend in the world.'
Thereupon, after filling Pontus with such glad tidings,
20   the goddess flew off elsewhere; but for me
these new joys banished my cares, and the iniquitous
        harshness of this place just fell away.
So, two-faced Janus, when you've opened the long-awaited
        year, when December's ousted by your sacred month,
25   the purple of highest office will robe my Pompey,
        ensure that his titles are complete.
Already I seem to see your halls crowded to bursting,
        folk trampled through lack of space,
you making your first visit to the Tarpeian temples,

30   the gods responding propitiously to your prayers.
          I see the oxen, grazed on Falerii's lush pastures,
                offering their throats to the sure axe;
          and when you pray to the gods, it's Jupiter and Caesar
                whose favour you'll most particularly seek.
35   You'll be received in the Senate, the Fathers assembled
                in traditional fashion will hang upon your words,
          and when you've delighted them with your eloquence, when custom
                has pronounced the lucky formulas for the day,
          and you've given due thanks to the gods on high, and to Caesar
40   (who'll give you cause to repeat them, time and again),
          you'll go home in procession with the whole Senate for escort,
                and the public's homage will overflow your house.
          My bad luck that I won't be seen in that crowd, that my eyes won't
                be able to feast on the sight!
45   What I *can* do is visualize a mental image of you
                in your absence: at least my mind will gaze
          on its dear consul's face. At some time too, God willing,
                you'll remember my name. 'Poor man,
          what's he up to these days?' you'll ask. If I get such a message,
50   I'll concede at once that my exile's more easily borne.

4.16: Ovid's Mortality

Compare this poem with Ovid's parting words in other works. There the poet typically insists on his immortality and lasting fame. He does so here as well, but punctuating his fame now are reminders of his own impending mortality.

          Envious wretch, why bother to savage a dead man's poems?
                Ovid is gone. As a rule no talent is hurt
          by death: fame grows after the ashes—and I enjoyed a
                reputation when I was alive still, when Marsus lived,
5   and bombastic Rabirius, Macer the Trojan War buff,
                Pedo up there among the stars,
           Carus (whose *Hercules* would have offended Juno, had its
                hero not already been Juno's son-in-law),
           Severus, who treated Rome to his *Royal Cantos*,
10   finicky Numa, Priscus A and B,
          Montanus, known as the two-metre man, adequate
                at epic and elegiacs both;
          Sabinus, who made Ulysses write back to Penelope
                during his ten-year traipse through choppy seas,
15   and whose premature death left his local battle-epic unfinished,

not to mention an almanac in verse;
Largus, whose large genius matched his surname, who trotted
　　old Phrygian what's-his-name off to the fields of Gaul,
Camerinus, who settled Troy's business after Hector's downfall,
20　　　Tuscus (a name for his *Phyllis*)—and what about
that old sea-dog of a poet, whose works might well have
　　been slapped together by the gods of the sea?
Or the other fellow who versified Rome's wars in Libya,
　　or Marius, the pro who could turn out *anything?*
25　Don't forget our Sicilian friend, mulling over his *Perseid,*
　　or Lupus on Menelaus and Helen's return,
or the litterateur who adapted Homer's Phaeacian sequence,
　　or Rufus, one-man performer upon Pindar's lyre,
or Turranius' Muse, propped up on her tragic buskins,
30　　or the Muse of Melissus with her comic clogs.
While Varius and Graccus wrote fierce fustian for tyrants,
　　Proculus trod Callimachus' primrose path,
Passer resummoned Tityrus to his ancient pastures,
　　Grattius wrote hot tips for hunting buffs,
35　Fontanus tossed off the amours of nymphs and satyrs,
　　Capella crammed phrases in the elegiac mould.
There were plenty more, though I don't have time to mention
　　all their names (but their works are in public vogue),
not to mention the youngsters whose efforts remain unpublished,
40　　and don't, thus, belong in my list
(though for you, Cotta Maximus, I have to make an exception,
　　the Muses' jewel and guardian of the courts,
endowed with a double nobility—your father's Messallan
　　ancestry, plus the Cottas on your mother's side).
455　If it's seemly to say so, my talent was distinguished,
　　and among all that competition, I was *fit to be read.*
So, Malice, sheathe your bloody claws, spare this poor exile,
　　don't scatter my ashes after death!
I have lost all: only bare life remains to quicken
50　　the awareness and substance of my pain.
What pleasure do you get from stabbing this dead body?
　　There is no space in me now for another wound.

Adkins, Lesley and Roy Adkins. *Handbook to Life in Ancient Rome.* New York: Facts on File, 1994.

Ahl, Frederick. *Metaformations: Soundplay and Wordplay in Ovid and Other Classical Poets.* Ithaca, NY: Cornell University Press, 1985.

Armstrong, David. "Horatius Eques et Scriba: Satires 1.6 and 2.7." *Transactions of the American Philological Association* 116 (1986): 255–88.

Balsdon, J.P.V.D. *Life and Leisure in Ancient Rome.* London: Phoenix, 2002.

———. *Roman Women: Their History and Habits.* New York: John Day, 2004.

Barrett, Anthony. *Livia: First Lady of Imperial Rome.* New Haven, CT: Yale University Press, 2002.

Beard, Mary. "Writing Ritual: The Triumph of Ovid." In *Rituals in Ink: A Conference on Religion and Literary Production in Ancient Rome Held at Stanford University in February 2002,* edited by Alessandro Barchiesi, Jörg Rüpke, and Susan Stephens, 115–26. Stuttgart: Steiner, 2004.

Beard, Mary, and Michael Crawford. *Rome in the Late Republic: Problems and Interpretations.* 2nd ed. London: Duckworth, 1999.

Boyle, A.J. *An Introduction to Roman Tragedy.* London: Routledge, 2006.

Bull, Malcolm. *The Mirror of the Gods.* Oxford: Oxford University Press, 2005.

Byatt, A.S. "Arachne." In *Ovid Metamorphosed,* edited by Philip Terry, 131–57. London: Chatto and Windus, 2000.

Calvino, Italo. "Ovid and Universal Contiguity." In *The Literature Machine,* translated by Patrick Creagh, 146–61. London: Secker and Warburg, 1989.

Cameron, Alan. "The First Edition of Ovid's *Amores.*" *Classical Quarterly* 18 (1968): 320–33.

Carcopino, Jérôme. *Daily Life in Ancient Rome.* Edited with bibliography and notes by H.T. Rowell. Translated by E.O. Lorimer. New Haven: Yale University Press, 1964.

Casson, Lionel. *Travel in the Ancient World.* London: Allen and Unwin, 1974.

Claridge, Amanda. *Rome: An Oxford Archeological Guide.* With contributions by Judith Toms and Tony Cubberley. 2nd ed. Oxford: Oxford University Press, 2010.

Clarke, John R. *The Houses of Roman Italy, 100 B.C.–A.D. 250: Ritual, Space, and Decoration.* Berkeley: University of California Press, 1991.

Conway, R.S. *The Italic Dialects.* Cambridge University Press, 1897.

Dalby, Andrew. *Empire of Pleasures: Luxury and Indulgence in the Roman World.* London: Routledge, 2000.

Davies, Ceri. "Poetry in the 'Circle' of Messalla." *Greece and Rome* 20 (1973): 25–35.

Dupont, Florence. *Daily Life in Ancient Rome.* Oxford: Blackwell, 1992.

———. "The Grammar of Roman Dining." In *Food: A Culinary History from Antiquity to the Present,* edited by Jean Louis Flandrin, Massimo Montanari, and Albert Sonnenfeld, 113–27. New York: Columbia University Press, 1999.

Everitt, Anthony. *Augustus: The Life of Rome's First Emperor.* New York: Random House, 2006.

Feeney, Denis. "I Shall Be Read." *London Review of Books,* August 17, 2006.

Gaisser, Julia H. "Tibullus 1.7: A Tribute to Messalla." *Classical Philology* 66 (1971): 221–9.

Gozzini Giacosa, Ilaria. *A Taste of Ancient Rome.* Translated by Anna Herklotz. Chicago: University of Chicago Press, 1992.

Green, Peter. Introduction to *The Erotic Poems* by Ovid, 15–81. Translated by Peter Green. Harmondsworth, UK: Penguin Books, 1982.

———. Introduction to *The Poems of Exile: Tristia and the Black Sea Letters* by Ovid, xix–lx. Translated by Peter Green. Berkeley: University of California Press, 2005.

Harlow, Mary, and Ray Laurence. *Growing Up and Growing Old in Ancient Rome: A Life Course Approach.* London: Routledge, 2002.

Herescu, N.I., ed. *Ovidiana: Recherches sur Ovide.* Paris: Les Belles Lettres, 1958.

Higham, T.F. "Ovid and Rhetoric." In Herescu, *Ovidiana,* 32–48.

Hölkeskamp, Karl-Joachim. "Under Roman Roofs: Family, House and Household." In *The Cambridge Companion to the Roman Republic,* edited by Harriet I. Flower, 113–38. Cambridge: Cambridge University Press, 2004.

Holzberg, Niklas. "Playing with His Life: Ovid's 'Autobiographical' References." In *Oxford Readings in Ovid,* edited by Peter E. Knox, 51–68. New York: Oxford University Press, 2006. Previously published in *Lampas* 30 (1997), 4–19.

Horace (Quintus Horatius Flaccus). *The Satires and Epistles of Horace: A Modern English Verse Translation*. Translated by Smith Palmer Bovie. Chicago: University of Chicago Press, 1959.

Hyde, Walter Woodburn. "The Volcanic History of Etna." *Geographical Review* 1 (1916): 401–18.

Lane Fox, Robin. *The Classical World: An Epic History from Homer to Hadrian*. London: Penguin Books, 2005.

Lyall, Sarah. "Historical Discovery? Well, Yes and No." *New York Times*, May 30, 2005.

Maas, Martha, and Jane McIntosh Snyder. *Stringed Instruments of Ancient Greece*. New Haven, CT: Yale University Press, 1989.

Marrou, H.I. *A History of Education in Antiquity*. Translated by George Lamb. New York: Sheed and Ward, 1956.

Moller, Herbert. "The Accelerated Development of Youth: Beard Growth as a Biological Marker." *Comparative Studies in Society and History* 29 (1987): 748–62.

Oliver, Revilo P. "The First Edition of the *Amores*." *Transactions and Proceedings of the American Philological Association* 76 (1945): 191–215.

Orr, David G. "Roman Domestic Religion: The Evidence of the Household Shrines." *Aufstieg und Niedergang der Römischen Welt* II.16.2 (1978): 1557–91.

Ovid (Publius Ovidius Naso). *The Erotic Poems*. Translated by Peter Green. Harmondsworth, UK: Penguin Books, 1982.

———. *Metamorphoses I–IV*. Edited and translated by D.E. Hill. Oak Park, IL: Bolchazy-Carducci Publishers, 1985.

———. *Tristia; Ex Ponto*. Translated and edited by A.L. Wheeler and G.P. Goold. 2nd ed. Cambridge, MA: Harvard University Press, 1988.

———. *Ovid's Fasti: Roman Holidays*. Translated by Betty Rose Nagle. Bloomington: Indiana University Press, 1995.

———. *Fasti*. Translated by Anthony J. Boyle and Roger D. Woodard. London: Penguin Books, 2004.

———. *Metamorphoses: A New Verse Translation*. Translated by David A. Raeburn. London: Penguin Books, 2004.

———. *The Poems of Exile: Tristia and the Black Sea Letters*. Translated by Peter Green. Berkeley: University of California Press, 2005.

[Hole, S.R.] *Thaumaturgia; or, Elucidations of the Marvellous*. By "An Oxonian." London: Schulze and Co., 1835.

Pindar. *Pindar's Victory Songs*. Translated, with introduction and prefaces, by Frank J. Nisetich. Baltimore: Johns Hopkins University Press, 1980.

Propertius, Sextus. *The Poems*. Translated by W.G. Shepherd. Harmondsworth, UK: Penguin Books, 1985.

Radford, R.S. "Tibullus and Ovid: The Authorship of the Sulpicia and Cornutus Elegies in the Tibullan Corpus." *American Journal of Philology* 44 (1923): 1–26.

Richmond, O.L. "The Augustan Palatium." *Journal of Roman Studies* 4 (1914): 193–226.

Salmon, E T. "S.M.P.E." In Herescu, *Ovidiana*, 3–20.

———. "The Cause of the Social War." *Phoenix* 16 (1962): 107–19.

Saylor, Steven. *Catilina's Riddle*. London: Robinson, 2005.

Shelton, Jo-Ann. *As the Romans Did: A Sourcebook in Roman Social History.* 2nd ed. New York: Oxford University Press, 1998.

Soranus. *Gynecology*. Translated by Owsei Temkin. Baltimore: Johns Hopkins University Press, 1991.

Speidel, Michael P., and Alexandra Dimitrova-Milčeva. "The Cult of the *Genii* in the Roman Army and a New Military Deity." *Aufstieg und Niedergang der Römischen Welt* II.16.2 (1978): 1542–55.

Syme, Ronald. *The Augustan Aristocracy*. New York: Oxford University Press, 1986.

———. *The Roman Revolution*. London: Oxford University Press, 1960.

Tibullus, Albius. *Poems: With the Tibullan Collection*. Translated by Philip Dunlop. Harmondsworth, UK: Penguin Books, 1982.

Treggiari, Susan. *Roman Marriage: Iusti Coniuges from the Time of Cicero to the Time of Ulpian*. New York: Oxford University Press, 1991.

Wallace-Hadrill, Andrew. *Houses and Society in Pompeii and Herculaneum*. Princeton: Princeton University Press, 1994.

Wheeler, Arthur L. "Topics from the Life of Ovid." *American Journal of Philology* 46 (1925): 1–28.

Witherstine, Ruth. "Where the Romans Lived in the First Century B.C." *Classical Journal* 21 (1926): 566–79.

1   All quotations from the *Metamorphoses* are from the translation of Raeburn (2004).

2   For a brief discussion of Ovid's survival, see Bull 2005, 17–21.

3   The only contemporary of Ovid is Seneca the Elder (circa 50 BC–circa AD 40), who left an eyewitness account of Ovid's performance as an orator: *Controversiae* 2.2.8–12.

4   All quotations from the *Tristia* and the *Epistulae ex Ponto* are from the translation of Green, *The Poems of Exile* (University of California Press, 2005).

5   By the time of his exile, Ovid was "unquestionably the most famous poet in the empire": Feeney 2006, 13.

6   Green 2005, xxv.

7   The *Amores* were probably first in circulation in the year 25 BC. Ovid refers to reading the earliest poems to audiences when he was about eighteen. However, the version that has come down to us was significantly revised after its publication around 15 BC: Green 2005, xx, and Oliver 1945, 192–3.

8   Boyle 2006, 167. Holzberg 2006, 63–7, is skeptical of the sources that assume Ovid wrote anything for the theater.

9   "Epilogue: Ovid in His Prime"—Ovid's forty-sixth birthday—has been compiled from passages of a chapter from the original biographical project.

10   Ovid, in reporting that he and his older brother shared a birthday, notes the appearance of the morning star on both days ("*Lucifer amborum natalibus affuit idem,*" *Tristia* 4.10.11).

11   Dupont 1992, 110.

12   Ibid., 222.

13   Clarke 1991, 10.

14   Details about the birthing process in this invented scene are drawn from the *Gynecology* of Soranus, a medical practitioner born (probably) in the second half of the first century AD. Books 1 and 2 of his treatise give practical advice about choosing a midwife and about best practices in assisting labor, delivery, and care of the young.

15   Harlow and Laurence 2002, 39.

16   Balsdon 2002, 91.

17   Hölkeskamp 2004, 126.

18 [Hole] 1835, 97–98.

19 Details about family ritual are extracted from Speidel and Dimitrova-Milčeva 1978 and Orr 1978.

20 Polybius, *Histories* 3.88.

21 On the origins and early history of the Paeligni, see Salmon 1958, 10–18.

22 Conway 1897, 234.

23 Salmon 1958, 14.

24 Salmon 1962, 119.

25 Ibid., 113–14.

26 91 BC: Ibid., 107. Other sources give 90 BC.

27 Syme 1960, 87.

28 Salmon 1958, 18, noting that despite the upgrade Sulmo "does not seem to have become a town of very real consequence."

29 Ibid., 7–9.

30 All quotations of the *Amores* are from the translation of Green, *The Erotic Poems* (1982).

31 Wheeler 1925, 2.

32 Dupont 1992, 36.

33 *Amores* 2.16.7–10, quoted presently.

34 Dupont 1999, 119.

35 Dupont 1992, 46.

36 Shelton 1998, 321.

37 Lane Fox 2005, 119.

38 Harlow and Laurence 2002, 61–3.

39 All quotations from the *Fasti* are from the translation of Boyle and Woodard (2004).

40 Maas and Snyder 1989, 34.

41 Ahl 1985, 226.

42 These birds are the former Pierides, or daughters of Pierus, who were transformed into magpies after losing a singing contest with the Muses (*Metamorphoses* 5.662–78).

43 For contemporary meditations on the myth of Arachne, see Byatt 2000 and Calvino 1989, 151–3.

44 Although Ovid does not explicitly say which sister became which bird, the name Itys was meant to resonate the song of the nightingale, who in older versions of the myth is the transformed Procne calling for her child.

45 Witherstine 1926.

46 Syme 1960, 10: "The two *consuls* remained at the head of the government, but policy was largely directed by ex-*consuls*."

47 Ibid., 18. See also Beard and Crawford 1999, 52–9.

48 Marrou 1956, 262.

49 Beard and Crawford 1999, 12–13.

50 Everitt 2006, 165.

51 Higham 1958, 35.

52 Ibid., 41.

53 Ibid., 47.

54 Ibid., 34.

55 Green 1982, 20.

56 Syme 1986, 201–2.

57 Armstrong 1986, 287.

58 Syme 1986, 207.

59 Ibid., 207–8.

60 Ibid., 207; Syme 1960, 291.

61 Syme 1960, 302.

62 She was paraded in effigy, according to Beard 2002, 116.

63 Syme 1960, 303.

64 Green 1982, 22.

65 Syme 1986, 200, notes that Messalla (and his contemporary, Asinius Pollio) "stood out as the shining glories of Augustan eloquence."

66 Cicero, *Ad Brutum* 23.1.

67 Gaisser 1971, 222.

68 Radford 1923 argues that the poems of Sulpicia were actually written by Ovid.

69 From the translation of Dunlop (1982).

70 Davies 1973, 31.

71 Barrett 2002, 177.

72 On the topography of the Augustan Palatine, see Richmond 1914.

73 Saylor's novel, *Catilina's Riddle* (2005), chapters 16–20, inspired the description of this day.

74 On the Tabularium, see Claridge 2010, 271–2.

75 The names Delia and Cynthia relate to Apollo, the god of music and the Muses. According to tradition, Apollo was born on the isle of Delos — more specifically, on Mount Cynthos.

76 From the translation of Shepherd (1985).

77 Green 1982, 30.

78 *Inberbis iuvenis* was the Latin label. On the transition from beardless youth to bearded manhood, see Harlow and Laurence 2002, 72–5.

79 From the translation of Bovie, *The Satires and Epistles of Horace* (University of Chicago Press, 1959).

80 Carcopino 1964, 160–1.

81   As translated in Harlow and Laurence 2002, 72.

82   *Ars Amatoria* 3.382–6.

83   Green 1982, 28.

84   Balsdon 2002, 21–4, describes the devolution of the *salutatio* from, under the republic, a business transaction between patron and client to, under the empire, a display of degradation.

85   Green 1982, 70n.

86   Treggiari 1991, 89.

87   Ibid., 445.

88   Recall the "spoilt beauty" of *Amores* 2.17.11, previously quoted.

89   Treggiari 1991, 414.

90   Harlow and Laurence 2002, 63.

91   Treggiari 1991, 169.

92   Ibid., 400.

93   Adkins and Adkins 1994, 340. On divorce in the republic and empire see Carcopino 1964, 109–15.

94   Carcopino 1964, 113.

95   Wheeler 1925, 16.

96   Cameron 1968, 326.

97   Casson 1974, 256.

98   Ibid., 248.

99   From the translation of Nisetich (1980).

100 Hyde 1916, 403–4.

101 See Green, Introduction to *The Erotic Poems*.

102 Ovid describes the birthday ritual from the bitter perspective of exile in *Tristia* 3.13.13–18.

103 On Ovid's enthusiasm for the gardens of his youth and their care, see *Epistulae ex Ponto* 1.8.39–62. See also Wallace-Hadrill 1994.

104 Dalby 2000, 244–7, discusses the importance of aromas to Roman sensuality.

105 Ovid commemorates his (unnamed) second wife in the *Tristia*: "a bride you could not find fault with, yet not destined / to warm my bed for long" (4.10.71–2). Green 2005, xx, speculates that she died in childbirth.

106 Lyall 2005.

107 Gozzini Giacosa 1992, 22.